INFINITY COUNTDOWN
DARKHAWK

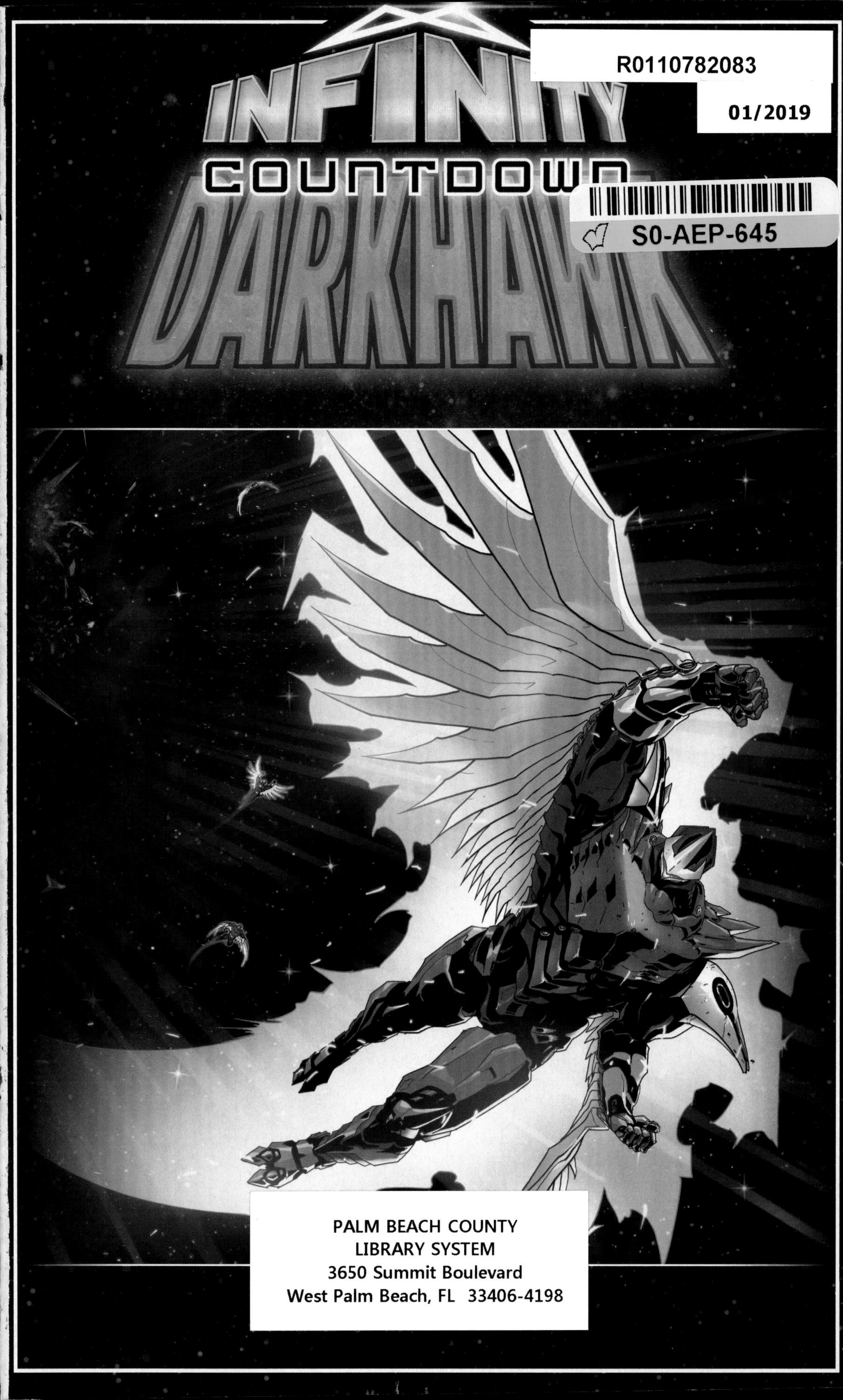

COLLECTION EDITOR **JENNIFER GRÜNWALD**
ASSISTANT EDITOR **CAITLIN O'CONNELL**
ASSOCIATE MANAGING EDITOR **KATERI WOODY**
EDITOR, SPECIAL PROJECTS **MARK D. BEAZLEY**
VP PRODUCTION & SPECIAL PROJECTS **JEFF YOUNGQUIST**
SVP PRINT, SALES & MARKETING **DAVID GABRIEL**

BOOK DESIGNERS **ADAM DEL RE** WITH **SALENA MAHINA**

EDITOR IN CHIEF **C.B. CEBULSKI**
CHIEF CREATIVE OFFICER **JOE QUESADA**
PRESIDENT **DAN BUCKLEY**
EXECUTIVE PRODUCER **ALAN FINE**

INFINITY COUNTDOWN: DARKHAWK. Contains material originally published in magazine form as INFINITY COUNTDOWN: DARKHAWK #1-4 and DARKHAWK #51. First printing 2018. ISBN 978-1-302-91493-6. Published by MARVEL WORLDWIDE, INC., a subsidiary of MARVEL ENTERTAINMENT, LLC. OFFICE OF PUBLICATION: 135 West 50th Street, New York, NY 10020. Copyright © 2018 MARVEL No similarity between any of the names, characters, persons, and/or institutions in this magazine with those of any living or dead person or institution is intended, and any such similarity which may exist is purely coincidental. **Printed in Canada.** DAN BUCKLEY, President, Marvel Entertainment; JOHN NEE, Publisher; JOE QUESADA, Chief Creative Officer; TOM BREVOORT, SVP of Publishing; DAVID BOGART, SVP of Business Affairs & Operations, Publishing & Partnership; DAVID GABRIEL, SVP of Sales & Marketing, Publishing; JEFF YOUNGQUIST, VP of Production & Special Projects; DAN CARR, Executive Director of Publishing Technology; ALEX MORALES, Director of Publishing Operations; DAN EDINGTON, Managing Editor; SUSAN CRESPI, Production Manager; STAN LEE, Chairman Emeritus. For information regarding advertising in Marvel Comics or on Marvel.com, please contact Vit DeBellis, Custom Solutions & Integrated Advertising Manager, at vdebellis@marvel.com. For Marvel subscription inquiries, please call 888-511-5480. **Manufactured between 7/27/2018 and 8/28/2018 by SOLISCO PRINTERS, SCOTT, QC, CANADA.**

10 9 8 7 6 5 4 3 2 1

INFINITY COUNTDOWN DARKHAWK

Chris Powell didn't know where the amulet came from or why it appeared in the old amusement park.
All he knew was that when he grasped it, he transformed into a being of great power. When he was young,
he used that power to defeat crime —— but it has been a long time since Chris was Darkhawk.

WRITERS
CHAD BOWERS & CHRIS SIMS

DARKHAWK #51

ARTIST
KEV WALKER

COLOR ARTIST
JAVA TARTAGLIA

COVER ART
DAVID NAKAYAMA

INFINITY COUNTDOWN: DARKHAWK #1-4

ARTIST
GANG HYUK LIM

COVER ART
SKAN

LETTERER
VC's TRAVIS LANHAM

ASSISTANT EDITORS
ANNALISE BISSA
WITH ALLISON STOCK (#51)

EDITORS
JORDAN D. WHITE
WITH CHARLES BEACHAM (#51)

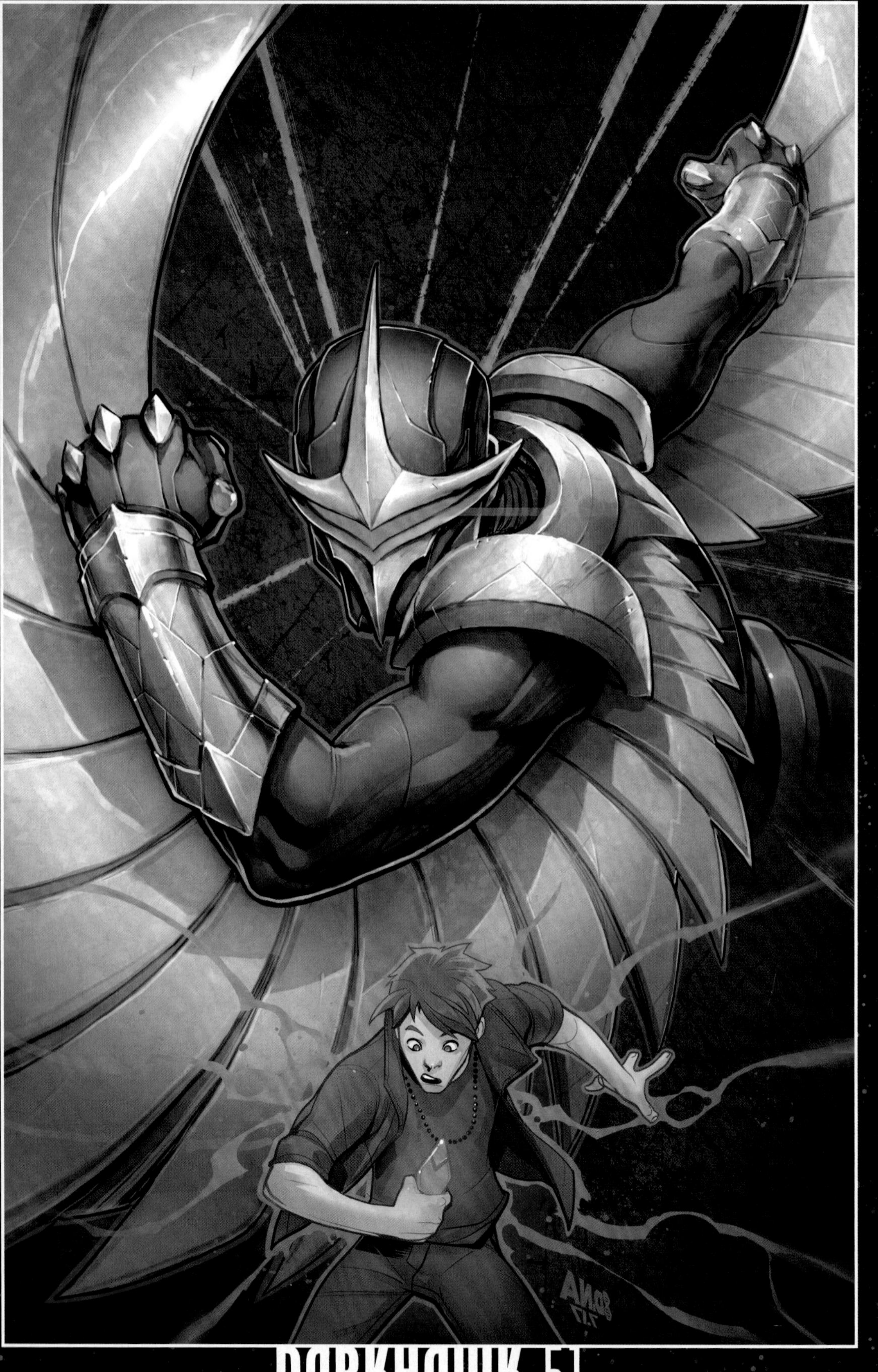

DARKHAWK 51

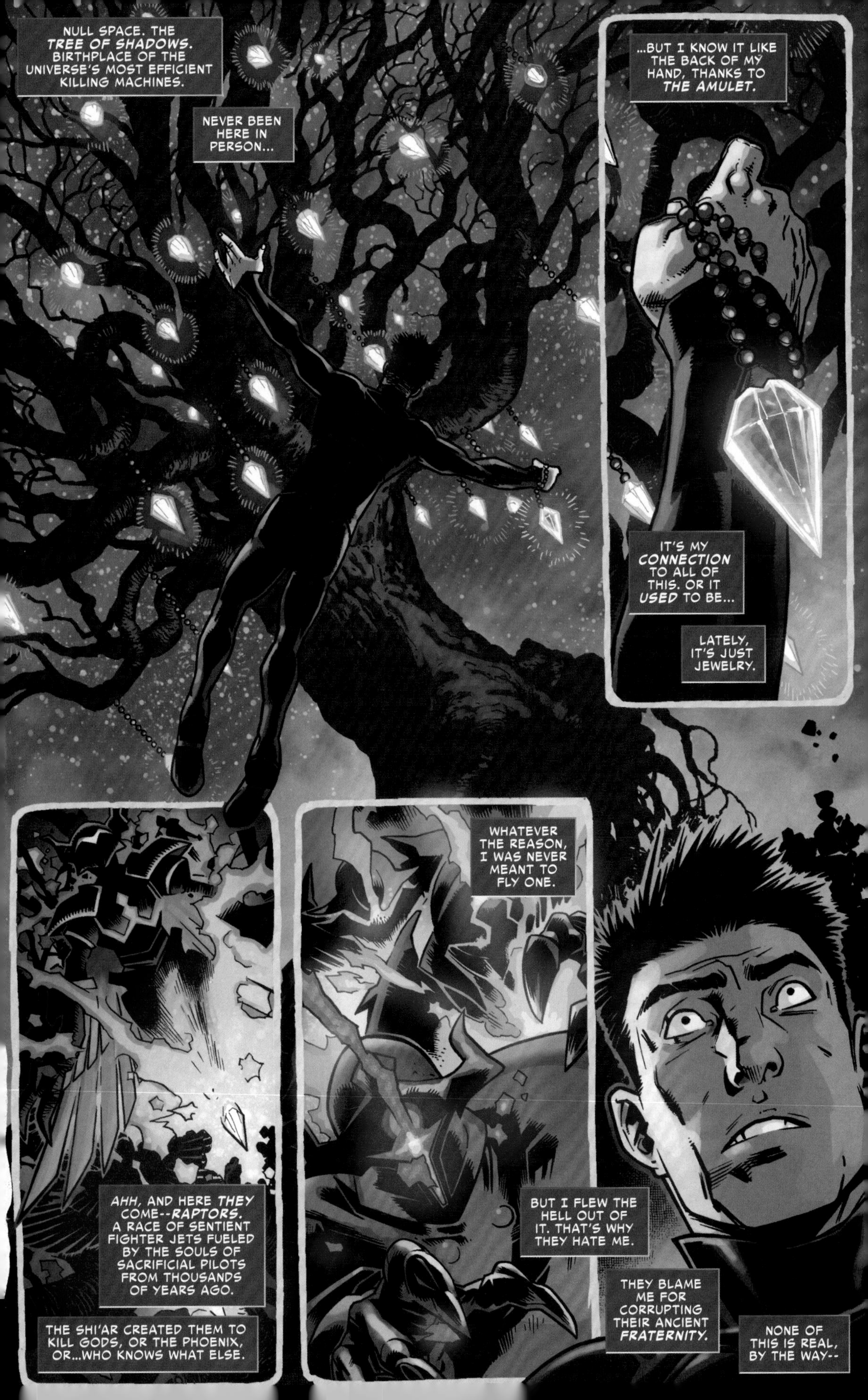
NULL SPACE. THE *TREE OF SHADOWS.* BIRTHPLACE OF THE UNIVERSE'S MOST EFFICIENT KILLING MACHINES.
NEVER BEEN HERE IN PERSON...
...BUT I KNOW IT LIKE THE BACK OF MY HAND, THANKS TO *THE AMULET.*
IT'S MY *CONNECTION* TO ALL OF THIS. OR IT *USED* TO BE...
LATELY, IT'S JUST JEWELRY.
AHH, AND HERE *THEY* COME--*RAPTORS.* A RACE OF SENTIENT FIGHTER JETS FUELED BY THE SOULS OF SACRIFICIAL PILOTS FROM THOUSANDS OF YEARS AGO.
THE SHI'AR CREATED THEM TO KILL GODS, OR THE PHOENIX, OR...WHO KNOWS WHAT ELSE.
WHATEVER THE REASON, I WAS NEVER MEANT TO FLY ONE.
BUT I FLEW THE HELL OUT OF IT. THAT'S WHY THEY HATE ME.
THEY BLAME ME FOR CORRUPTING THEIR ANCIENT *FRATERNITY.*
NONE OF THIS IS REAL, BY THE WAY--

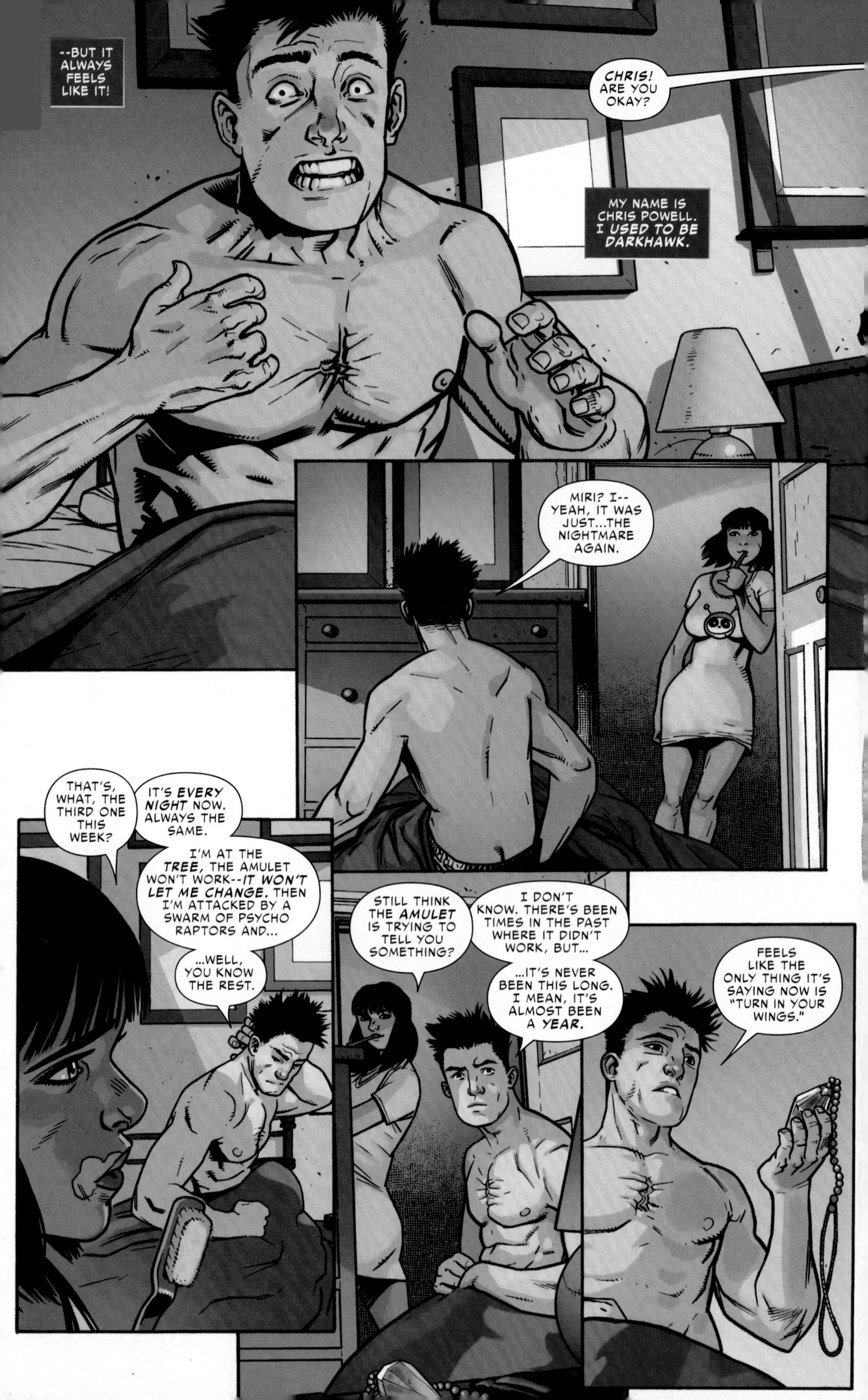

--BUT IT ALWAYS FEELS LIKE IT!
CHRIS! ARE YOU OKAY?
MY NAME IS CHRIS POWELL. I USED TO BE DARKHAWK.
MIRI? I-- YEAH, IT WAS JUST...THE NIGHTMARE AGAIN.
THAT'S, WHAT, THE THIRD ONE THIS WEEK?
IT'S EVERY NIGHT NOW. ALWAYS THE SAME.
I'M AT THE TREE, THE AMULET WON'T WORK--IT WON'T LET ME CHANGE. THEN I'M ATTACKED BY A SWARM OF PSYCHO RAPTORS AND...
...WELL, YOU KNOW THE REST.
STILL THINK THE AMULET IS TRYING TO TELL YOU SOMETHING?
I DON'T KNOW. THERE'S BEEN TIMES IN THE PAST WHERE IT DIDN'T WORK, BUT...
...IT'S NEVER BEEN THIS LONG. I MEAN, IT'S ALMOST BEEN A YEAR.
FEELS LIKE THE ONLY THING IT'S SAYING NOW IS "TURN IN YOUR WINGS."

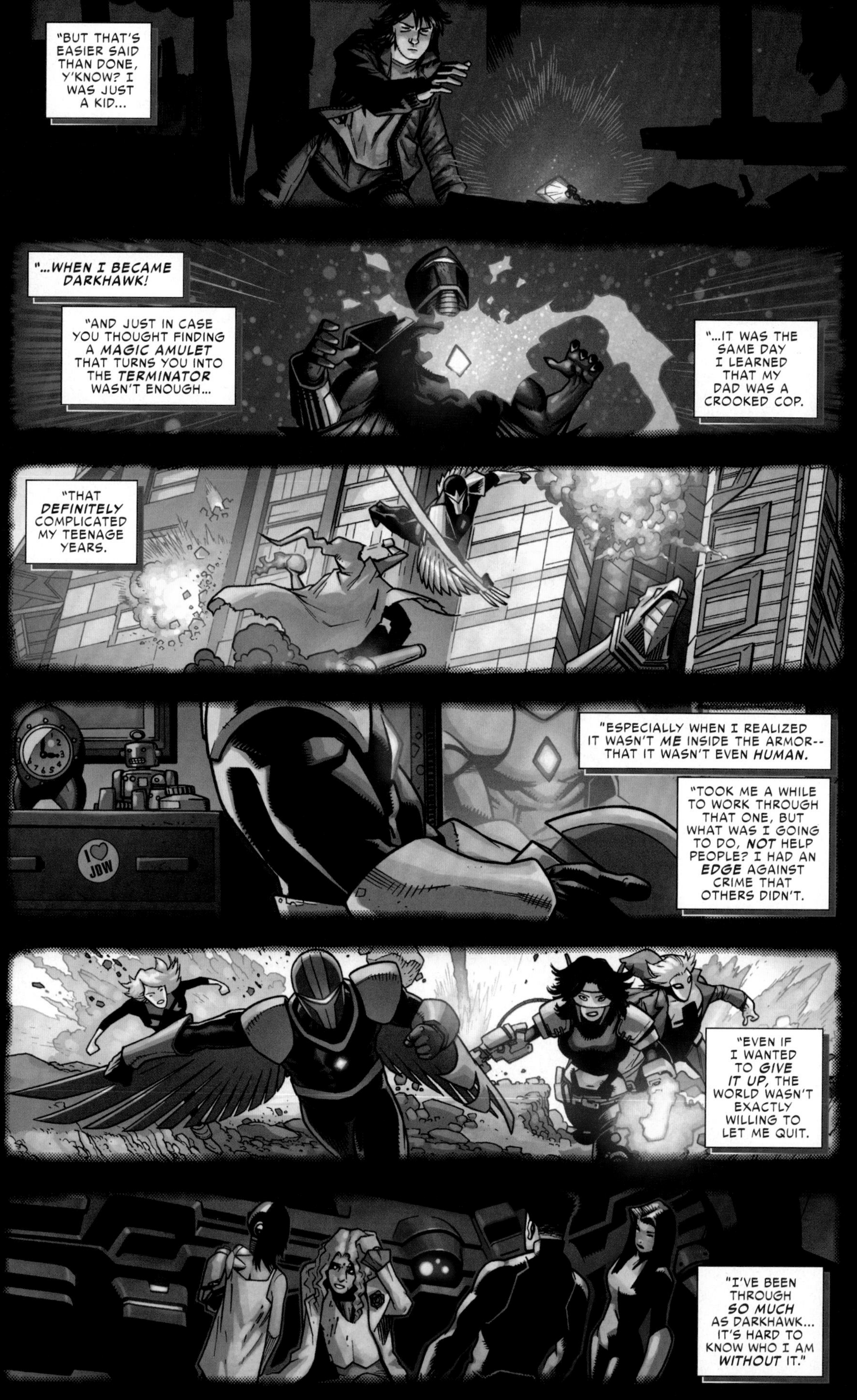

"BUT THAT'S EASIER SAID THAN DONE, Y'KNOW? I WAS JUST A KID...
"...WHEN I BECAME DARKHAWK!
"AND JUST IN CASE YOU THOUGHT FINDING A MAGIC AMULET THAT TURNS YOU INTO THE TERMINATOR WASN'T ENOUGH...
"...IT WAS THE SAME DAY I LEARNED THAT MY DAD WAS A CROOKED COP.
"THAT DEFINITELY COMPLICATED MY TEENAGE YEARS.
"ESPECIALLY WHEN I REALIZED IT WASN'T ME INSIDE THE ARMOR-- THAT IT WASN'T EVEN HUMAN.
"TOOK ME A WHILE TO WORK THROUGH THAT ONE, BUT WHAT WAS I GOING TO DO, NOT HELP PEOPLE? I HAD AN EDGE AGAINST CRIME THAT OTHERS DIDN'T.
I ♥ JDW
"EVEN IF I WANTED TO GIVE IT UP, THE WORLD WASN'T EXACTLY WILLING TO LET ME QUIT.
"I'VE BEEN THROUGH SO MUCH AS DARKHAWK... IT'S HARD TO KNOW WHO I AM WITHOUT IT."

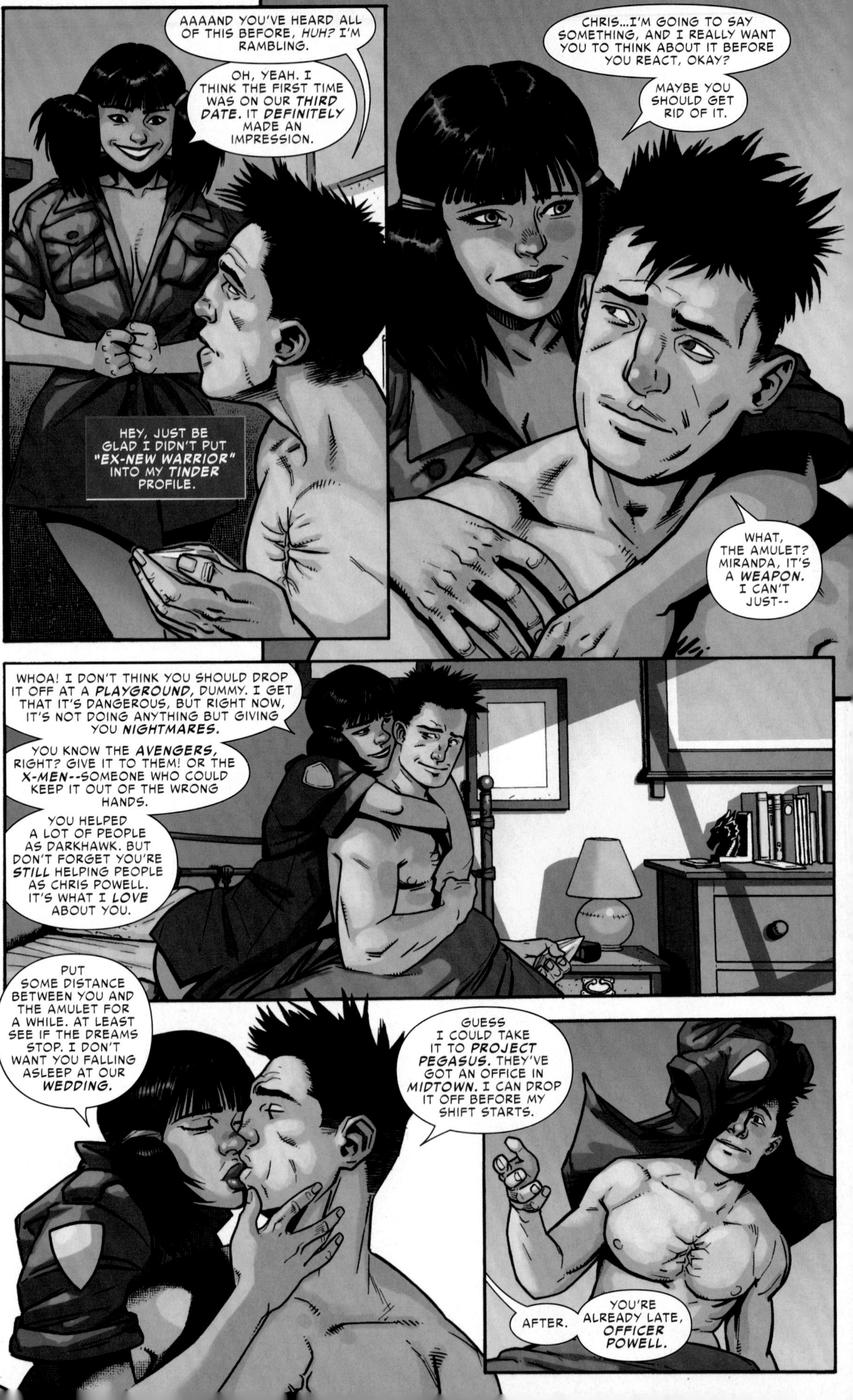
AAAAND YOU'VE HEARD ALL OF THIS BEFORE, HUH? I'M RAMBLING.
OH, YEAH. I THINK THE FIRST TIME WAS ON OUR THIRD DATE. IT DEFINITELY MADE AN IMPRESSION.
HEY, JUST BE GLAD I DIDN'T PUT "EX-NEW WARRIOR" INTO MY TINDER PROFILE.
CHRIS...I'M GOING TO SAY SOMETHING, AND I REALLY WANT YOU TO THINK ABOUT IT BEFORE YOU REACT, OKAY?
MAYBE YOU SHOULD GET RID OF IT.
WHAT, THE AMULET? MIRANDA, IT'S A WEAPON. I CAN'T JUST--
WHOA! I DON'T THINK YOU SHOULD DROP IT OFF AT A PLAYGROUND, DUMMY. I GET THAT IT'S DANGEROUS, BUT RIGHT NOW, IT'S NOT DOING ANYTHING BUT GIVING YOU NIGHTMARES.
YOU KNOW THE AVENGERS, RIGHT? GIVE IT TO THEM! OR THE X-MEN--SOMEONE WHO COULD KEEP IT OUT OF THE WRONG HANDS.
YOU HELPED A LOT OF PEOPLE AS DARKHAWK. BUT DON'T FORGET YOU'RE STILL HELPING PEOPLE AS CHRIS POWELL. IT'S WHAT I LOVE ABOUT YOU.
PUT SOME DISTANCE BETWEEN YOU AND THE AMULET FOR A WHILE. AT LEAST SEE IF THE DREAMS STOP. I DON'T WANT YOU FALLING ASLEEP AT OUR WEDDING.
GUESS I COULD TAKE IT TO PROJECT PEGASUS. THEY'VE GOT AN OFFICE IN MIDTOWN. I CAN DROP IT OFF BEFORE MY SHIFT STARTS.
AFTER.
YOU'RE ALREADY LATE, OFFICER POWELL.

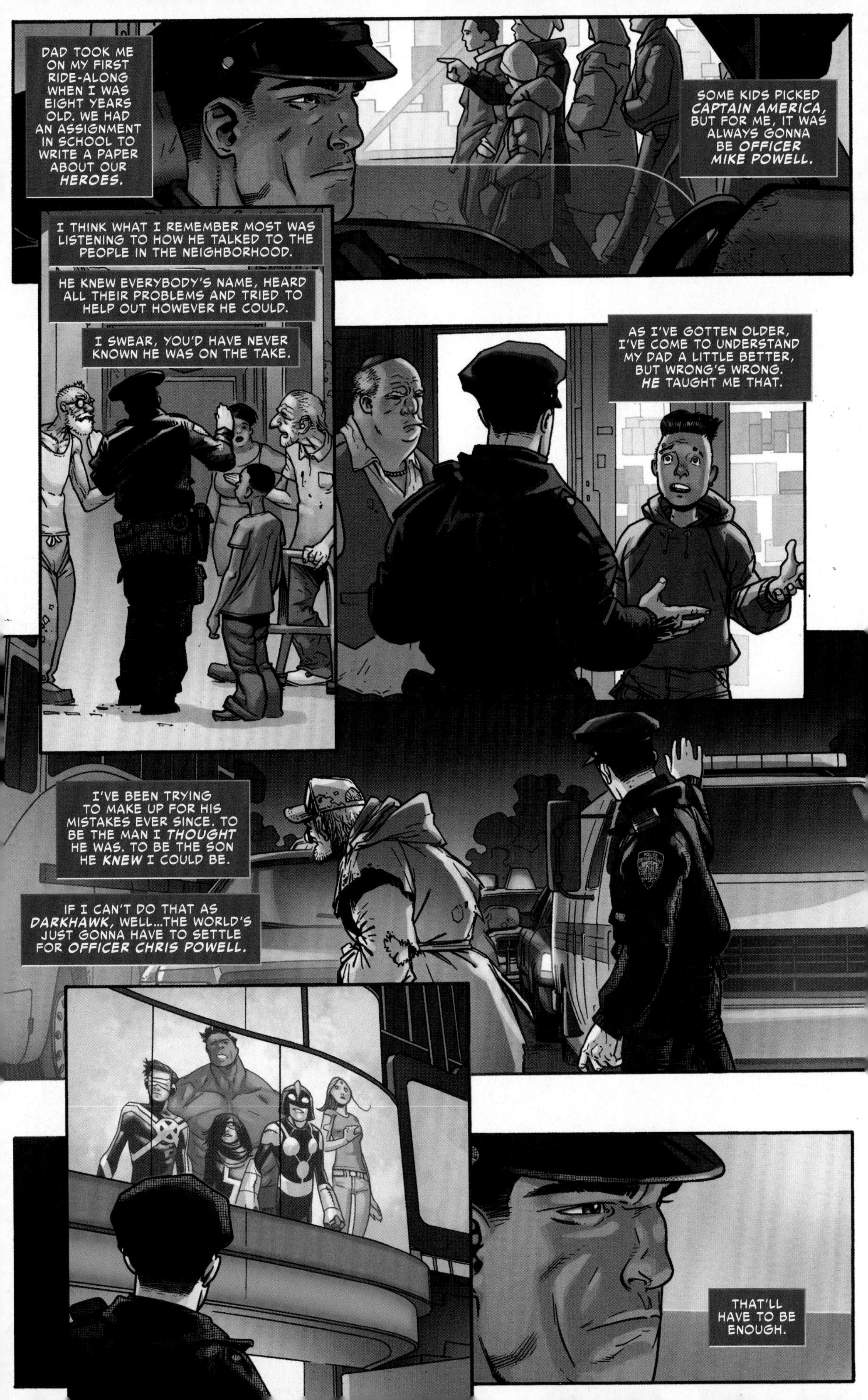
DAD TOOK ME ON MY FIRST RIDE-ALONG WHEN I WAS EIGHT YEARS OLD. WE HAD AN ASSIGNMENT IN SCHOOL TO WRITE A PAPER ABOUT OUR *HEROES*.
SOME KIDS PICKED *CAPTAIN AMERICA*, BUT FOR ME, IT WAS ALWAYS GONNA BE *OFFICER MIKE POWELL*.
I THINK WHAT I REMEMBER MOST WAS LISTENING TO HOW HE TALKED TO THE PEOPLE IN THE NEIGHBORHOOD.
HE KNEW EVERYBODY'S NAME, HEARD ALL THEIR PROBLEMS AND TRIED TO HELP OUT HOWEVER HE COULD.
I SWEAR, YOU'D HAVE NEVER KNOWN HE WAS ON THE TAKE.
AS I'VE GOTTEN OLDER, I'VE COME TO UNDERSTAND MY DAD A LITTLE BETTER, BUT WRONG'S WRONG. *HE* TAUGHT ME THAT.
I'VE BEEN TRYING TO MAKE UP FOR HIS MISTAKES EVER SINCE. TO BE THE MAN I *THOUGHT* HE WAS. TO BE THE SON HE *KNEW* I COULD BE.
IF I CAN'T DO THAT AS *DARKHAWK*, WELL...THE WORLD'S JUST GONNA HAVE TO SETTLE FOR *OFFICER CHRIS POWELL*.
THAT'LL HAVE TO BE ENOUGH.

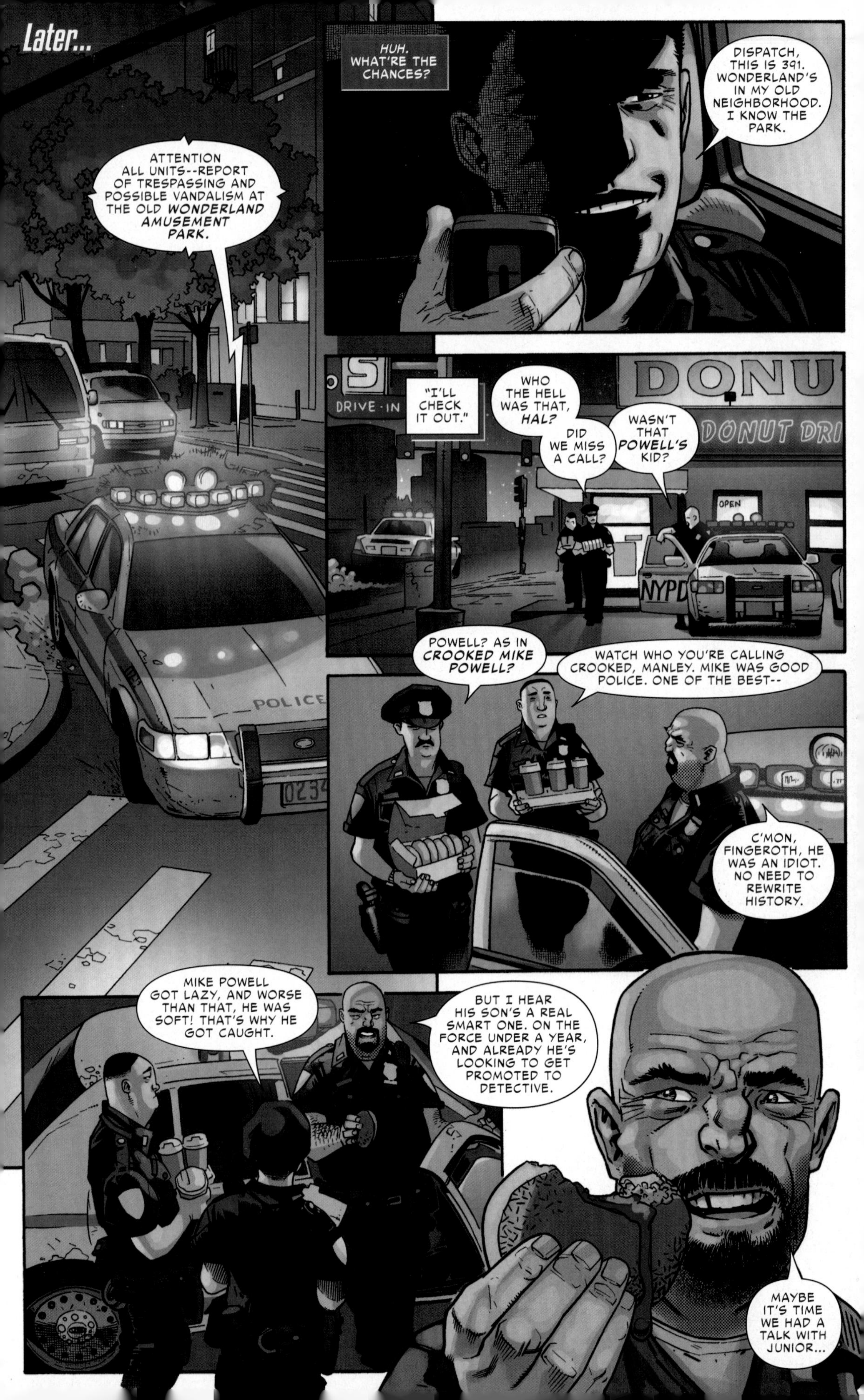
Later...
ATTENTION ALL UNITS--REPORT OF TRESPASSING AND POSSIBLE VANDALISM AT THE OLD WONDERLAND AMUSEMENT PARK.
HUH. WHAT'RE THE CHANCES?
DISPATCH, THIS IS 391. WONDERLAND'S IN MY OLD NEIGHBORHOOD. I KNOW THE PARK.
"I'LL CHECK IT OUT."
WHO THE HELL WAS THAT, HAL?
DID WE MISS A CALL?
WASN'T THAT POWELL'S KID?
POWELL? AS IN CROOKED MIKE POWELL?
WATCH WHO YOU'RE CALLING CROOKED, MANLEY. MIKE WAS GOOD POLICE. ONE OF THE BEST--
C'MON, FINGEROTH, HE WAS AN IDIOT. NO NEED TO REWRITE HISTORY.
MIKE POWELL GOT LAZY, AND WORSE THAN THAT, HE WAS SOFT! THAT'S WHY HE GOT CAUGHT.
BUT I HEAR HIS SON'S A REAL SMART ONE. ON THE FORCE UNDER A YEAR, AND ALREADY HE'S LOOKING TO GET PROMOTED TO DETECTIVE.
MAYBE IT'S TIME WE HAD A TALK WITH JUNIOR...

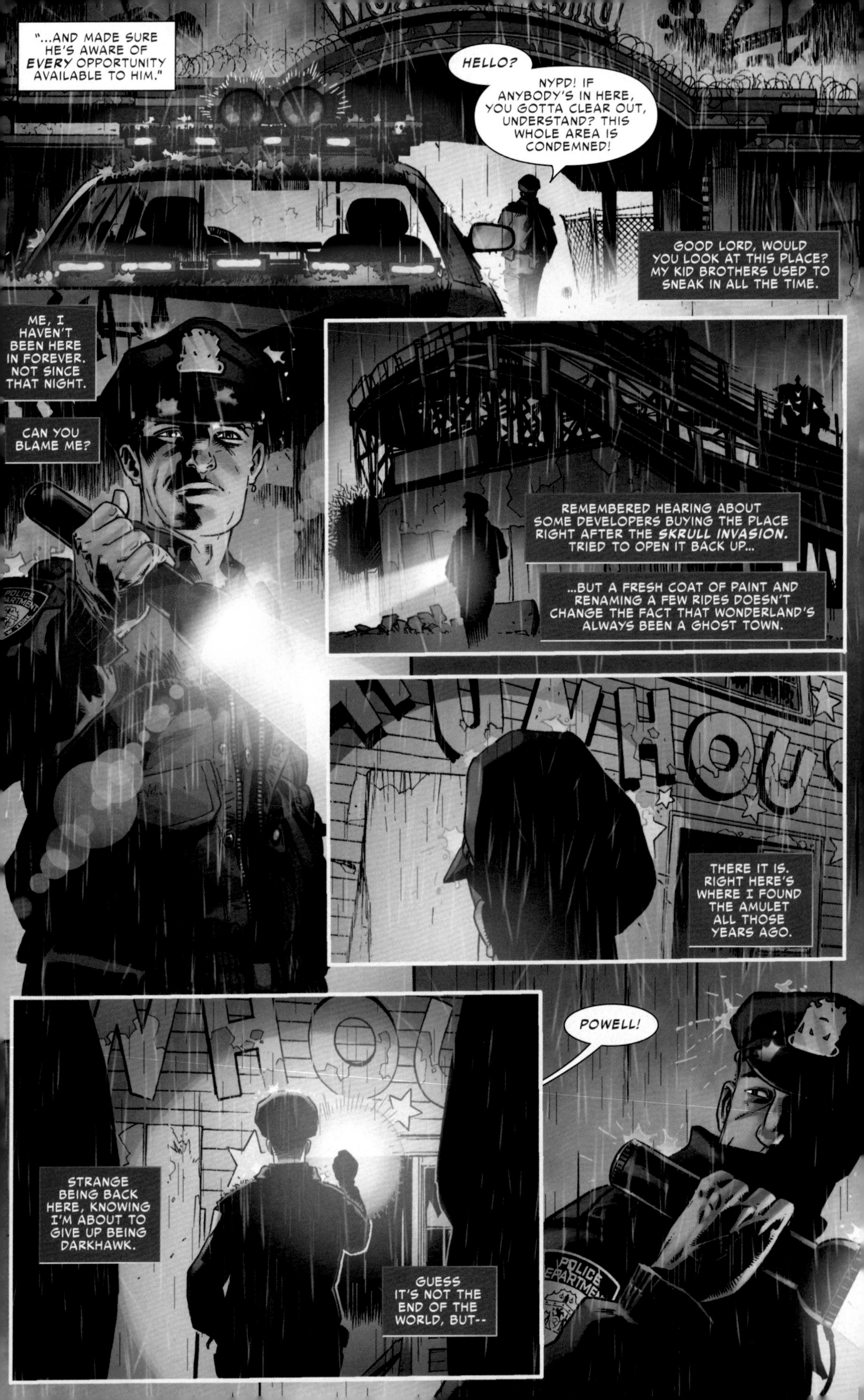
"...AND MADE SURE HE'S AWARE OF EVERY OPPORTUNITY AVAILABLE TO HIM."
HELLO?
NYPD! IF ANYBODY'S IN HERE, YOU GOTTA CLEAR OUT, UNDERSTAND? THIS WHOLE AREA IS CONDEMNED!
GOOD LORD, WOULD YOU LOOK AT THIS PLACE? MY KID BROTHERS USED TO SNEAK IN ALL THE TIME.
ME, I HAVEN'T BEEN HERE IN FOREVER. NOT SINCE THAT NIGHT.
CAN YOU BLAME ME?
REMEMBERED HEARING ABOUT SOME DEVELOPERS BUYING THE PLACE RIGHT AFTER THE SKRULL INVASION. TRIED TO OPEN IT BACK UP...
...BUT A FRESH COAT OF PAINT AND RENAMING A FEW RIDES DOESN'T CHANGE THE FACT THAT WONDERLAND'S ALWAYS BEEN A GHOST TOWN.
THERE IT IS. RIGHT HERE'S WHERE I FOUND THE AMULET ALL THOSE YEARS AGO.
STRANGE BEING BACK HERE, KNOWING I'M ABOUT TO GIVE UP BEING DARKHAWK.
GUESS IT'S NOT THE END OF THE WORLD, BUT--
POWELL!

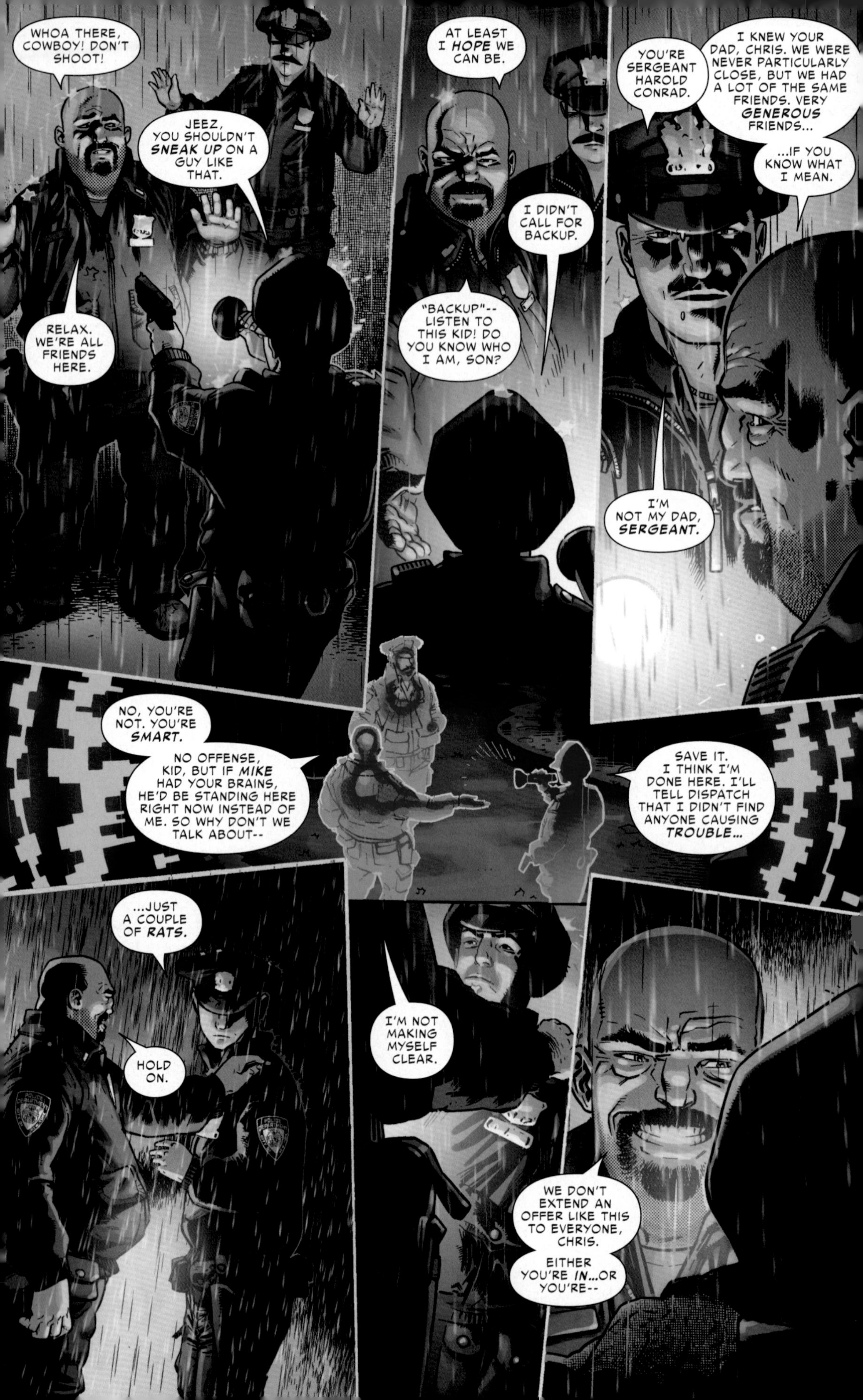
WHOA THERE, COWBOY! DON'T SHOOT!
JEEZ, YOU SHOULDN'T SNEAK UP ON A GUY LIKE THAT.
RELAX. WE'RE ALL FRIENDS HERE.
AT LEAST I HOPE WE CAN BE.
I DIDN'T CALL FOR BACKUP.
"BACKUP"-- LISTEN TO THIS KID! DO YOU KNOW WHO I AM, SON?
YOU'RE SERGEANT HAROLD CONRAD.
I KNEW YOUR DAD, CHRIS. WE WERE NEVER PARTICULARLY CLOSE, BUT WE HAD A LOT OF THE SAME FRIENDS. VERY GENEROUS FRIENDS...
...IF YOU KNOW WHAT I MEAN.
I'M NOT MY DAD, SERGEANT.
NO, YOU'RE NOT. YOU'RE SMART.
NO OFFENSE, KID, BUT IF MIKE HAD YOUR BRAINS, HE'D BE STANDING HERE RIGHT NOW INSTEAD OF ME. SO WHY DON'T WE TALK ABOUT--
SAVE IT. I THINK I'M DONE HERE. I'LL TELL DISPATCH THAT I DIDN'T FIND ANYONE CAUSING TROUBLE...
...JUST A COUPLE OF RATS.
HOLD ON.
I'M NOT MAKING MYSELF CLEAR.
WE DON'T EXTEND AN OFFER LIKE THIS TO EVERYONE, CHRIS.
EITHER YOU'RE IN...OR YOU'RE--

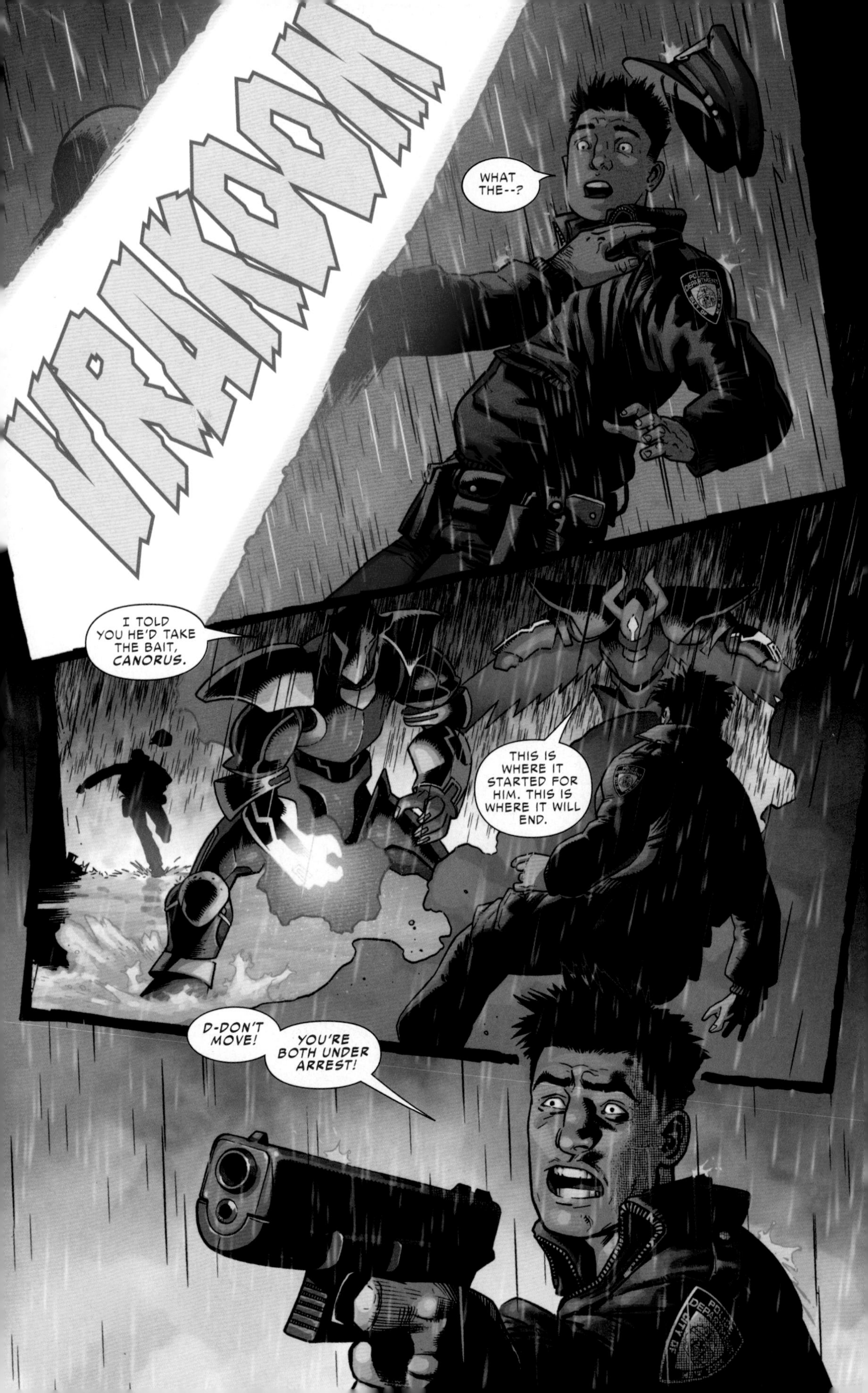

VRAKOOM
WHAT THE--?
I TOLD YOU HE'D TAKE THE BAIT, CANORUS.
THIS IS WHERE IT STARTED FOR HIM. THIS IS WHERE IT WILL END.
D-DON'T MOVE!
YOU'RE BOTH UNDER ARREST!

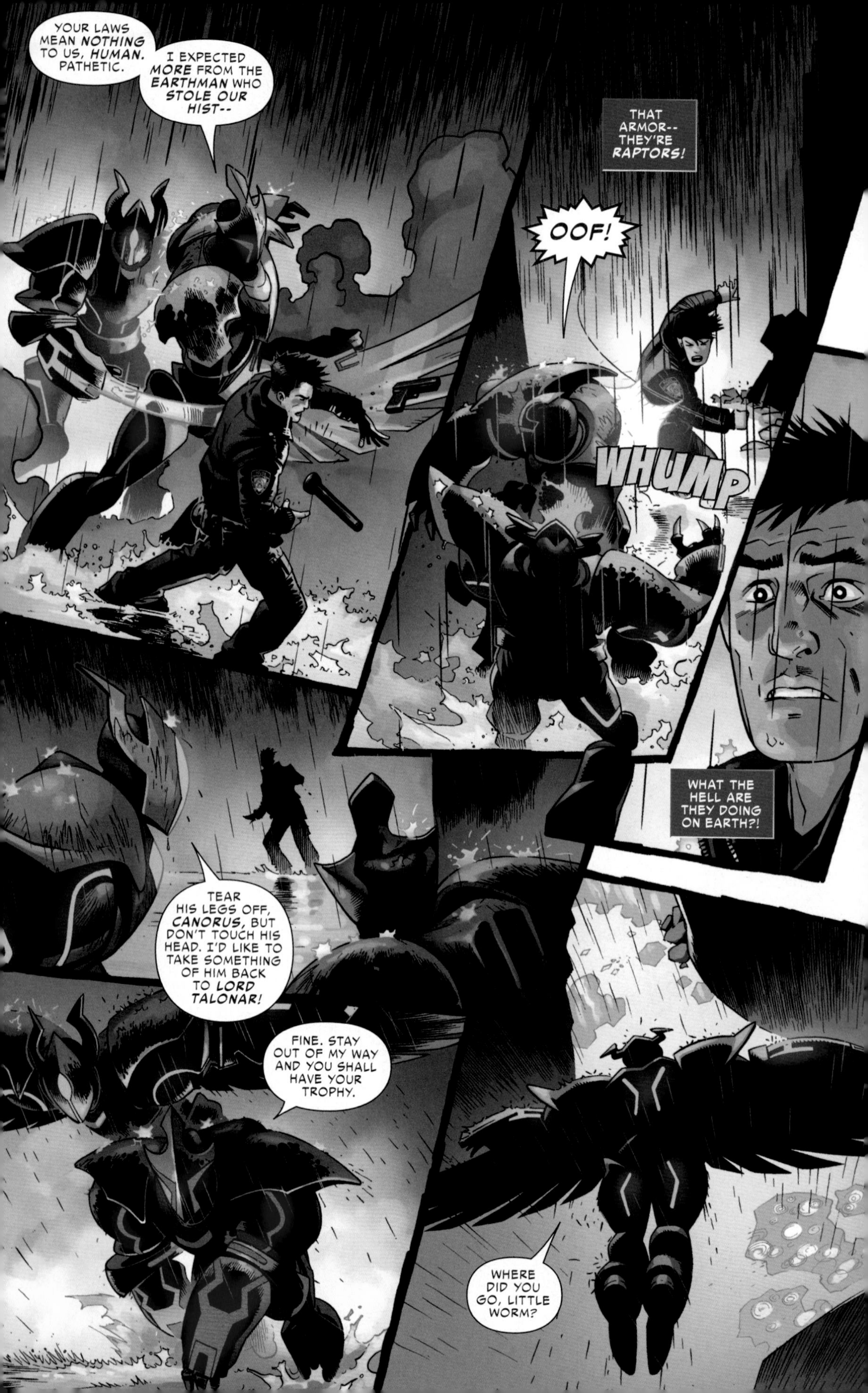

YOUR LAWS MEAN NOTHING TO US, HUMAN. PATHETIC.
I EXPECTED MORE FROM THE EARTHMAN WHO STOLE OUR HIST--
THAT ARMOR-- THEY'RE RAPTORS!
OOF!
WHUMP
WHAT THE HELL ARE THEY DOING ON EARTH?!
TEAR HIS LEGS OFF, CANORUS, BUT DON'T TOUCH HIS HEAD. I'D LIKE TO TAKE SOMETHING OF HIM BACK TO LORD TALONAR!
FINE. STAY OUT OF MY WAY AND YOU SHALL HAVE YOUR TROPHY.
WHERE DID YOU GO, LITTLE WORM?

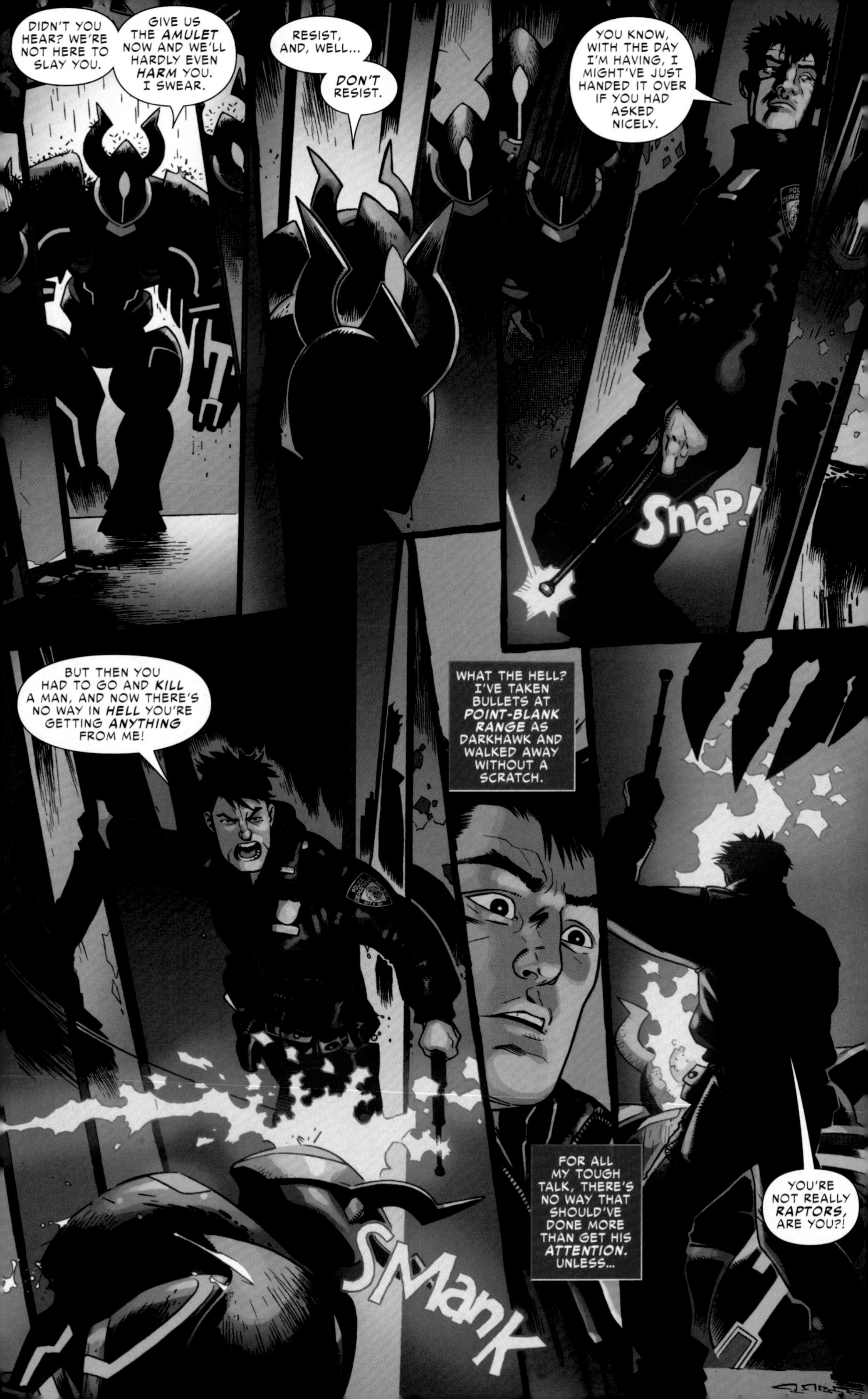

DIDN'T YOU HEAR? WE'RE NOT HERE TO SLAY YOU.
GIVE US THE *AMULET* NOW AND WE'LL HARDLY EVEN *HARM* YOU. I SWEAR.
RESIST, AND, WELL...
DON'T RESIST.
YOU KNOW, WITH THE DAY I'M HAVING, I MIGHT'VE JUST HANDED IT OVER IF YOU HAD ASKED NICELY.
SNAP!
BUT THEN YOU HAD TO GO AND *KILL* A MAN, AND NOW THERE'S NO WAY IN *HELL* YOU'RE GETTING *ANYTHING* FROM ME!
SMANK
WHAT THE HELL? I'VE TAKEN BULLETS AT *POINT-BLANK RANGE* AS DARKHAWK AND WALKED AWAY WITHOUT A SCRATCH.
FOR ALL MY TOUGH TALK, THERE'S NO WAY THAT SHOULD'VE DONE MORE THAN GET HIS *ATTENTION*. UNLESS...
YOU'RE NOT REALLY *RAPTORS*, ARE YOU?!

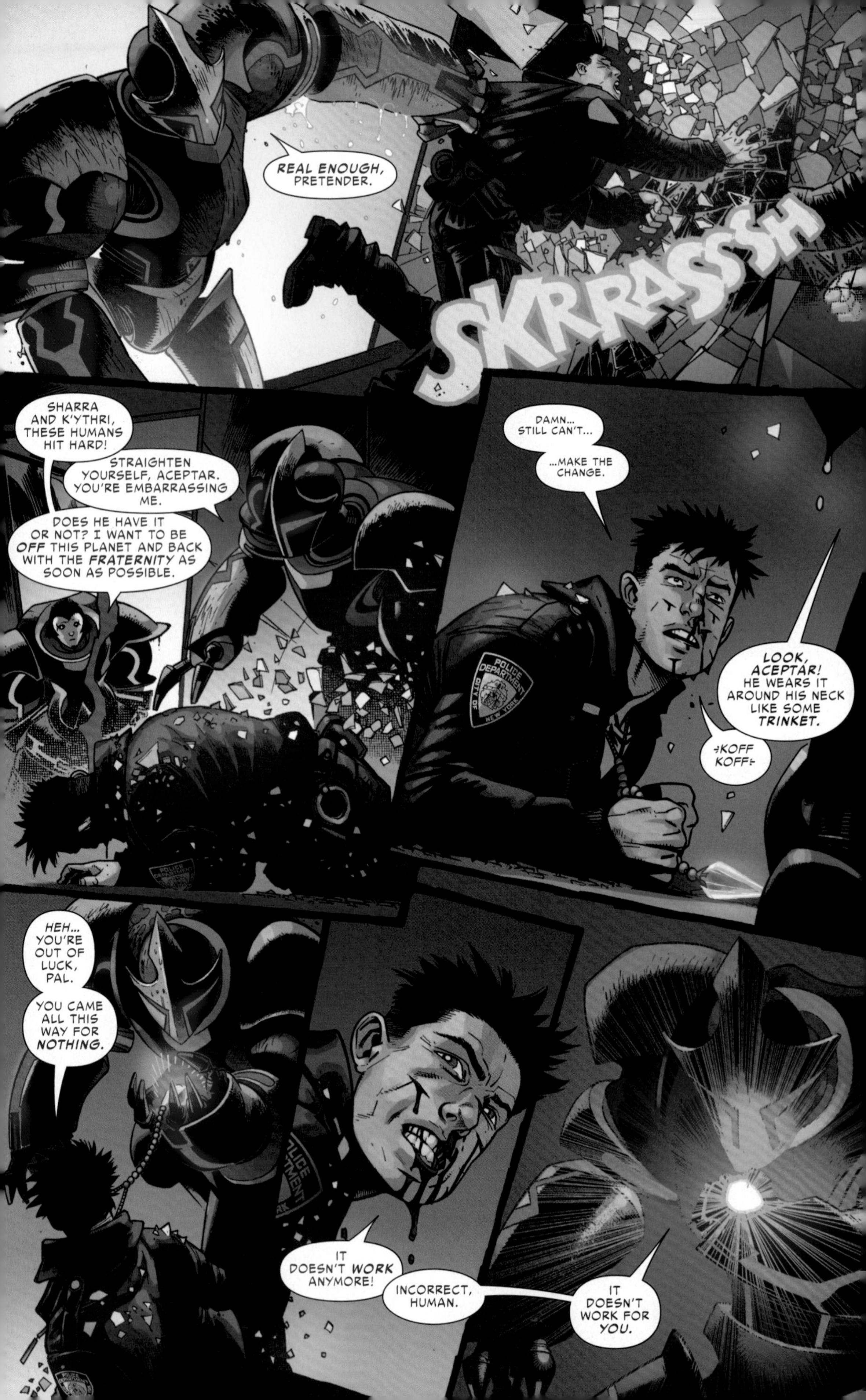
REAL ENOUGH, PRETENDER.
SKRRASSH
SHARRA AND K'YTHRI, THESE HUMANS HIT HARD!
STRAIGHTEN YOURSELF, ACEPTAR. YOU'RE EMBARRASSING ME.
DOES HE HAVE IT OR NOT? I WANT TO BE OFF THIS PLANET AND BACK WITH THE FRATERNITY AS SOON AS POSSIBLE.
DAMN... STILL CAN'T...
...MAKE THE CHANGE.
LOOK, ACEPTAR! HE WEARS IT AROUND HIS NECK LIKE SOME TRINKET.
KOFF KOFF
HEH... YOU'RE OUT OF LUCK, PAL.
YOU CAME ALL THIS WAY FOR NOTHING.
IT DOESN'T WORK ANYMORE!
INCORRECT, HUMAN.
IT DOESN'T WORK FOR YOU.

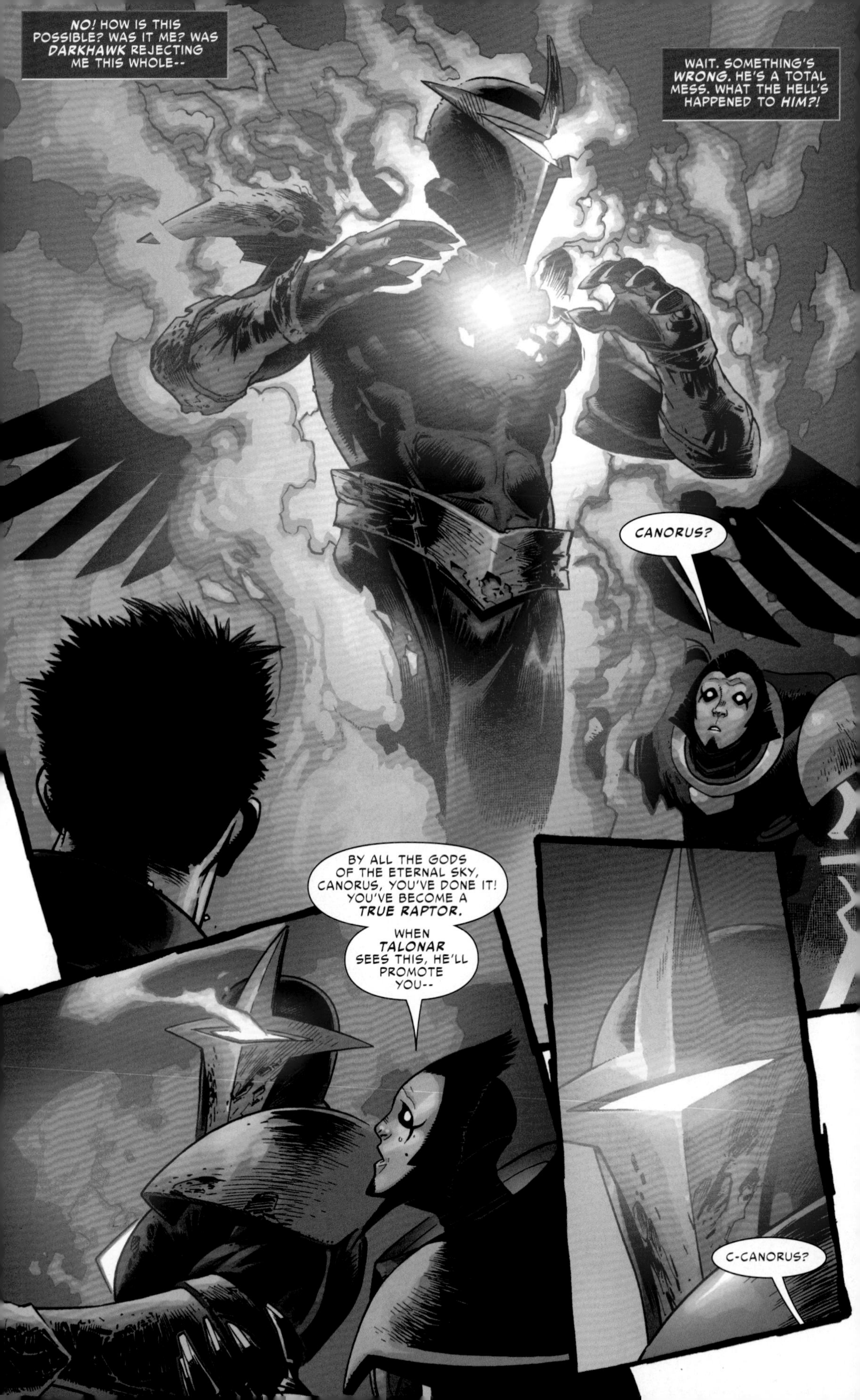
NO! HOW IS THIS POSSIBLE? WAS IT ME? WAS DARKHAWK REJECTING ME THIS WHOLE--
WAIT. SOMETHING'S WRONG. HE'S A TOTAL MESS. WHAT THE HELL'S HAPPENED TO HIM?!
CANORUS?
BY ALL THE GODS OF THE ETERNAL SKY, CANORUS, YOU'VE DONE IT! YOU'VE BECOME A TRUE RAPTOR.
WHEN TALONAR SEES THIS, HE'LL PROMOTE YOU--
C-CANORUS?

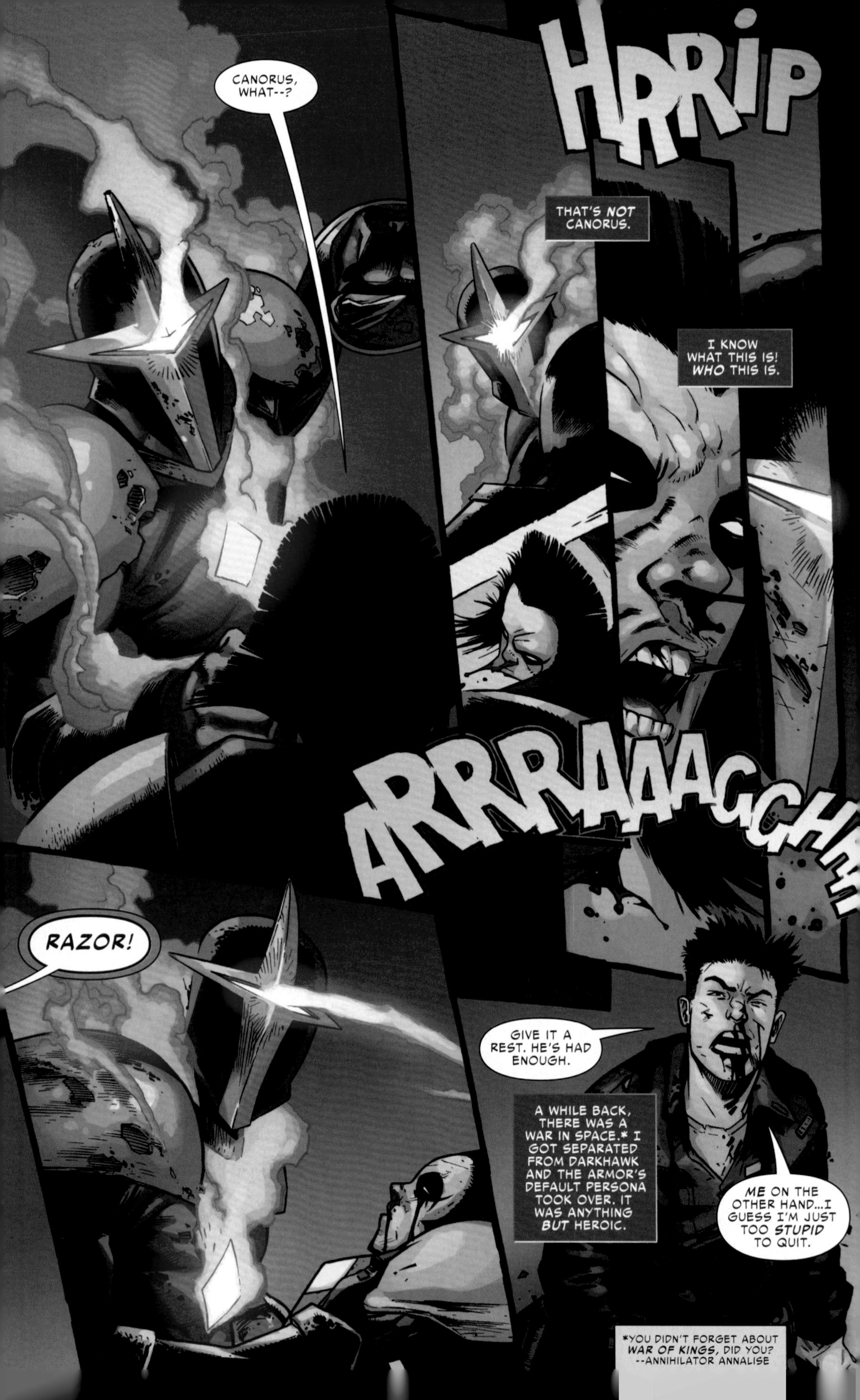
CANORUS, WHAT--?
HRRIP
THAT'S NOT CANORUS.
I KNOW WHAT THIS IS! WHO THIS IS.
ARRRAAAGCHH!
RAZOR!
GIVE IT A REST. HE'S HAD ENOUGH.
A WHILE BACK, THERE WAS A WAR IN SPACE.* I GOT SEPARATED FROM DARKHAWK AND THE ARMOR'S DEFAULT PERSONA TOOK OVER. IT WAS ANYTHING BUT HEROIC.
ME ON THE OTHER HAND...I GUESS I'M JUST TOO STUPID TO QUIT.
*YOU DIDN'T FORGET ABOUT WAR OF KINGS, DID YOU? --ANNIHILATOR ANNALISE

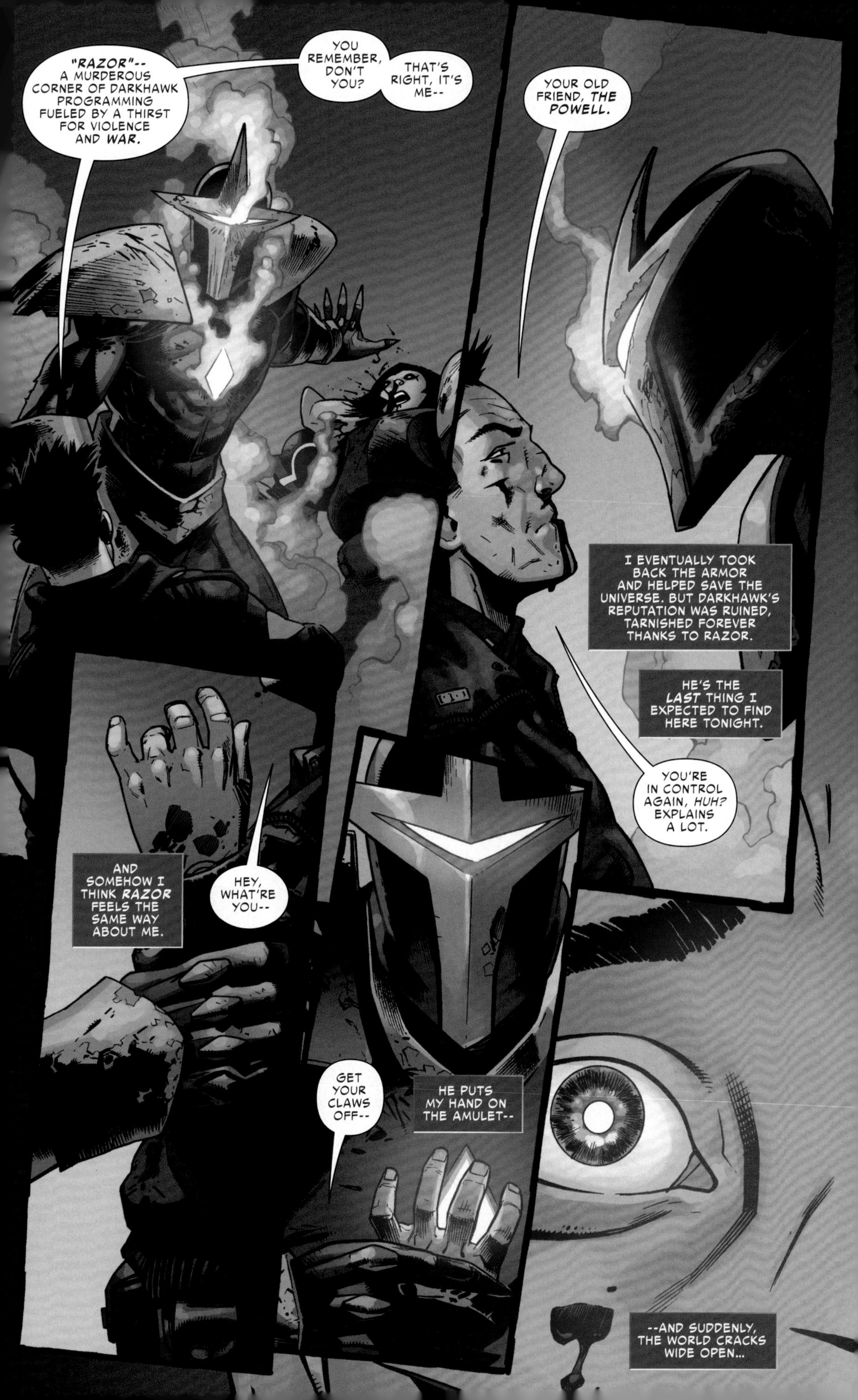
"RAZOR"-- A MURDEROUS CORNER OF DARKHAWK PROGRAMMING FUELED BY A THIRST FOR VIOLENCE AND WAR.
YOU REMEMBER, DON'T YOU?
THAT'S RIGHT, IT'S ME--
YOUR OLD FRIEND, THE POWELL.
I EVENTUALLY TOOK BACK THE ARMOR AND HELPED SAVE THE UNIVERSE. BUT DARKHAWK'S REPUTATION WAS RUINED, TARNISHED FOREVER THANKS TO RAZOR.
HE'S THE LAST THING I EXPECTED TO FIND HERE TONIGHT.
YOU'RE IN CONTROL AGAIN, HUH? EXPLAINS A LOT.
AND SOMEHOW I THINK RAZOR FEELS THE SAME WAY ABOUT ME.
HEY, WHAT'RE YOU--
GET YOUR CLAWS OFF--
HE PUTS MY HAND ON THE AMULET--
--AND SUDDENLY, THE WORLD CRACKS WIDE OPEN...

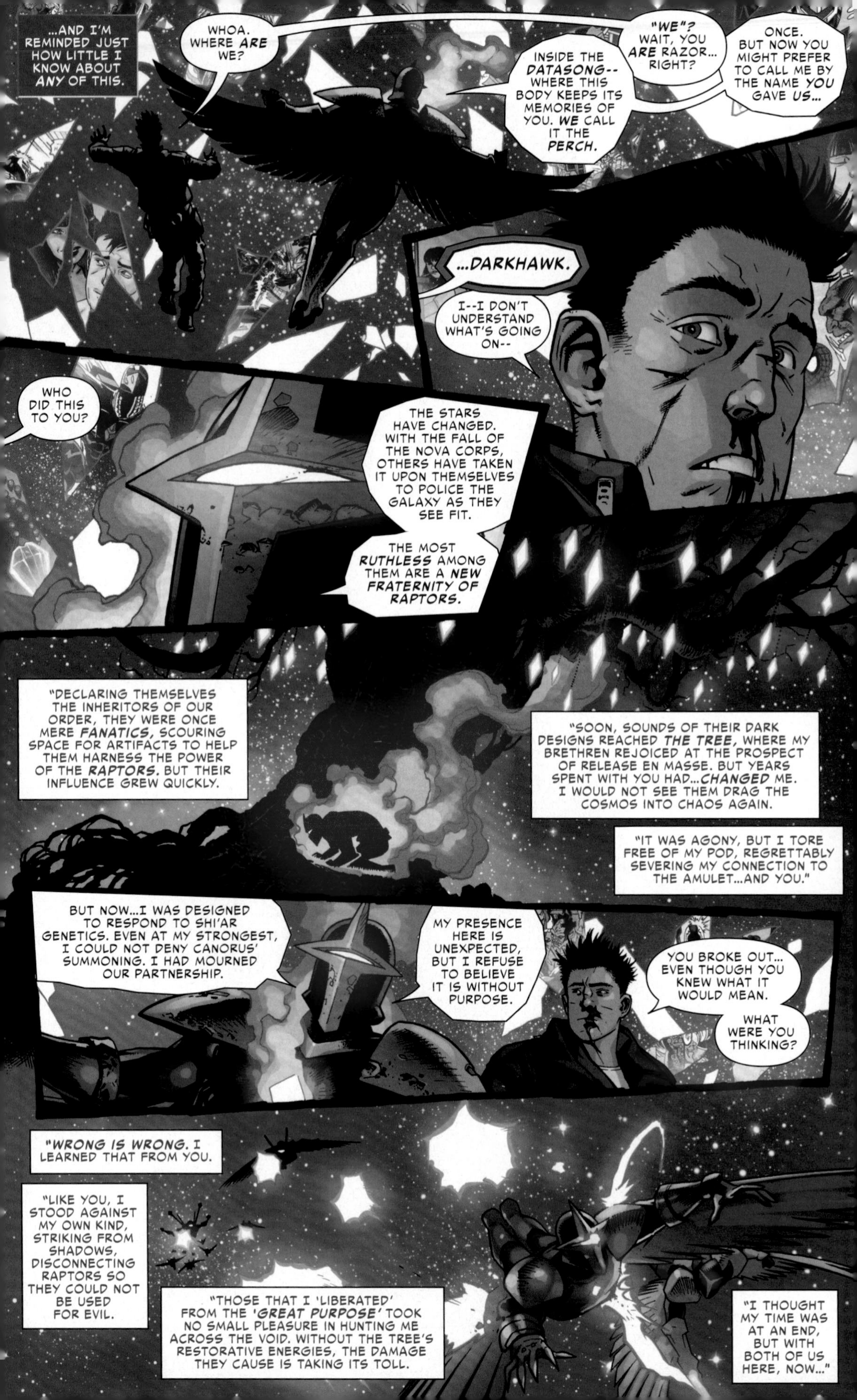
...AND I'M REMINDED JUST HOW LITTLE I KNOW ABOUT ANY OF THIS.
WHOA. WHERE ARE WE?
INSIDE THE DATASONG-- WHERE THIS BODY KEEPS ITS MEMORIES OF YOU. WE CALL IT THE PERCH.
"WE"? WAIT, YOU ARE RAZOR... RIGHT?
ONCE. BUT NOW YOU MIGHT PREFER TO CALL ME BY THE NAME YOU GAVE US...
...DARKHAWK.
I--I DON'T UNDERSTAND WHAT'S GOING ON--
WHO DID THIS TO YOU?
THE STARS HAVE CHANGED. WITH THE FALL OF THE NOVA CORPS, OTHERS HAVE TAKEN IT UPON THEMSELVES TO POLICE THE GALAXY AS THEY SEE FIT.
THE MOST RUTHLESS AMONG THEM ARE A NEW FRATERNITY OF RAPTORS.
"DECLARING THEMSELVES THE INHERITORS OF OUR ORDER, THEY WERE ONCE MERE FANATICS, SCOURING SPACE FOR ARTIFACTS TO HELP THEM HARNESS THE POWER OF THE RAPTORS. BUT THEIR INFLUENCE GREW QUICKLY.
"SOON, SOUNDS OF THEIR DARK DESIGNS REACHED THE TREE, WHERE MY BRETHREN REJOICED AT THE PROSPECT OF RELEASE EN MASSE. BUT YEARS SPENT WITH YOU HAD...CHANGED ME. I WOULD NOT SEE THEM DRAG THE COSMOS INTO CHAOS AGAIN.
"IT WAS AGONY, BUT I TORE FREE OF MY POD, REGRETTABLY SEVERING MY CONNECTION TO THE AMULET...AND YOU."
BUT NOW...I WAS DESIGNED TO RESPOND TO SHI'AR GENETICS. EVEN AT MY STRONGEST, I COULD NOT DENY CANORUS' SUMMONING. I HAD MOURNED OUR PARTNERSHIP.
MY PRESENCE HERE IS UNEXPECTED, BUT I REFUSE TO BELIEVE IT IS WITHOUT PURPOSE.
YOU BROKE OUT... EVEN THOUGH YOU KNEW WHAT IT WOULD MEAN.
WHAT WERE YOU THINKING?
"WRONG IS WRONG. I LEARNED THAT FROM YOU.
"LIKE YOU, I STOOD AGAINST MY OWN KIND, STRIKING FROM SHADOWS, DISCONNECTING RAPTORS SO THEY COULD NOT BE USED FOR EVIL.
"THOSE THAT I 'LIBERATED' FROM THE 'GREAT PURPOSE' TOOK NO SMALL PLEASURE IN HUNTING ME ACROSS THE VOID. WITHOUT THE TREE'S RESTORATIVE ENERGIES, THE DAMAGE THEY CAUSE IS TAKING ITS TOLL.
"I THOUGHT MY TIME WAS AT AN END, BUT WITH BOTH OF US HERE, NOW..."

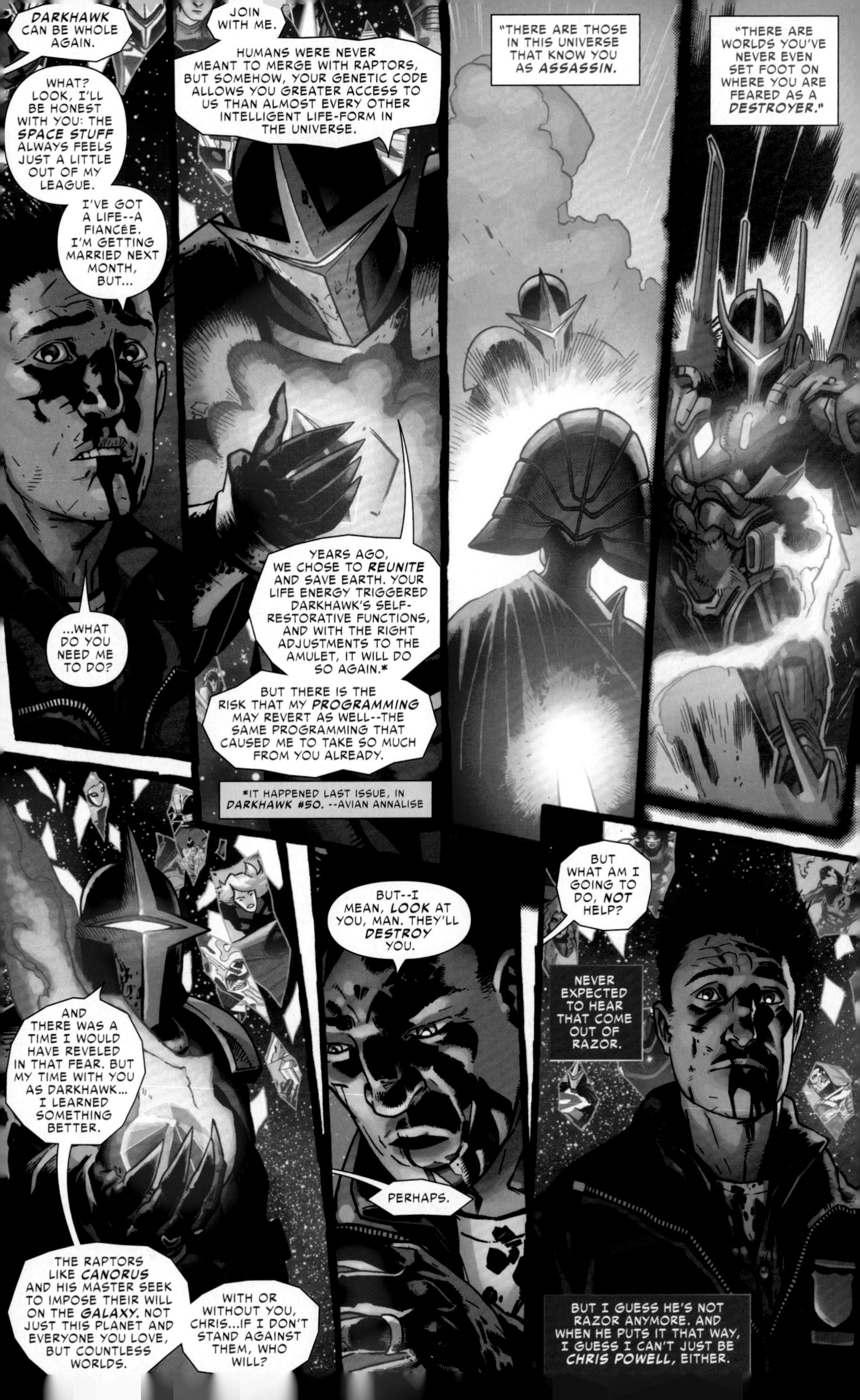

DARKHAWK CAN BE WHOLE AGAIN.
JOIN WITH ME.
HUMANS WERE NEVER MEANT TO MERGE WITH RAPTORS, BUT SOMEHOW, YOUR GENETIC CODE ALLOWS YOU GREATER ACCESS TO US THAN ALMOST EVERY OTHER INTELLIGENT LIFE-FORM IN THE UNIVERSE.
WHAT? LOOK, I'LL BE HONEST WITH YOU: THE SPACE STUFF ALWAYS FEELS JUST A LITTLE OUT OF MY LEAGUE.
I'VE GOT A LIFE--A FIANCÉE. I'M GETTING MARRIED NEXT MONTH, BUT...
...WHAT DO YOU NEED ME TO DO?
YEARS AGO, WE CHOSE TO REUNITE AND SAVE EARTH. YOUR LIFE ENERGY TRIGGERED DARKHAWK'S SELF-RESTORATIVE FUNCTIONS, AND WITH THE RIGHT ADJUSTMENTS TO THE AMULET, IT WILL DO SO AGAIN.*
BUT THERE IS THE RISK THAT MY PROGRAMMING MAY REVERT AS WELL--THE SAME PROGRAMMING THAT CAUSED ME TO TAKE SO MUCH FROM YOU ALREADY.
*IT HAPPENED LAST ISSUE, IN DARKHAWK #50. --AVIAN ANNALISE
"THERE ARE THOSE IN THIS UNIVERSE THAT KNOW YOU AS ASSASSIN.
"THERE ARE WORLDS YOU'VE NEVER EVEN SET FOOT ON WHERE YOU ARE FEARED AS A DESTROYER."
AND THERE WAS A TIME I WOULD HAVE REVELED IN THAT FEAR. BUT MY TIME WITH YOU AS DARKHAWK... I LEARNED SOMETHING BETTER.
THE RAPTORS LIKE CANORUS AND HIS MASTER SEEK TO IMPOSE THEIR WILL ON THE GALAXY. NOT JUST THIS PLANET AND EVERYONE YOU LOVE, BUT COUNTLESS WORLDS.
WITH OR WITHOUT YOU, CHRIS...IF I DON'T STAND AGAINST THEM, WHO WILL?
BUT--I MEAN, LOOK AT YOU, MAN. THEY'LL DESTROY YOU.
PERHAPS.
BUT WHAT AM I GOING TO DO, NOT HELP?
NEVER EXPECTED TO HEAR THAT COME OUT OF RAZOR.
BUT I GUESS HE'S NOT RAZOR ANYMORE. AND WHEN HE PUTS IT THAT WAY, I GUESS I CAN'T JUST BE CHRIS POWELL, EITHER.

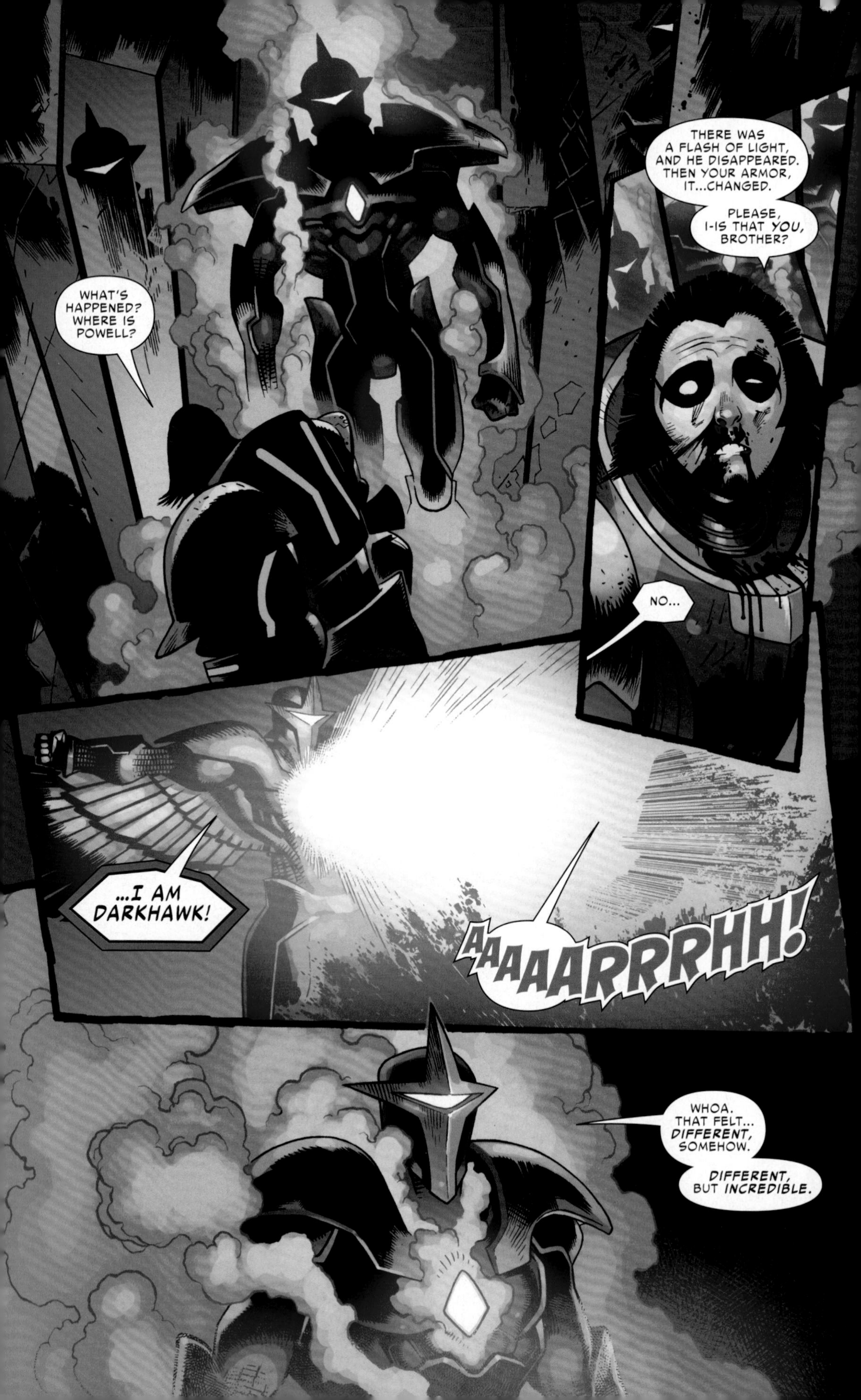

WHAT'S HAPPENED? WHERE IS POWELL?
THERE WAS A FLASH OF LIGHT, AND HE DISAPPEARED. THEN YOUR ARMOR, IT...CHANGED.
PLEASE, I-IS THAT YOU, BROTHER?
NO...
...I AM DARKHAWK!
AAAAARRRRHH!
WHOA. THAT FELT... DIFFERENT, SOMEHOW.
DIFFERENT, BUT INCREDIBLE.

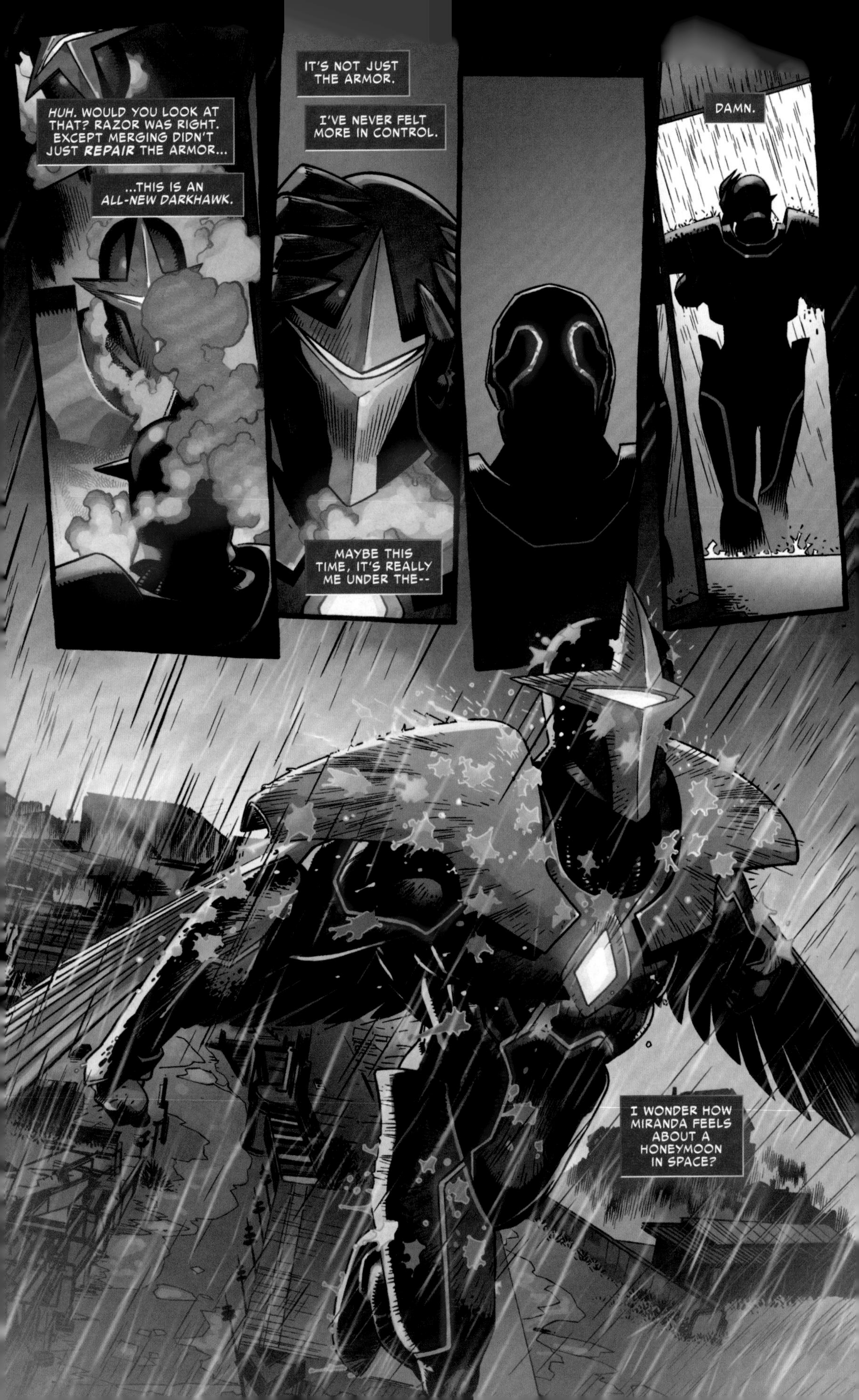
HUH. WOULD YOU LOOK AT THAT? RAZOR WAS RIGHT. EXCEPT MERGING DIDN'T JUST REPAIR THE ARMOR...
...THIS IS AN ALL-NEW DARKHAWK.
IT'S NOT JUST THE ARMOR.
I'VE NEVER FELT MORE IN CONTROL.
MAYBE THIS TIME, IT'S REALLY ME UNDER THE--
DAMN.
I WONDER HOW MIRANDA FEELS ABOUT A HONEYMOON IN SPACE?

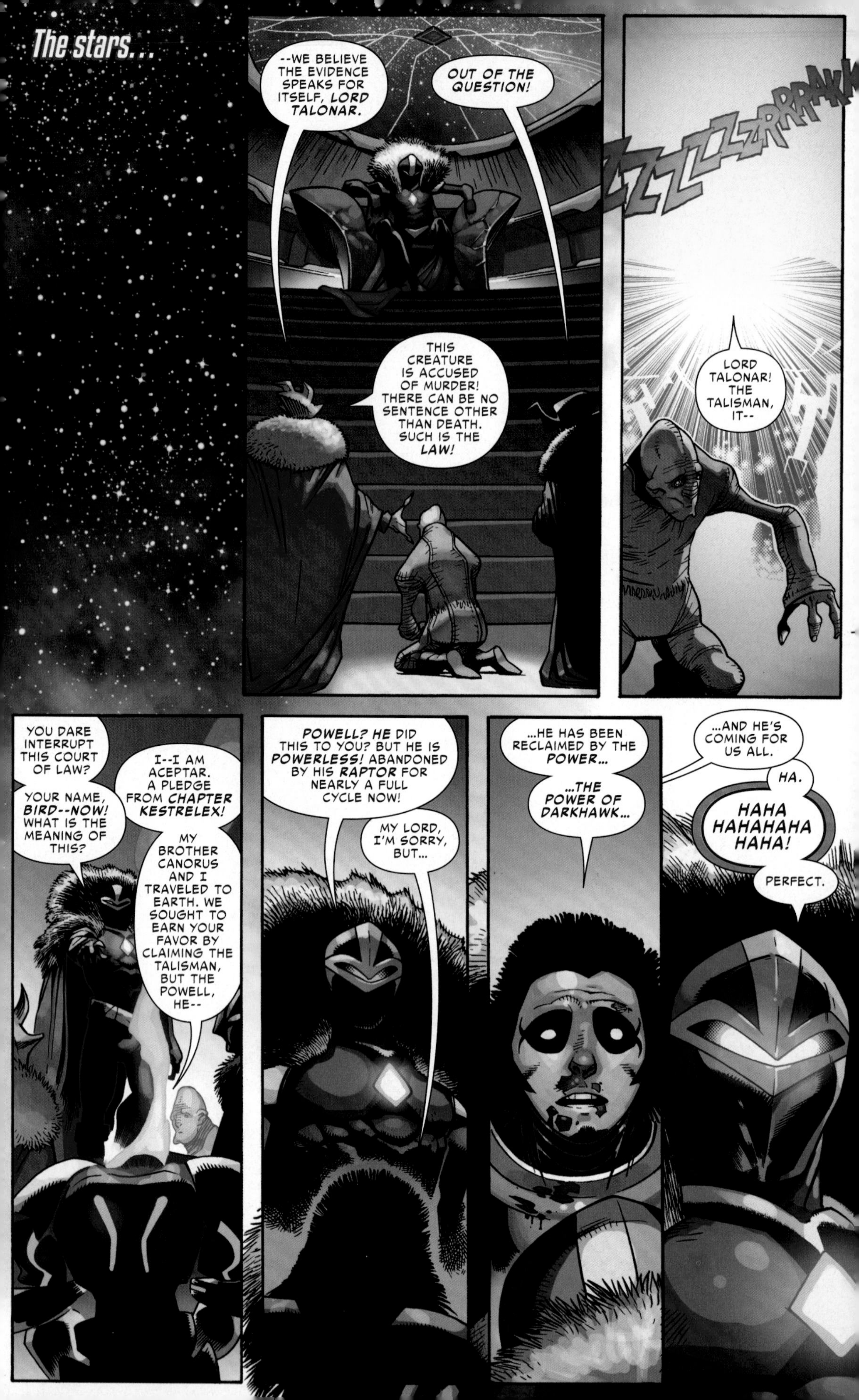
The stars...
--WE BELIEVE THE EVIDENCE SPEAKS FOR ITSELF, LORD TALONAR.
OUT OF THE QUESTION!
THIS CREATURE IS ACCUSED OF MURDER! THERE CAN BE NO SENTENCE OTHER THAN DEATH. SUCH IS THE LAW!
ZZZZZZRRRAKK
LORD TALONAR! THE TALISMAN, IT--
YOU DARE INTERRUPT THIS COURT OF LAW?
YOUR NAME, BIRD--NOW! WHAT IS THE MEANING OF THIS?
I--I AM ACEPTAR. A PLEDGE FROM CHAPTER KESTRELEX!
MY BROTHER CANORUS AND I TRAVELED TO EARTH. WE SOUGHT TO EARN YOUR FAVOR BY CLAIMING THE TALISMAN, BUT THE POWELL, HE--
POWELL? HE DID THIS TO YOU? BUT HE IS POWERLESS! ABANDONED BY HIS RAPTOR FOR NEARLY A FULL CYCLE NOW!
MY LORD, I'M SORRY, BUT...
...HE HAS BEEN RECLAIMED BY THE POWER...
...THE POWER OF DARKHAWK...
...AND HE'S COMING FOR US ALL.
HA.
HAHA HAHAHAHA HAHA!
PERFECT.

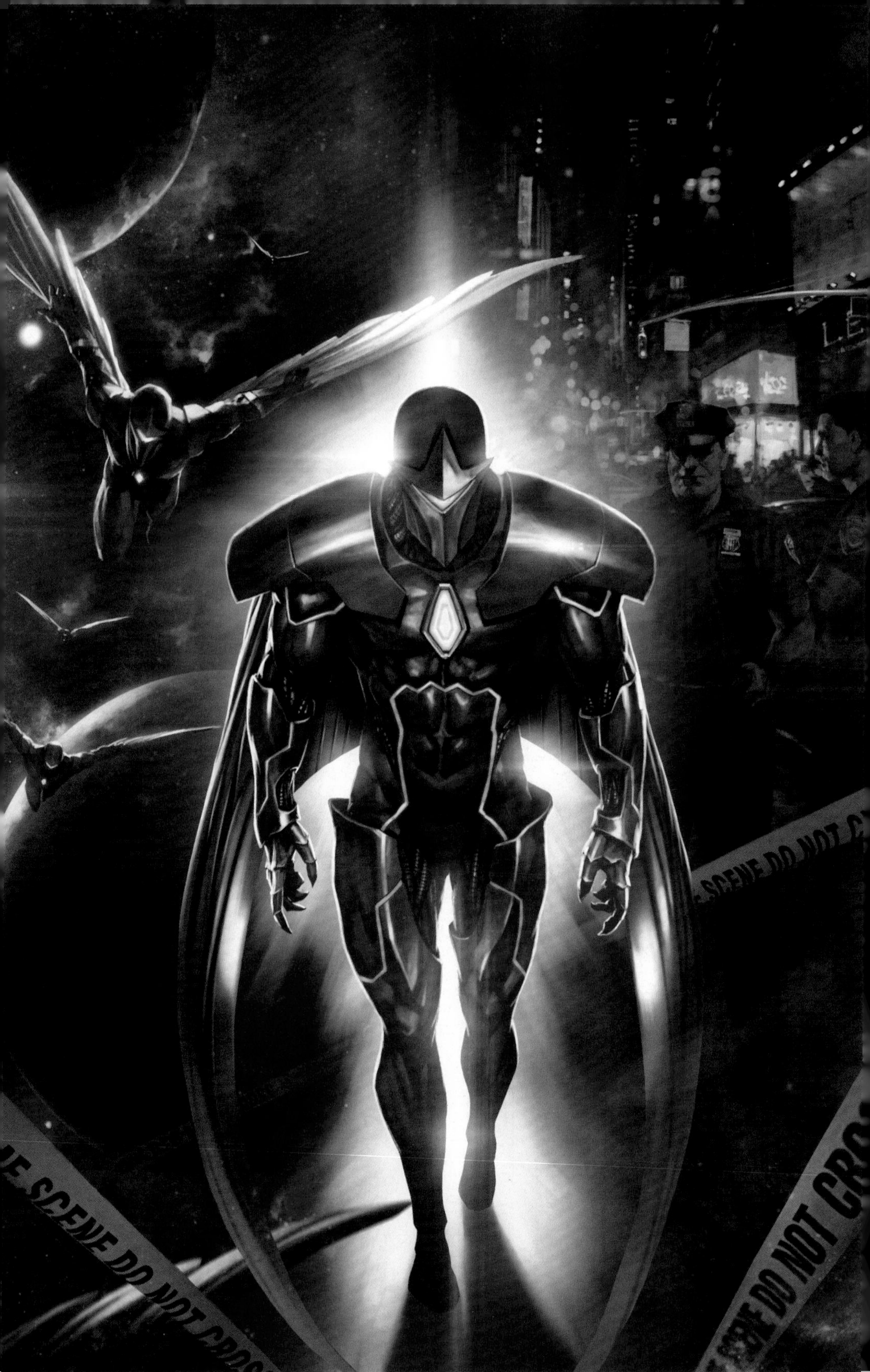
SCENE DO NOT
SCENE DO NOT
SCENE DO NOT CRO

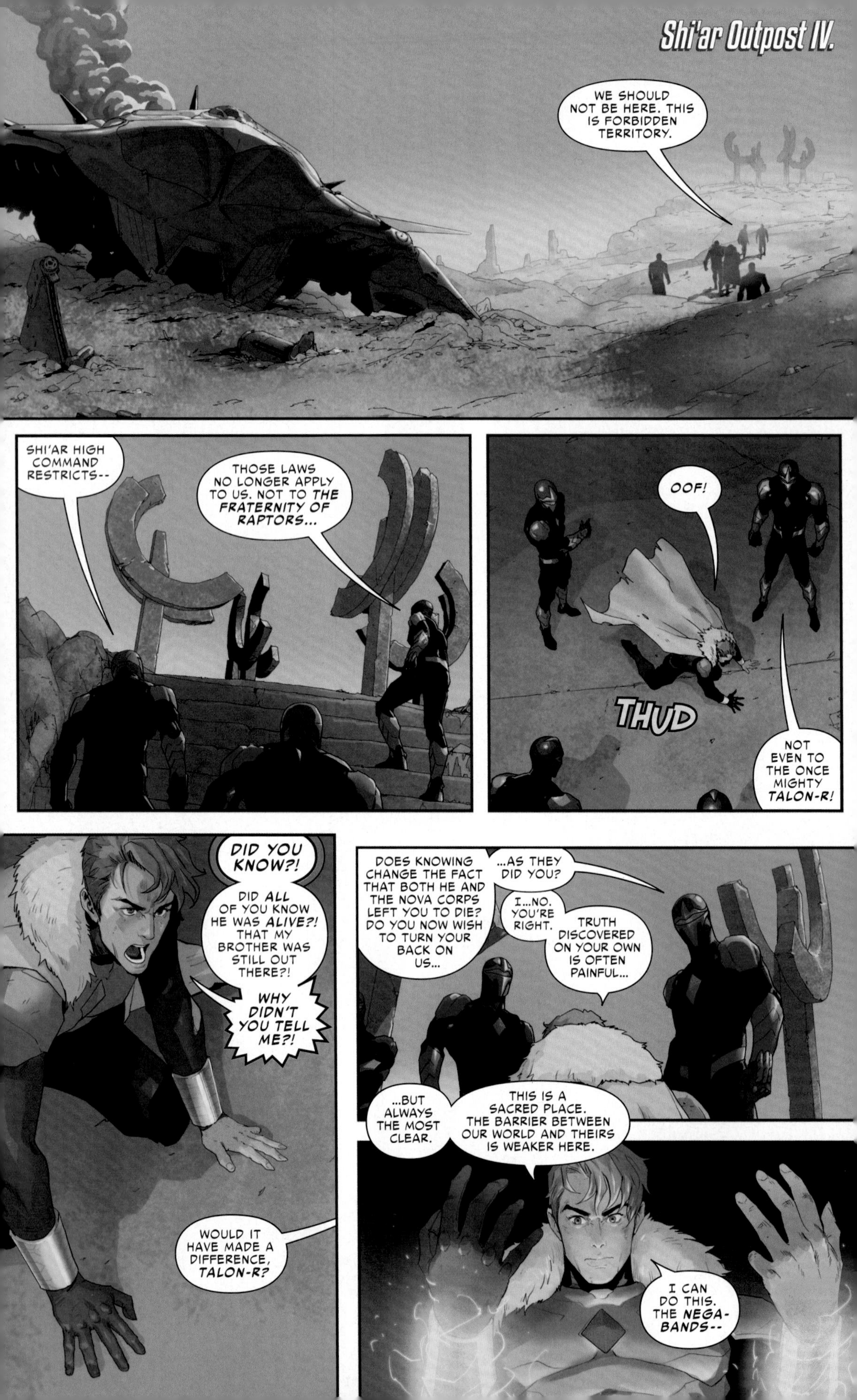

Shi'ar Outpost IV.
WE SHOULD NOT BE HERE. THIS IS FORBIDDEN TERRITORY.
SHI'AR HIGH COMMAND RESTRICTS--
THOSE LAWS NO LONGER APPLY TO US. NOT TO THE FRATERNITY OF RAPTORS...
OOF!
THUD
NOT EVEN TO THE ONCE MIGHTY TALON-R!
DID YOU KNOW?!
DID ALL OF YOU KNOW HE WAS ALIVE?! THAT MY BROTHER WAS STILL OUT THERE?!
WHY DIDN'T YOU TELL ME?!
WOULD IT HAVE MADE A DIFFERENCE, TALON-R?
DOES KNOWING CHANGE THE FACT THAT BOTH HE AND THE NOVA CORPS LEFT YOU TO DIE? DO YOU NOW WISH TO TURN YOUR BACK ON US...
...AS THEY DID YOU?
I...NO. YOU'RE RIGHT.
TRUTH DISCOVERED ON YOUR OWN IS OFTEN PAINFUL...
...BUT ALWAYS THE MOST CLEAR.
THIS IS A SACRED PLACE. THE BARRIER BETWEEN OUR WORLD AND THEIRS IS WEAKER HERE.
I CAN DO THIS. THE NEGA-BANDS--

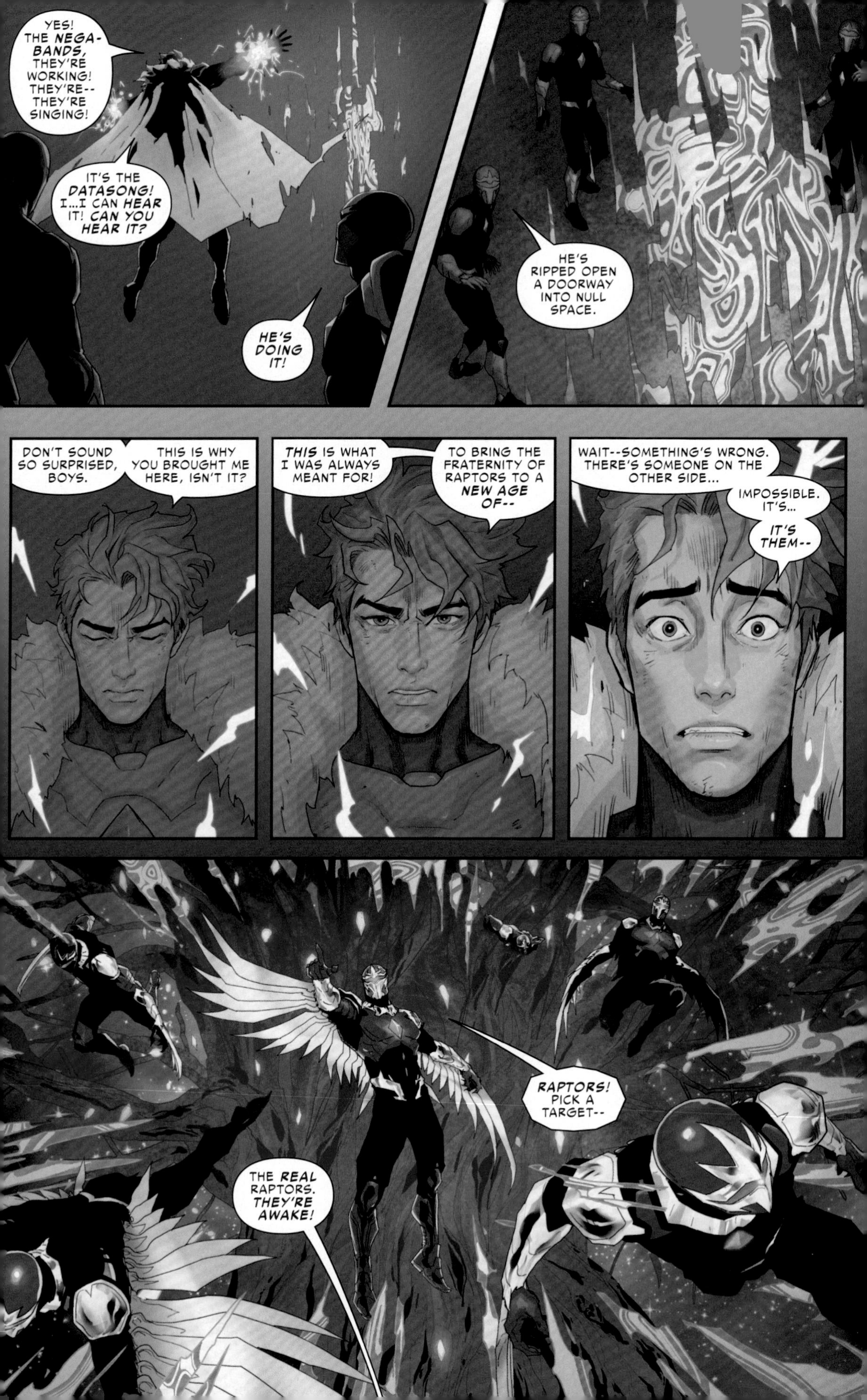
YES! THE NEGA-BANDS, THEY'RE WORKING! THEY'RE--THEY'RE SINGING!
IT'S THE DATASONG! I...I CAN HEAR IT! CAN YOU HEAR IT?
HE'S DOING IT!
HE'S RIPPED OPEN A DOORWAY INTO NULL SPACE.
DON'T SOUND SO SURPRISED, BOYS.
THIS IS WHY YOU BROUGHT ME HERE, ISN'T IT?
THIS IS WHAT I WAS ALWAYS MEANT FOR!
TO BRING THE FRATERNITY OF RAPTORS TO A NEW AGE OF--
WAIT--SOMETHING'S WRONG. THERE'S SOMEONE ON THE OTHER SIDE...
IMPOSSIBLE. IT'S...
IT'S THEM--
RAPTORS! PICK A TARGET--
THE REAL RAPTORS. THEY'RE AWAKE!

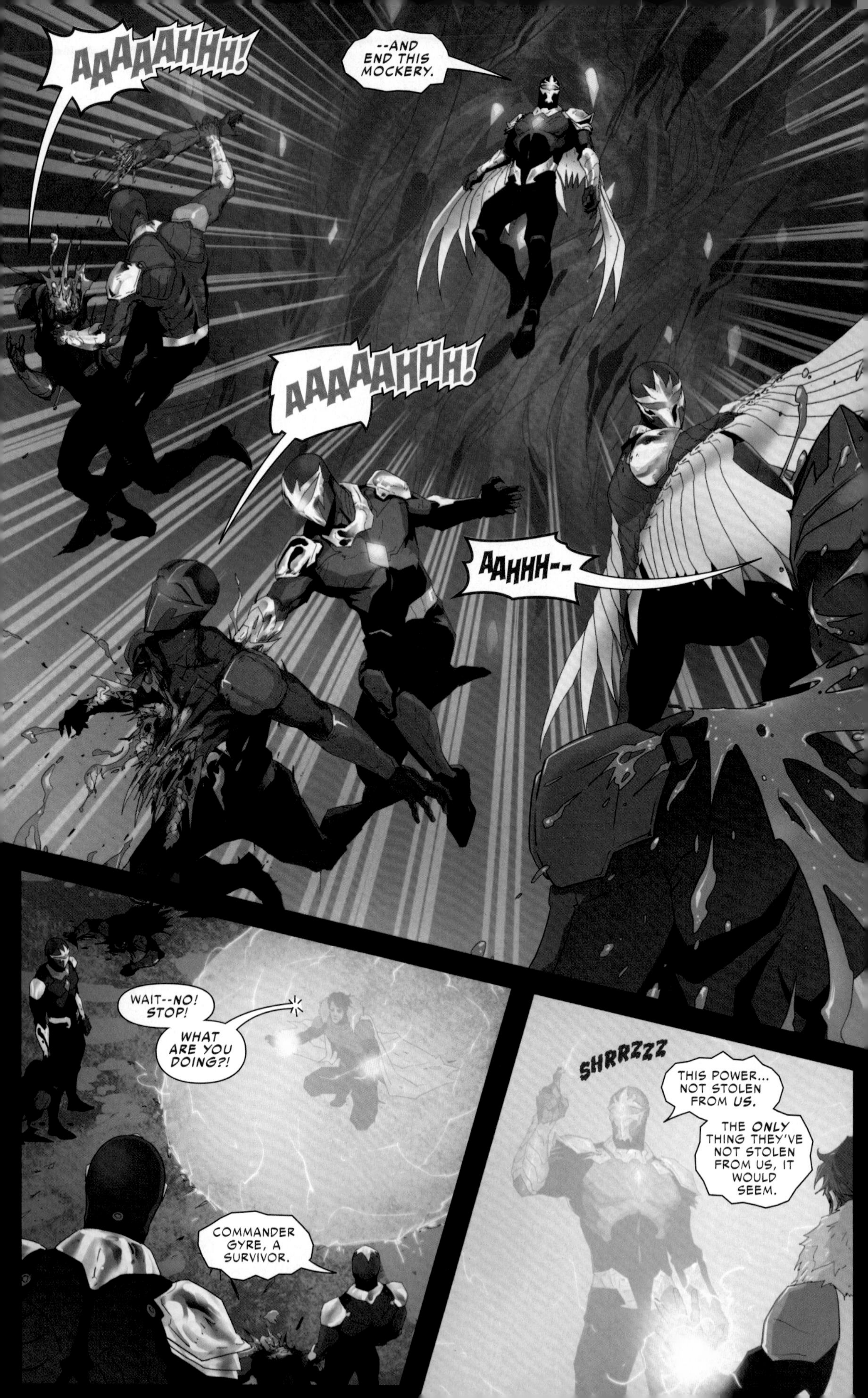
AAAAAHHH!
--AND END THIS MOCKERY.
AAAAAHHH!
AAHHH--
WAIT--NO! STOP!
WHAT ARE YOU DOING?!
COMMANDER GYRE, A SURVIVOR.
SHRRZZZ
THIS POWER... NOT STOLEN FROM US.
THE ONLY THING THEY'VE NOT STOLEN FROM US, IT WOULD SEEM.

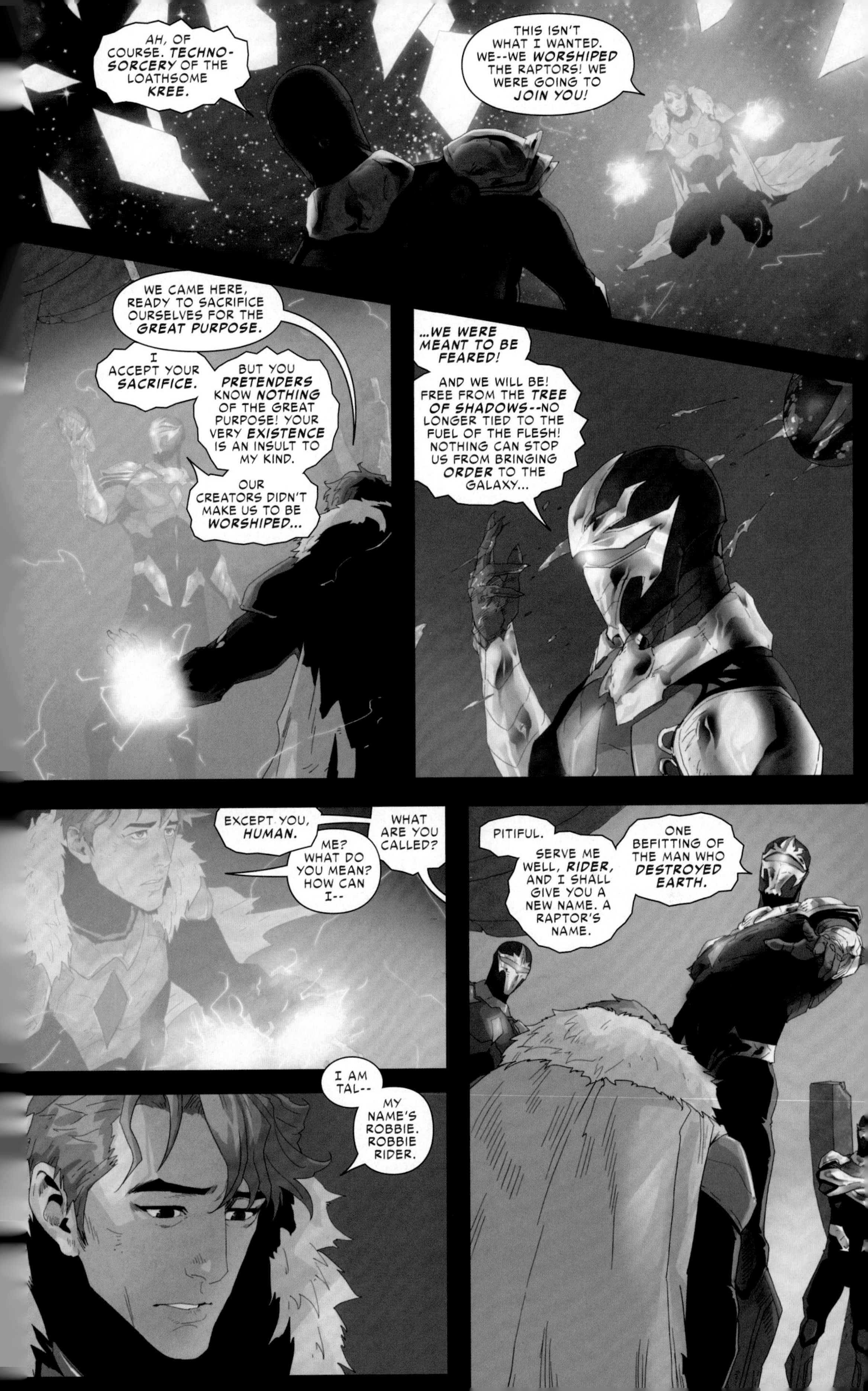
AH, OF COURSE. TECHNO-SORCERY OF THE LOATHSOME KREE.
THIS ISN'T WHAT I WANTED. WE--WE WORSHIPED THE RAPTORS! WE WERE GOING TO JOIN YOU!
WE CAME HERE, READY TO SACRIFICE OURSELVES FOR THE GREAT PURPOSE.
I ACCEPT YOUR SACRIFICE.
BUT YOU PRETENDERS KNOW NOTHING OF THE GREAT PURPOSE! YOUR VERY EXISTENCE IS AN INSULT TO MY KIND.
OUR CREATORS DIDN'T MAKE US TO BE WORSHIPED...
...WE WERE MEANT TO BE FEARED!
AND WE WILL BE! FREE FROM THE TREE OF SHADOWS--NO LONGER TIED TO THE FUEL OF THE FLESH! NOTHING CAN STOP US FROM BRINGING ORDER TO THE GALAXY...
EXCEPT YOU, HUMAN.
ME? WHAT DO YOU MEAN? HOW CAN I--
WHAT ARE YOU CALLED?
I AM TAL--
MY NAME'S ROBBIE. ROBBIE RIDER.
PITIFUL.
SERVE ME WELL, RIDER, AND I SHALL GIVE YOU A NEW NAME. A RAPTOR'S NAME.
ONE BEFITTING OF THE MAN WHO DESTROYED EARTH.

INFINITY
COUNTDOWN

CHRIS POWELL DIDN'T KNOW WHERE THE AMULET CAME FROM. ALL HE KNEW WAS THAT WHEN HE GRASPED IT, HE TRANSFORMED INTO A BEING OF GREAT POWER. WHEN HE WAS YOUNG, HE USED THAT POWER TO DEFEAT CRIME, BUT NOW HE KEEPS THE STREETS CLEAN AS A POLICE OFFICER. IT HAS BEEN A LONG TIME SINCE CHRIS WAS...

DARKHAWK

THE INFINITY STONES WERE REBORN AND SCATTERED, PASSING FROM HAND TO HAND ACROSS THE UNIVERSE AND THROUGH TIME, TRANSGRESSING THE BOUNDARIES BETWEEN WORLDS...

THE FRATERNITY OF RAPTORS RECENTLY FACED A MAJOR DEFEAT IN THEIR QUEST FOR THE STONES.

MEANWHILE, CHRIS HAD AN ENCOUNTER THAT NOT ONLY REAWAKENED HIS ABILITY TO TRANSFORM...IT CONNECTED CHRIS TO THE DARKHAWK ARMOR LIKE NEVER BEFORE!

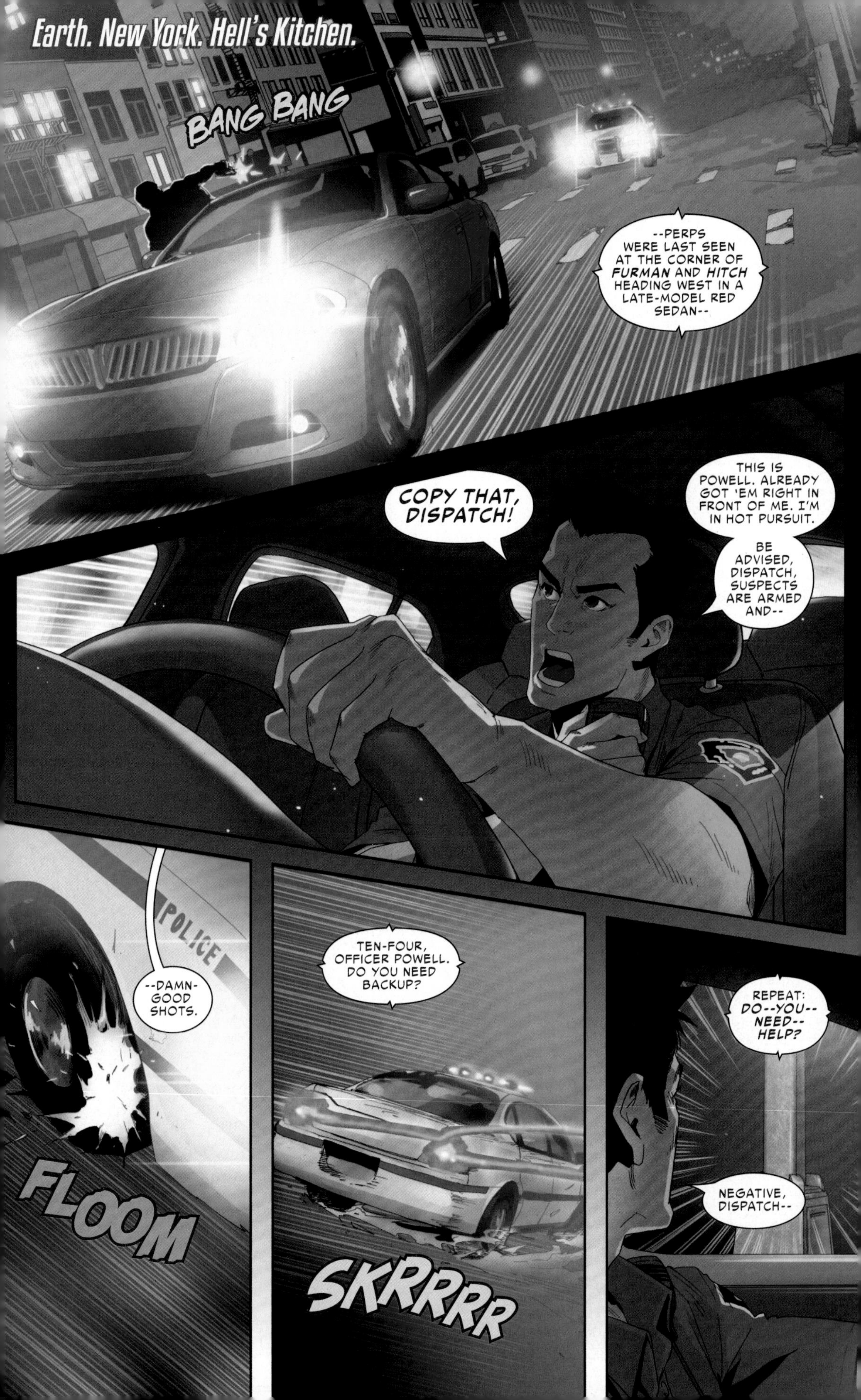
Earth. New York. Hell's Kitchen.
BANG BANG
--PERPS WERE LAST SEEN AT THE CORNER OF FURMAN AND HITCH HEADING WEST IN A LATE-MODEL RED SEDAN--
COPY THAT, DISPATCH!
THIS IS POWELL. ALREADY GOT 'EM RIGHT IN FRONT OF ME. I'M IN HOT PURSUIT.
BE ADVISED, DISPATCH, SUSPECTS ARE ARMED AND--
POLICE
--DAMN-GOOD SHOTS.
FLOOM
TEN-FOUR, OFFICER POWELL. DO YOU NEED BACKUP?
SKRRRR
REPEAT: DO--YOU--NEED--HELP?
NEGATIVE, DISPATCH--

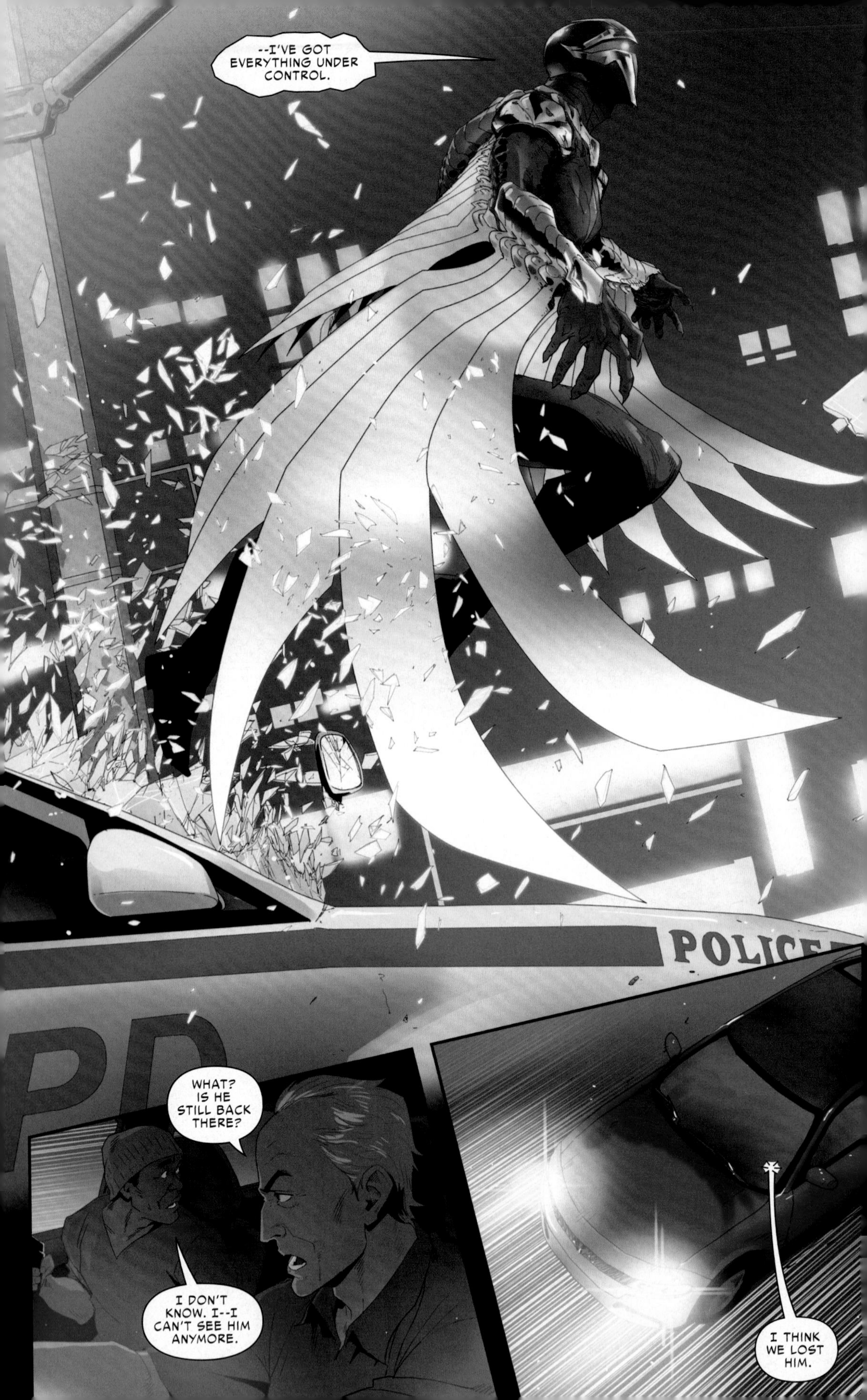
--I'VE GOT EVERYTHING UNDER CONTROL.
POLICE
PD
WHAT? IS HE STILL BACK THERE?
I DON'T KNOW. I--I CAN'T SEE HIM ANYMORE.
I THINK WE LOST HIM.

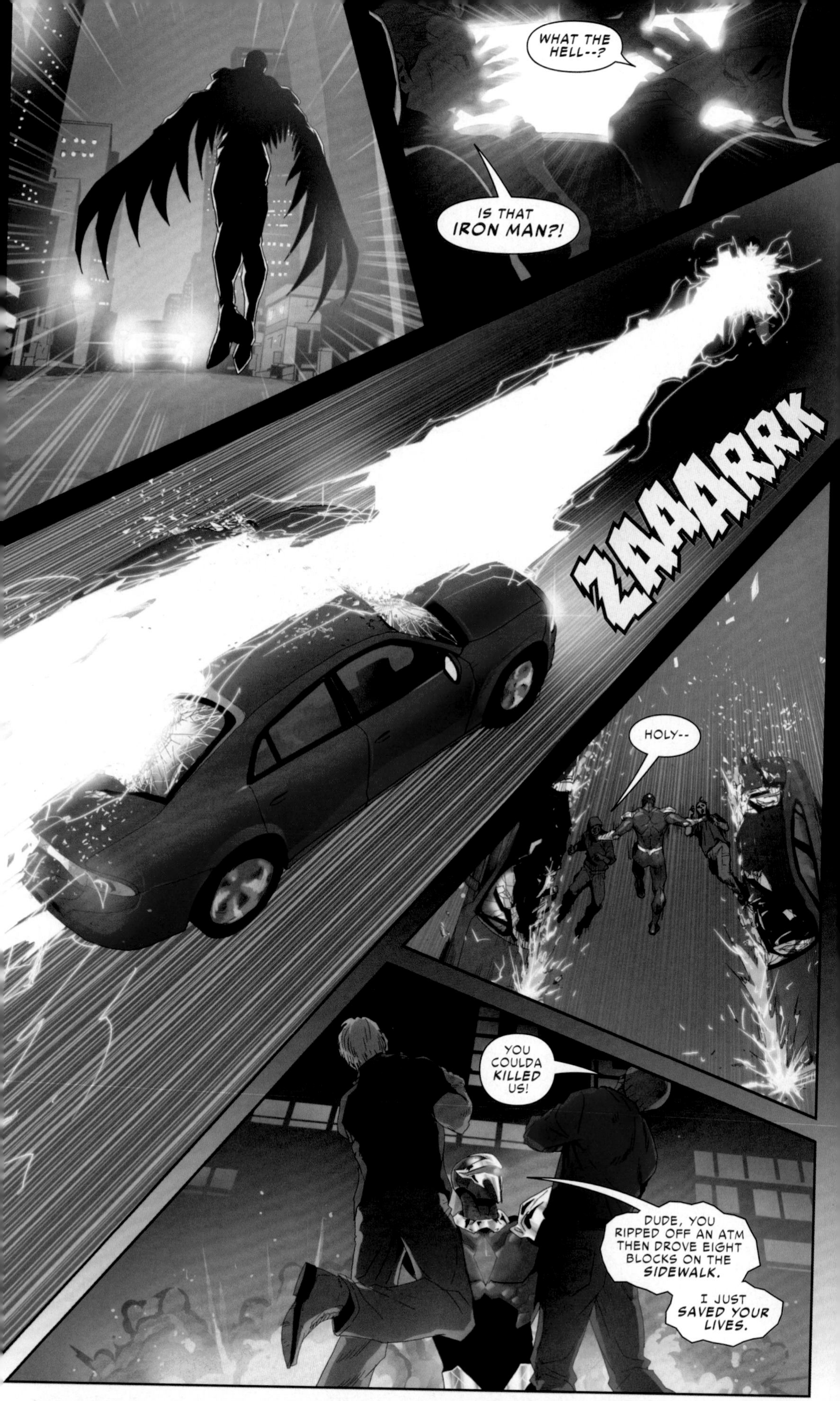
WHAT THE HELL--?
IS THAT IRON MAN?!
ZAAARRK
HOLY--
YOU COULDA KILLED US!
DUDE, YOU RIPPED OFF AN ATM THEN DROVE EIGHT BLOCKS ON THE SIDEWALK.
I JUST SAVED YOUR LIVES.

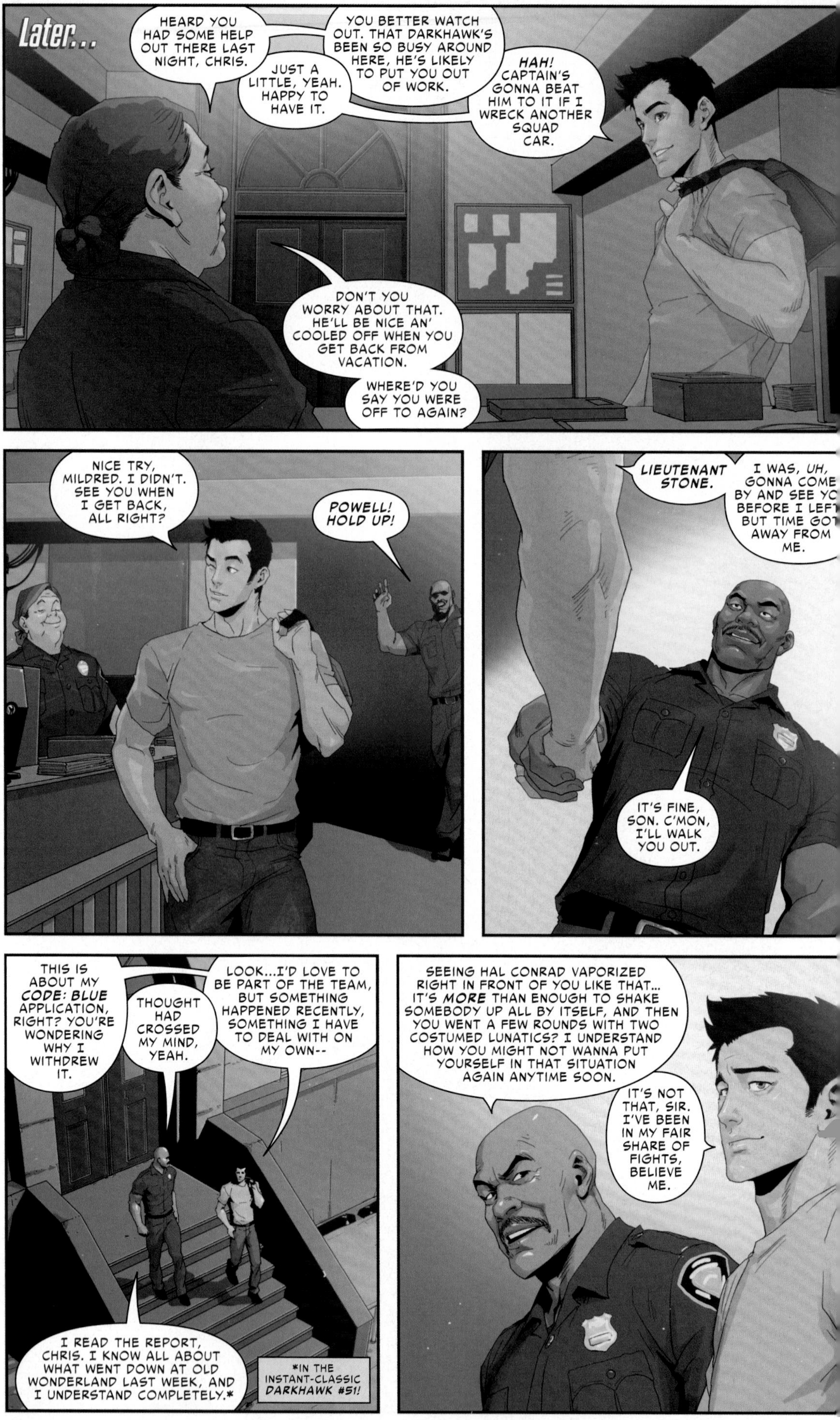
Later...
HEARD YOU HAD SOME HELP OUT THERE LAST NIGHT, CHRIS.
JUST A LITTLE, YEAH. HAPPY TO HAVE IT.
YOU BETTER WATCH OUT. THAT DARKHAWK'S BEEN SO BUSY AROUND HERE, HE'S LIKELY TO PUT YOU OUT OF WORK.
HAH! CAPTAIN'S GONNA BEAT HIM TO IT IF I WRECK ANOTHER SQUAD CAR.
DON'T YOU WORRY ABOUT THAT. HE'LL BE NICE AN' COOLED OFF WHEN YOU GET BACK FROM VACATION.
WHERE'D YOU SAY YOU WERE OFF TO AGAIN?
NICE TRY, MILDRED. I DIDN'T. SEE YOU WHEN I GET BACK, ALL RIGHT?
POWELL! HOLD UP!
LIEUTENANT STONE.
I WAS, UH, GONNA COME BY AND SEE YO BEFORE I LEF BUT TIME GOT AWAY FROM ME.
IT'S FINE, SON. C'MON, I'LL WALK YOU OUT.
THIS IS ABOUT MY CODE: BLUE APPLICATION, RIGHT? YOU'RE WONDERING WHY I WITHDREW IT.
THOUGHT HAD CROSSED MY MIND, YEAH.
LOOK...I'D LOVE TO BE PART OF THE TEAM, BUT SOMETHING HAPPENED RECENTLY, SOMETHING I HAVE TO DEAL WITH ON MY OWN--
I READ THE REPORT, CHRIS. I KNOW ALL ABOUT WHAT WENT DOWN AT OLD WONDERLAND LAST WEEK, AND I UNDERSTAND COMPLETELY.*
*IN THE INSTANT-CLASSIC DARKHAWK #51!
SEEING HAL CONRAD VAPORIZED RIGHT IN FRONT OF YOU LIKE THAT... IT'S MORE THAN ENOUGH TO SHAKE SOMEBODY UP ALL BY ITSELF, AND THEN YOU WENT A FEW ROUNDS WITH TWO COSTUMED LUNATICS? I UNDERSTAND HOW YOU MIGHT NOT WANNA PUT YOURSELF IN THAT SITUATION AGAIN ANYTIME SOON.
IT'S NOT THAT, SIR. I'VE BEEN IN MY FAIR SHARE OF FIGHTS, BELIEVE ME.

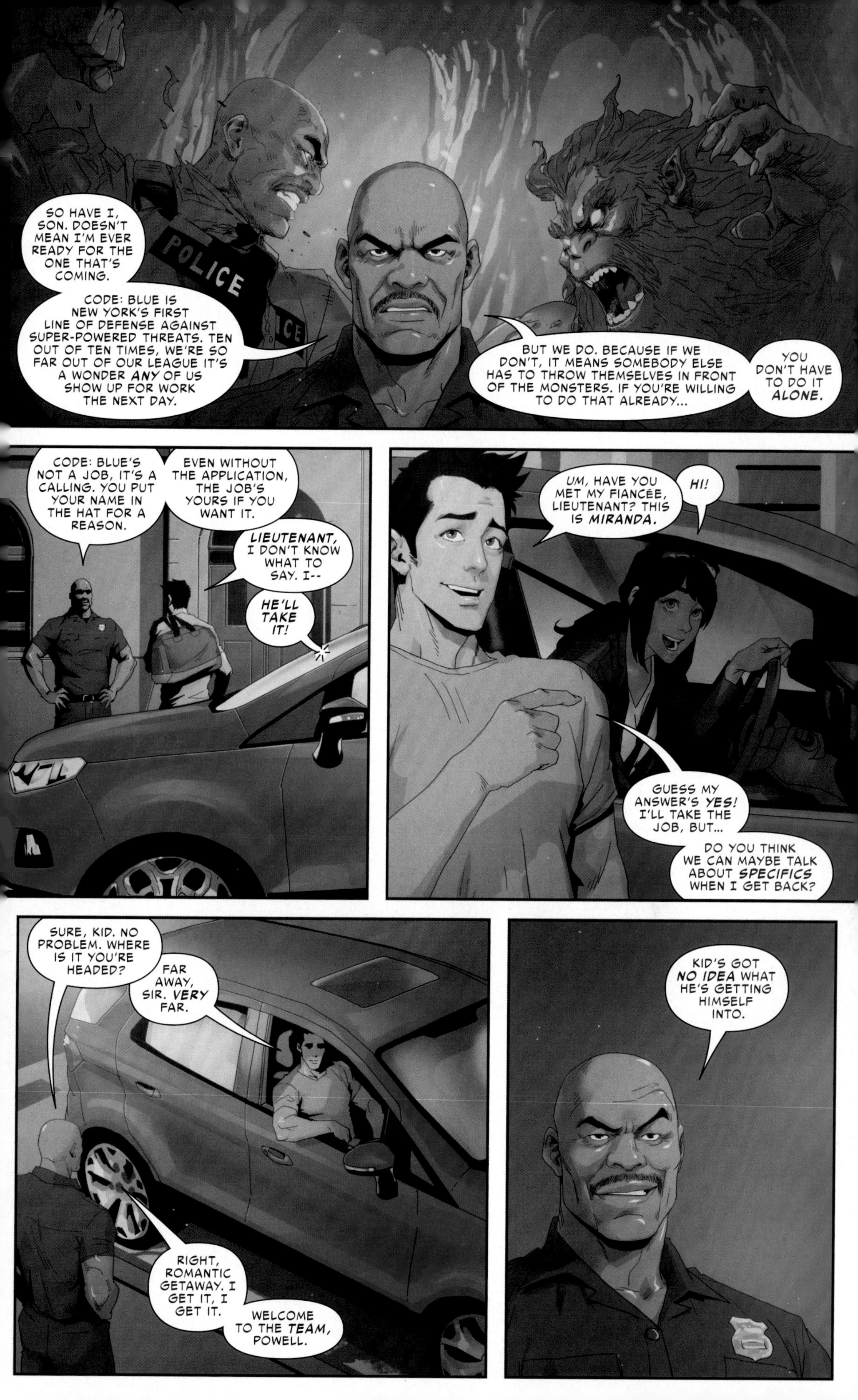
SO HAVE I, SON. DOESN'T MEAN I'M EVER READY FOR THE ONE THAT'S COMING.
CODE: BLUE IS NEW YORK'S FIRST LINE OF DEFENSE AGAINST SUPER-POWERED THREATS. TEN OUT OF TEN TIMES, WE'RE SO FAR OUT OF OUR LEAGUE IT'S A WONDER *ANY* OF US SHOW UP FOR WORK THE NEXT DAY.
BUT WE DO. BECAUSE IF WE DON'T, IT MEANS SOMEBODY ELSE HAS TO THROW THEMSELVES IN FRONT OF THE MONSTERS. IF YOU'RE WILLING TO DO THAT ALREADY...
YOU DON'T HAVE TO DO IT *ALONE.*
CODE: BLUE'S NOT A JOB, IT'S A CALLING. YOU PUT YOUR NAME IN THE HAT FOR A REASON.
EVEN WITHOUT THE APPLICATION, THE JOB'S YOURS IF YOU WANT IT.
LIEUTENANT, I DON'T KNOW WHAT TO SAY. I--
HE'LL TAKE IT!
UM, HAVE YOU MET MY FIANCÉE, LIEUTENANT? THIS IS *MIRANDA.*
HI!
GUESS MY ANSWER'S *YES!* I'LL TAKE THE JOB, BUT...
DO YOU THINK WE CAN MAYBE TALK ABOUT *SPECIFICS* WHEN I GET BACK?
SURE, KID. NO PROBLEM. WHERE IS IT YOU'RE HEADED?
FAR AWAY, SIR. *VERY* FAR.
RIGHT, ROMANTIC GETAWAY. I GET IT, I GET IT.
WELCOME TO THE *TEAM,* POWELL.
KID'S GOT *NO IDEA* WHAT HE'S GETTING HIMSELF INTO.

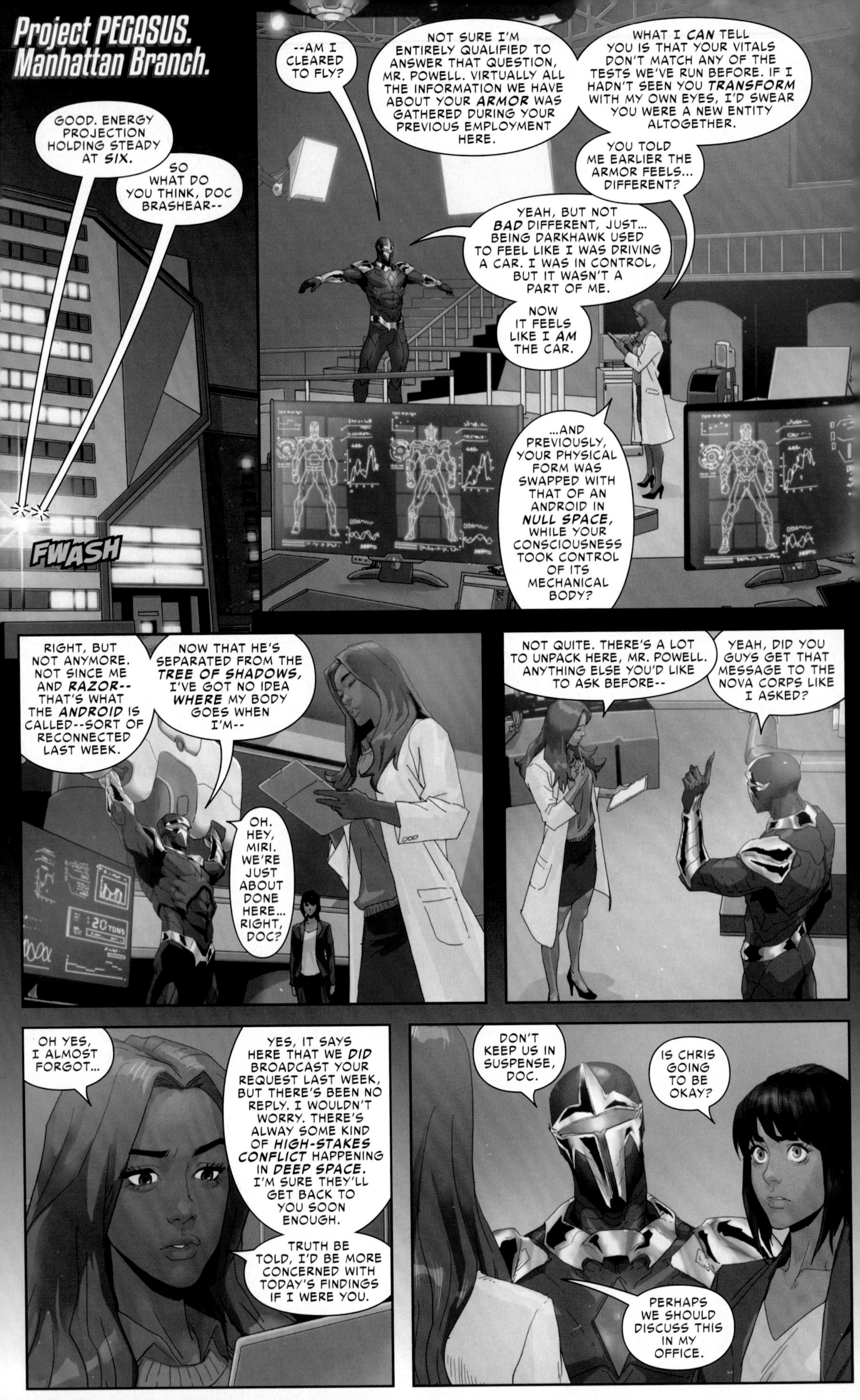
Project PEGASUS. Manhattan Branch.
GOOD. ENERGY PROJECTION HOLDING STEADY AT SIX.
SO WHAT DO YOU THINK, DOC BRASHEAR--
FWASH
--AM I CLEARED TO FLY?
NOT SURE I'M ENTIRELY QUALIFIED TO ANSWER THAT QUESTION, MR. POWELL. VIRTUALLY ALL THE INFORMATION WE HAVE ABOUT YOUR ARMOR WAS GATHERED DURING YOUR PREVIOUS EMPLOYMENT HERE.
WHAT I CAN TELL YOU IS THAT YOUR VITALS DON'T MATCH ANY OF THE TESTS WE'VE RUN BEFORE. IF I HADN'T SEEN YOU TRANSFORM WITH MY OWN EYES, I'D SWEAR YOU WERE A NEW ENTITY ALTOGETHER.
YOU TOLD ME EARLIER THE ARMOR FEELS... DIFFERENT?
YEAH, BUT NOT BAD DIFFERENT, JUST... BEING DARKHAWK USED TO FEEL LIKE I WAS DRIVING A CAR. I WAS IN CONTROL, BUT IT WASN'T A PART OF ME.
NOW IT FEELS LIKE I AM THE CAR.
...AND PREVIOUSLY, YOUR PHYSICAL FORM WAS SWAPPED WITH THAT OF AN ANDROID IN NULL SPACE, WHILE YOUR CONSCIOUSNESS TOOK CONTROL OF ITS MECHANICAL BODY?
RIGHT, BUT NOT ANYMORE. NOT SINCE ME AND RAZOR--THAT'S WHAT THE ANDROID IS CALLED--SORT OF RECONNECTED LAST WEEK.
NOW THAT HE'S SEPARATED FROM THE TREE OF SHADOWS, I'VE GOT NO IDEA WHERE MY BODY GOES WHEN I'M--
OH. HEY, MIRI. WE'RE JUST ABOUT DONE HERE... RIGHT, DOC?
20 TONS
NOT QUITE. THERE'S A LOT TO UNPACK HERE, MR. POWELL. ANYTHING ELSE YOU'D LIKE TO ASK BEFORE--
YEAH, DID YOU GUYS GET THAT MESSAGE TO THE NOVA CORPS LIKE I ASKED?
OH YES, I ALMOST FORGOT...
YES, IT SAYS HERE THAT WE DID BROADCAST YOUR REQUEST LAST WEEK, BUT THERE'S BEEN NO REPLY. I WOULDN'T WORRY. THERE'S ALWAY SOME KIND OF HIGH-STAKES CONFLICT HAPPENING IN DEEP SPACE. I'M SURE THEY'LL GET BACK TO YOU SOON ENOUGH.
TRUTH BE TOLD, I'D BE MORE CONCERNED WITH TODAY'S FINDINGS IF I WERE YOU.
DON'T KEEP US IN SUSPENSE, DOC.
IS CHRIS GOING TO BE OKAY?
PERHAPS WE SHOULD DISCUSS THIS IN MY OFFICE.

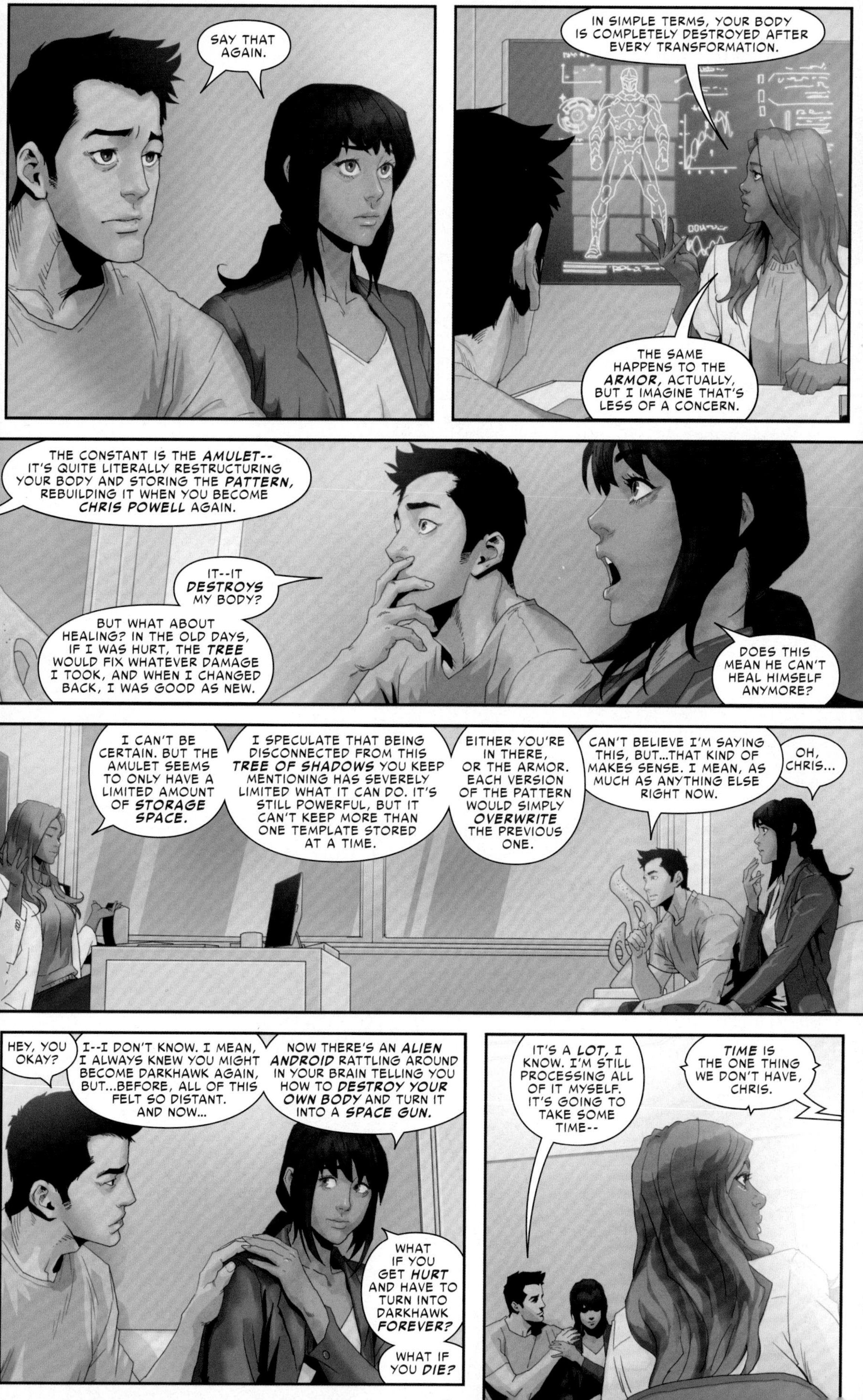
SAY THAT AGAIN.
IN SIMPLE TERMS, YOUR BODY IS COMPLETELY DESTROYED AFTER EVERY TRANSFORMATION.
THE SAME HAPPENS TO THE ARMOR, ACTUALLY, BUT I IMAGINE THAT'S LESS OF A CONCERN.
THE CONSTANT IS THE AMULET-- IT'S QUITE LITERALLY RESTRUCTURING YOUR BODY AND STORING THE PATTERN, REBUILDING IT WHEN YOU BECOME CHRIS POWELL AGAIN.
IT--IT DESTROYS MY BODY?
BUT WHAT ABOUT HEALING? IN THE OLD DAYS, IF I WAS HURT, THE TREE WOULD FIX WHATEVER DAMAGE I TOOK, AND WHEN I CHANGED BACK, I WAS GOOD AS NEW.
DOES THIS MEAN HE CAN'T HEAL HIMSELF ANYMORE?
I CAN'T BE CERTAIN. BUT THE AMULET SEEMS TO ONLY HAVE A LIMITED AMOUNT OF STORAGE SPACE.
I SPECULATE THAT BEING DISCONNECTED FROM THIS TREE OF SHADOWS YOU KEEP MENTIONING HAS SEVERELY LIMITED WHAT IT CAN DO. IT'S STILL POWERFUL, BUT IT CAN'T KEEP MORE THAN ONE TEMPLATE STORED AT A TIME.
EITHER YOU'RE IN THERE, OR THE ARMOR. EACH VERSION OF THE PATTERN WOULD SIMPLY OVERWRITE THE PREVIOUS ONE.
CAN'T BELIEVE I'M SAYING THIS, BUT...THAT KIND OF MAKES SENSE. I MEAN, AS MUCH AS ANYTHING ELSE RIGHT NOW.
OH, CHRIS...
HEY, YOU OKAY?
I--I DON'T KNOW. I MEAN, I ALWAYS KNEW YOU MIGHT BECOME DARKHAWK AGAIN, BUT...BEFORE, ALL OF THIS FELT SO DISTANT. AND NOW...
NOW THERE'S AN ALIEN ANDROID RATTLING AROUND IN YOUR BRAIN TELLING YOU HOW TO DESTROY YOUR OWN BODY AND TURN IT INTO A SPACE GUN.
WHAT IF YOU GET HURT AND HAVE TO TURN INTO DARKHAWK FOREVER?
WHAT IF YOU DIE?
IT'S A LOT, I KNOW. I'M STILL PROCESSING ALL OF IT MYSELF. IT'S GOING TO TAKE SOME TIME--
TIME IS THE ONE THING WE DON'T HAVE, CHRIS.

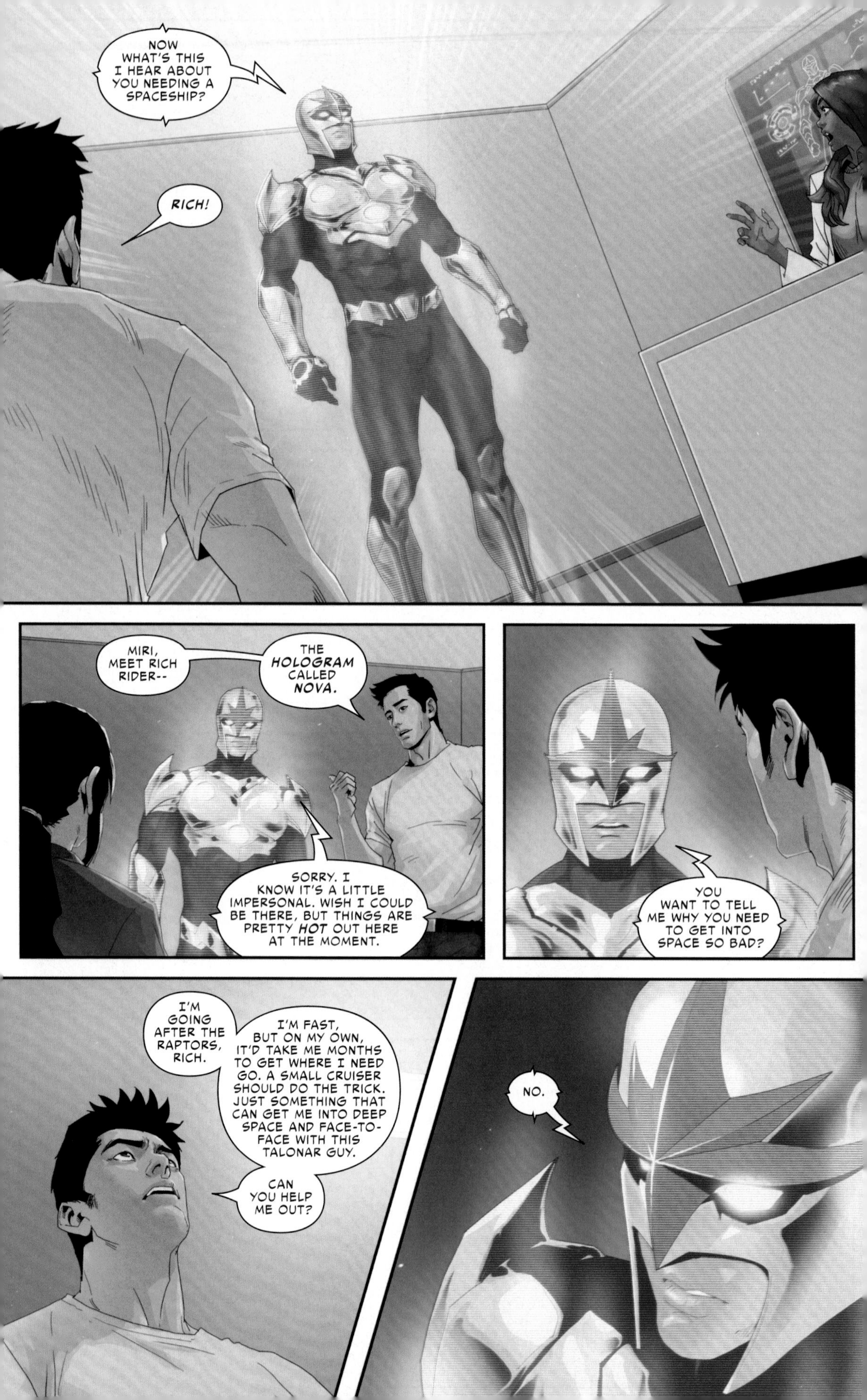
NOW WHAT'S THIS I HEAR ABOUT YOU NEEDING A SPACESHIP?
RICH!
MIRI, MEET RICH RIDER--
THE HOLOGRAM CALLED NOVA.
SORRY. I KNOW IT'S A LITTLE IMPERSONAL. WISH I COULD BE THERE, BUT THINGS ARE PRETTY HOT OUT HERE AT THE MOMENT.
YOU WANT TO TELL ME WHY YOU NEED TO GET INTO SPACE SO BAD?
I'M GOING AFTER THE RAPTORS, RICH.
I'M FAST, BUT ON MY OWN, IT'D TAKE ME MONTHS TO GET WHERE I NEED GO. A SMALL CRUISER SHOULD DO THE TRICK. JUST SOMETHING THAT CAN GET ME INTO DEEP SPACE AND FACE-TO-FACE WITH THIS TALONAR GUY.
CAN YOU HELP ME OUT?
NO.

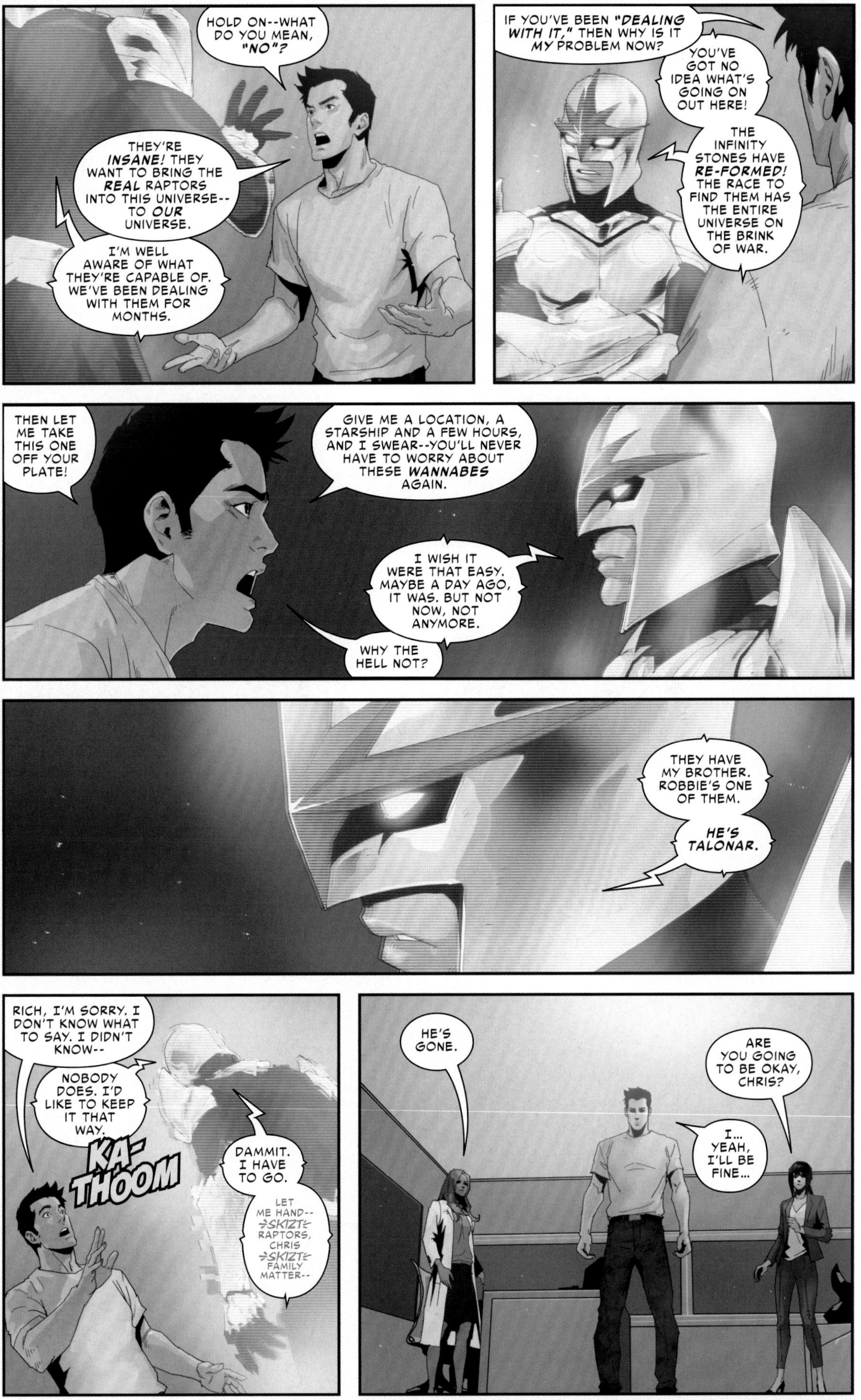
HOLD ON--WHAT DO YOU MEAN, "NO"?
THEY'RE INSANE! THEY WANT TO BRING THE REAL RAPTORS INTO THIS UNIVERSE--TO OUR UNIVERSE.
I'M WELL AWARE OF WHAT THEY'RE CAPABLE OF. WE'VE BEEN DEALING WITH THEM FOR MONTHS.
IF YOU'VE BEEN "DEALING WITH IT," THEN WHY IS IT MY PROBLEM NOW?
YOU'VE GOT NO IDEA WHAT'S GOING ON OUT HERE!
THE INFINITY STONES HAVE RE-FORMED! THE RACE TO FIND THEM HAS THE ENTIRE UNIVERSE ON THE BRINK OF WAR.
THEN LET ME TAKE THIS ONE OFF YOUR PLATE!
GIVE ME A LOCATION, A STARSHIP AND A FEW HOURS, AND I SWEAR--YOU'LL NEVER HAVE TO WORRY ABOUT THESE WANNABES AGAIN.
I WISH IT WERE THAT EASY. MAYBE A DAY AGO, IT WAS. BUT NOT NOW, NOT ANYMORE.
WHY THE HELL NOT?
THEY HAVE MY BROTHER. ROBBIE'S ONE OF THEM.
HE'S TALONAR.
RICH, I'M SORRY. I DON'T KNOW WHAT TO SAY. I DIDN'T KNOW--
NOBODY DOES. I'D LIKE TO KEEP IT THAT WAY.
KA-THOOM
DAMMIT. I HAVE TO GO.
LET ME HAND--SKIZT--RAPTORS, CHRIS--SKIZT--FAMILY MATTER--
HE'S GONE.
ARE YOU GOING TO BE OKAY, CHRIS?
I... YEAH, I'LL BE FINE...

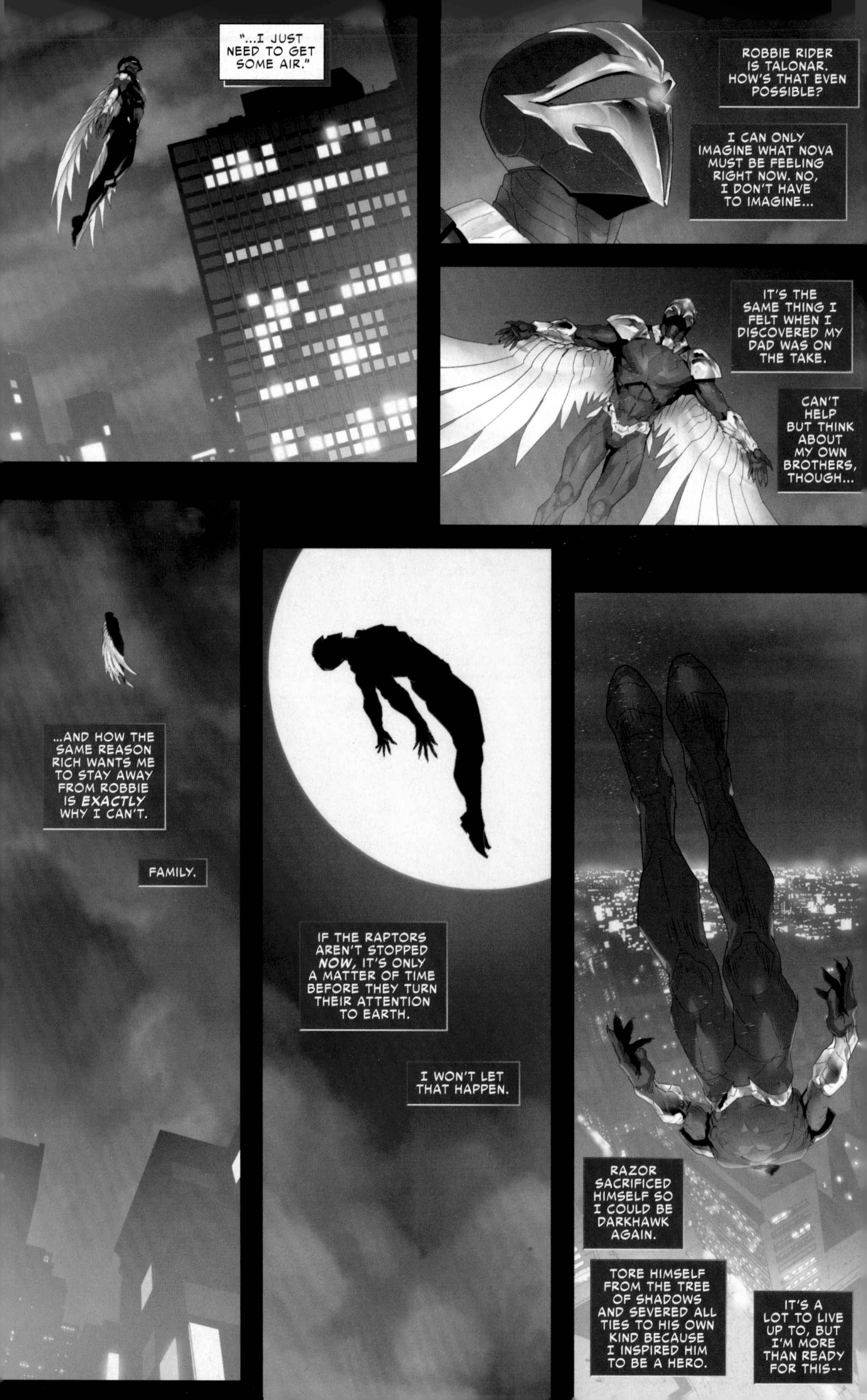
"...I JUST NEED TO GET SOME AIR."
ROBBIE RIDER IS TALONAR. HOW'S THAT EVEN POSSIBLE?
I CAN ONLY IMAGINE WHAT NOVA MUST BE FEELING RIGHT NOW. NO, I DON'T HAVE TO IMAGINE...
IT'S THE SAME THING I FELT WHEN I DISCOVERED MY DAD WAS ON THE TAKE.
CAN'T HELP BUT THINK ABOUT MY OWN BROTHERS, THOUGH...
...AND HOW THE SAME REASON RICH WANTS ME TO STAY AWAY FROM ROBBIE IS *EXACTLY* WHY I CAN'T.
FAMILY.
IF THE RAPTORS AREN'T STOPPED *NOW*, IT'S ONLY A MATTER OF TIME BEFORE THEY TURN THEIR ATTENTION TO EARTH.
I WON'T LET THAT HAPPEN.
RAZOR SACRIFICED HIMSELF SO I COULD BE DARKHAWK AGAIN.
TORE HIMSELF FROM THE TREE OF SHADOWS AND SEVERED ALL TIES TO HIS OWN KIND BECAUSE I INSPIRED HIM TO BE A HERO.
IT'S A LOT TO LIVE UP TO, BUT I'M MORE THAN READY FOR THIS--

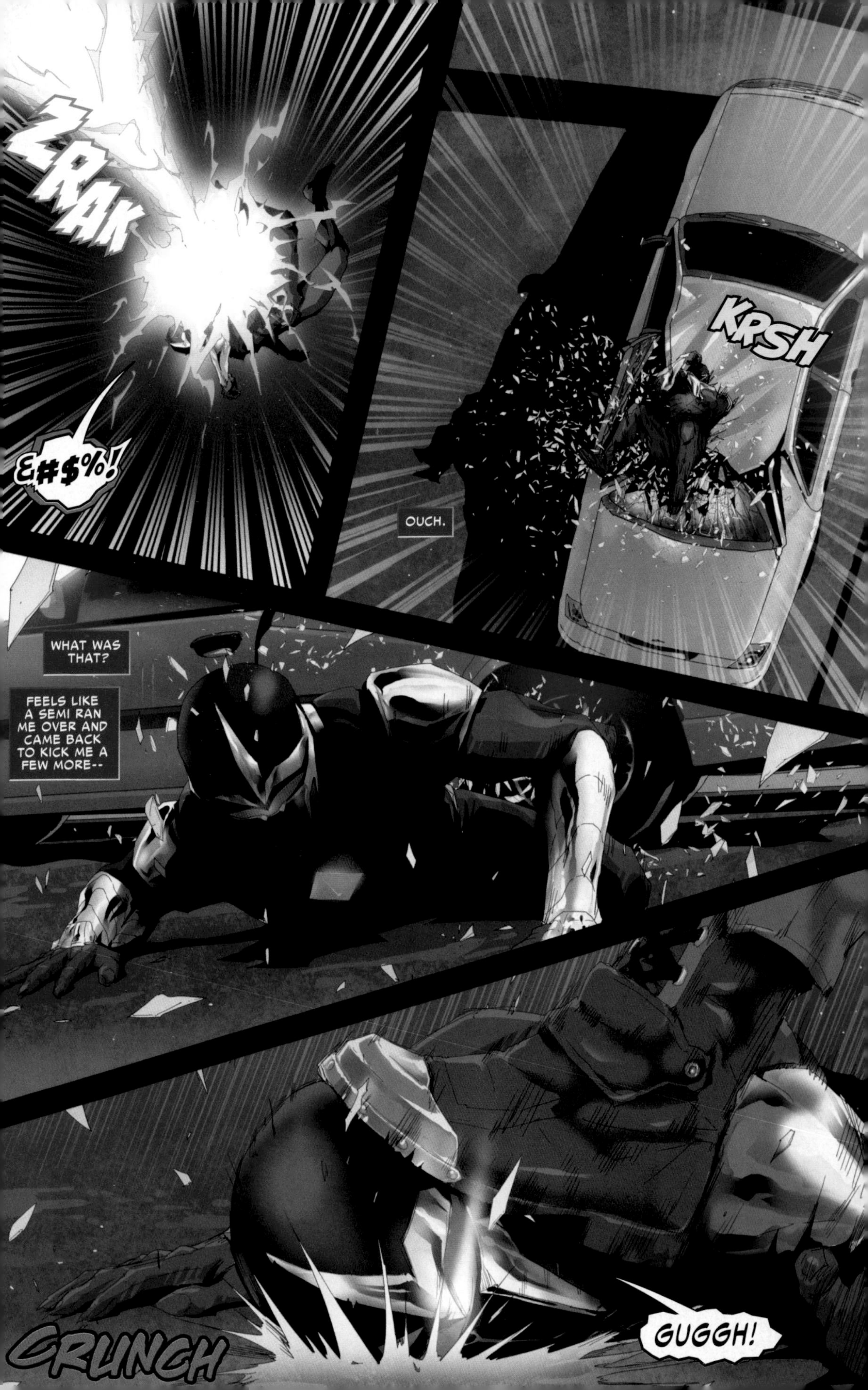
ZRAK
&#$%!
KRSH
OUCH.
WHAT WAS THAT?
FEELS LIKE A SEMI RAN ME OVER AND CAME BACK TO KICK ME A FEW MORE--
CRUNCH
GUGGH!

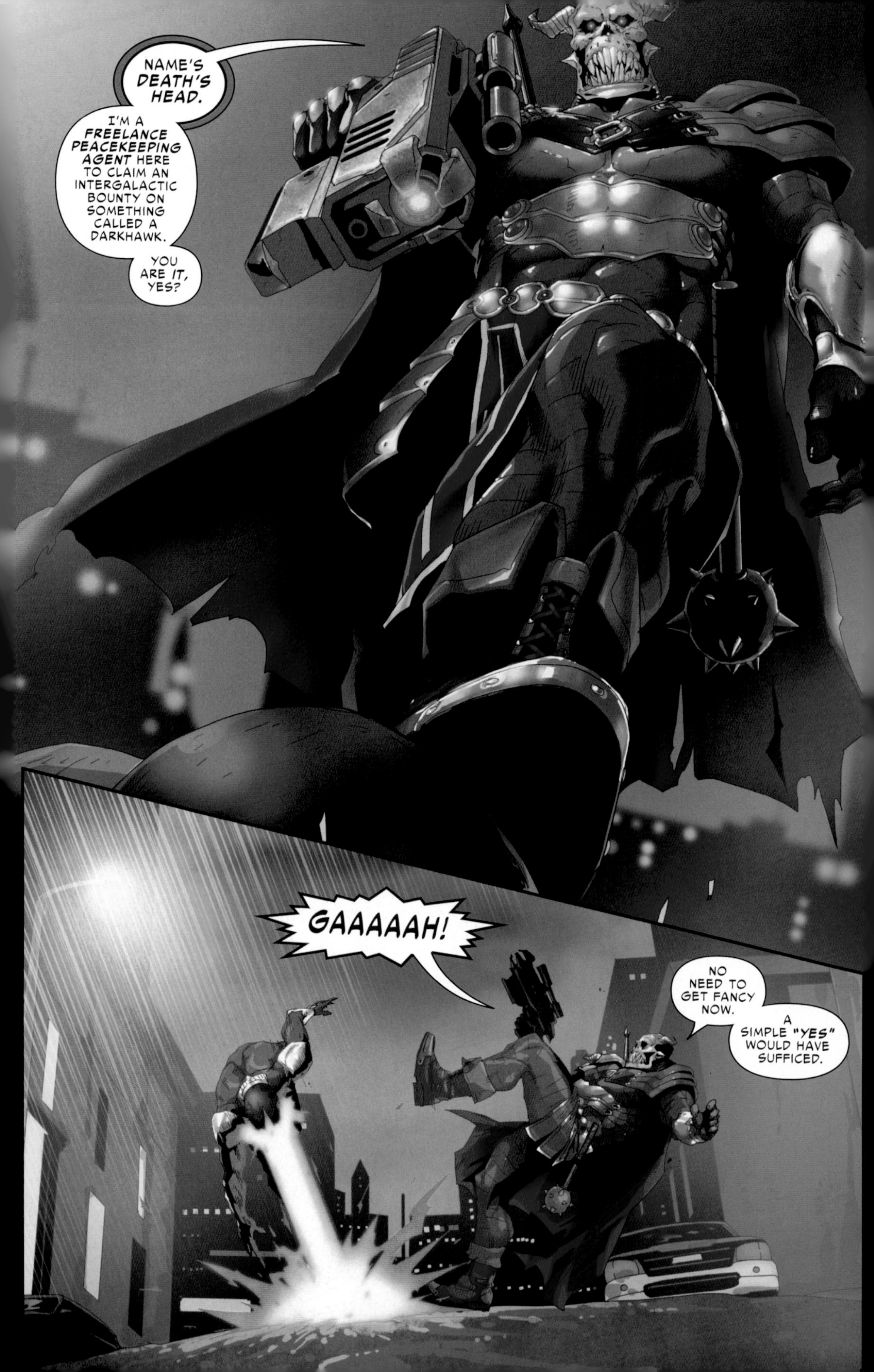
NAME'S DEATH'S HEAD.
I'M A FREELANCE PEACEKEEPING AGENT HERE TO CLAIM AN INTERGALACTIC BOUNTY ON SOMETHING CALLED A DARKHAWK.
YOU ARE IT, YES?
GAAAAAH!
NO NEED TO GET FANCY NOW.
A SIMPLE "YES" WOULD HAVE SUFFICED.

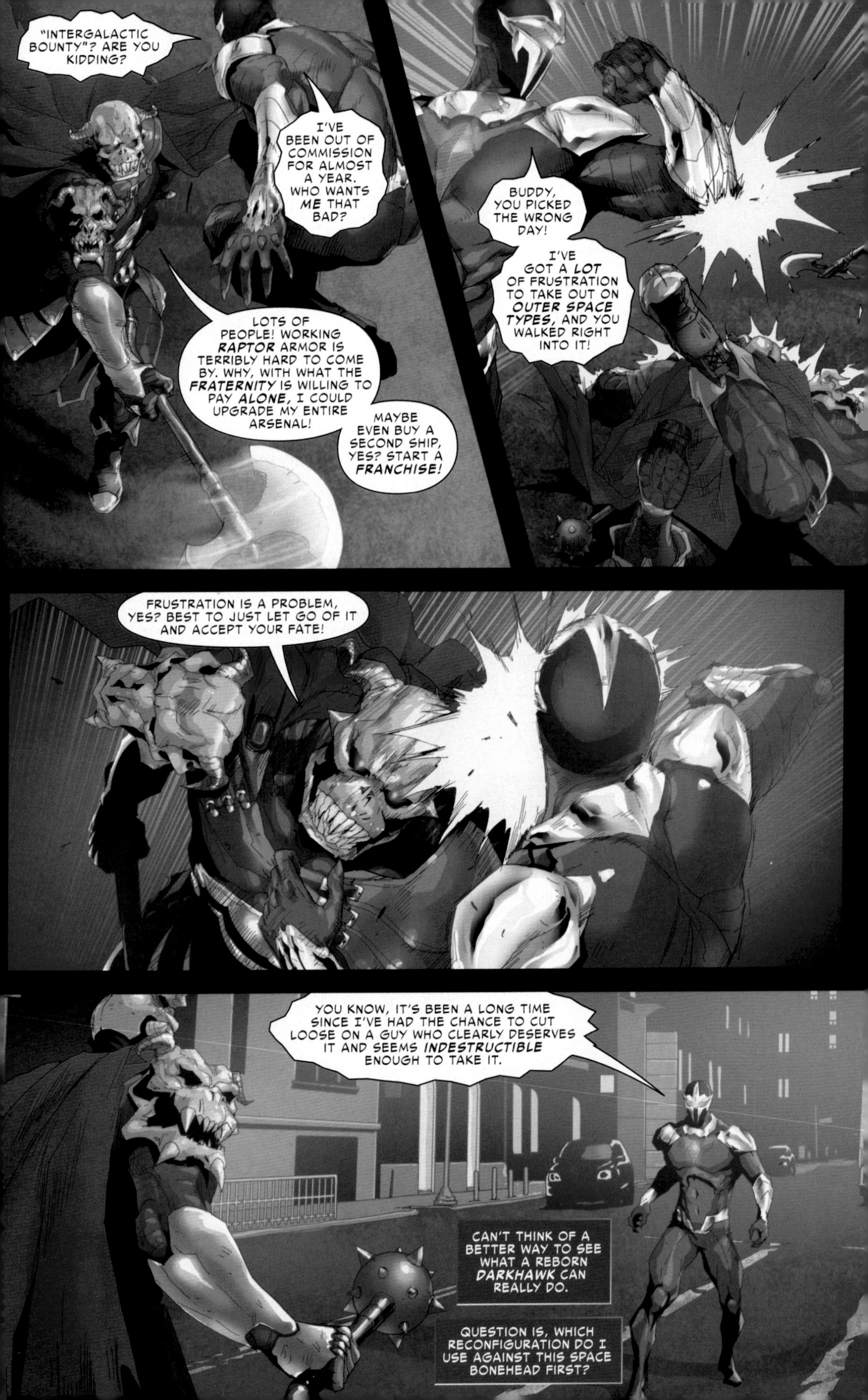
"INTERGALACTIC BOUNTY"? ARE YOU KIDDING?
I'VE BEEN OUT OF COMMISSION FOR ALMOST A YEAR. WHO WANTS *ME* THAT BAD?
LOTS OF PEOPLE! WORKING *RAPTOR* ARMOR IS TERRIBLY HARD TO COME BY. WHY, WITH WHAT THE *FRATERNITY* IS WILLING TO PAY *ALONE*, I COULD UPGRADE MY ENTIRE ARSENAL!
MAYBE EVEN BUY A SECOND SHIP, YES? START A *FRANCHISE!*
BUDDY, YOU PICKED THE WRONG DAY!
I'VE GOT A *LOT* OF FRUSTRATION TO TAKE OUT ON *OUTER SPACE TYPES*, AND YOU WALKED RIGHT INTO IT!
FRUSTRATION IS A PROBLEM, YES? BEST TO JUST LET GO OF IT AND ACCEPT YOUR FATE!
YOU KNOW, IT'S BEEN A LONG TIME SINCE I'VE HAD THE CHANCE TO CUT LOOSE ON A GUY WHO CLEARLY DESERVES IT AND SEEMS *INDESTRUCTIBLE* ENOUGH TO TAKE IT.
CAN'T THINK OF A BETTER WAY TO SEE WHAT A REBORN *DARKHAWK* CAN REALLY DO.
QUESTION IS, WHICH RECONFIGURATION DO I USE AGAINST THIS SPACE BONEHEAD FIRST?

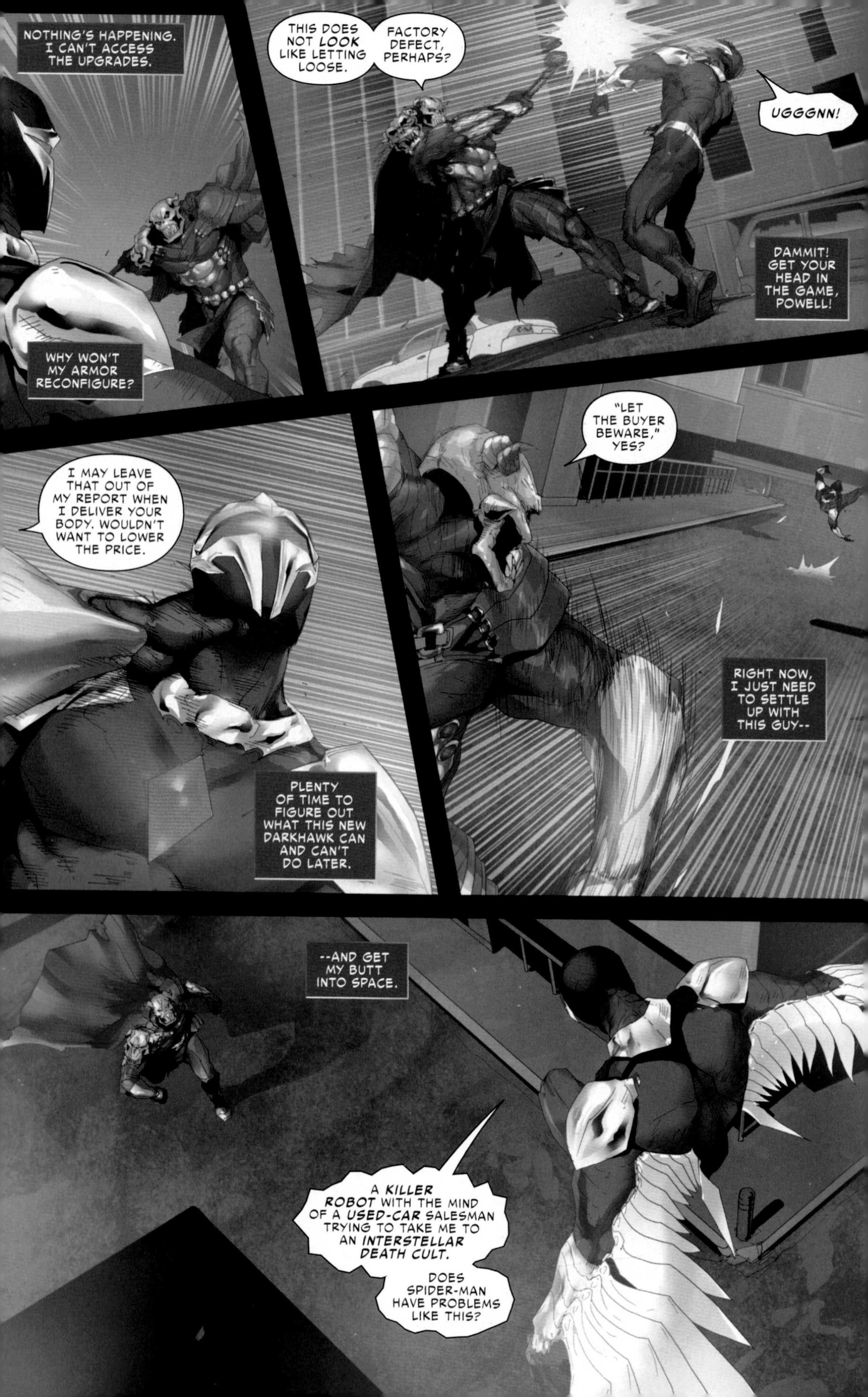
NOTHING'S HAPPENING. I CAN'T ACCESS THE UPGRADES.
WHY WON'T MY ARMOR RECONFIGURE?
THIS DOES NOT LOOK LIKE LETTING LOOSE.
FACTORY DEFECT, PERHAPS?
UGGGNN!
DAMMIT! GET YOUR HEAD IN THE GAME, POWELL!
I MAY LEAVE THAT OUT OF MY REPORT WHEN I DELIVER YOUR BODY. WOULDN'T WANT TO LOWER THE PRICE.
PLENTY OF TIME TO FIGURE OUT WHAT THIS NEW DARKHAWK CAN AND CAN'T DO LATER.
"LET THE BUYER BEWARE," YES?
RIGHT NOW, I JUST NEED TO SETTLE UP WITH THIS GUY--
--AND GET MY BUTT INTO SPACE.
A KILLER ROBOT WITH THE MIND OF A USED-CAR SALESMAN TRYING TO TAKE ME TO AN INTERSTELLAR DEATH CULT.
DOES SPIDER-MAN HAVE PROBLEMS LIKE THIS?

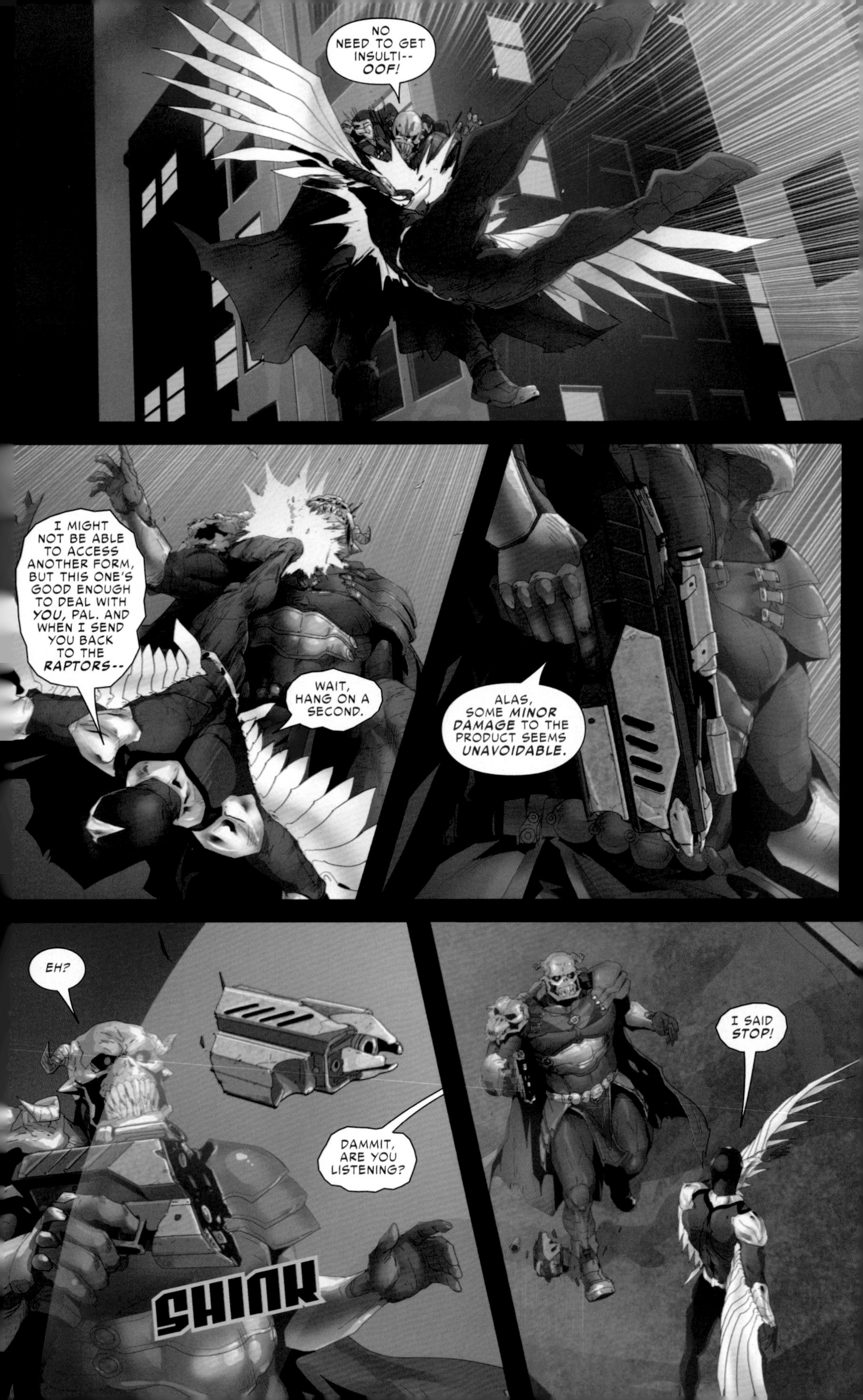
NO NEED TO GET INSULTI-- OOF!
I MIGHT NOT BE ABLE TO ACCESS ANOTHER FORM, BUT THIS ONE'S GOOD ENOUGH TO DEAL WITH YOU, PAL. AND WHEN I SEND YOU BACK TO THE RAPTORS--
WAIT, HANG ON A SECOND.
ALAS, SOME MINOR DAMAGE TO THE PRODUCT SEEMS UNAVOIDABLE.
EH?
DAMMIT, ARE YOU LISTENING?
SHINK
I SAID STOP!

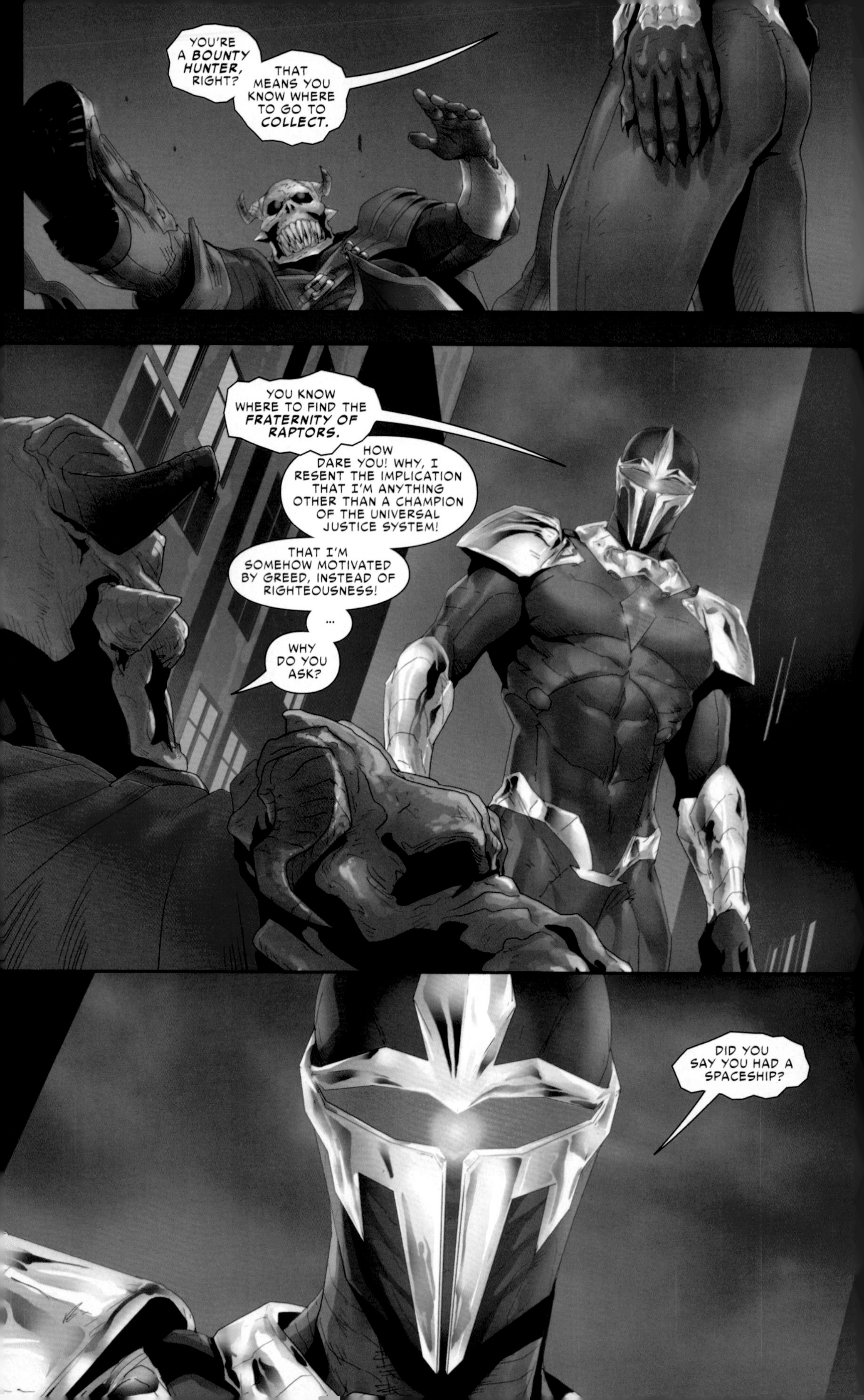

YOU'RE A BOUNTY HUNTER, RIGHT?
THAT MEANS YOU KNOW WHERE TO GO TO COLLECT.
YOU KNOW WHERE TO FIND THE FRATERNITY OF RAPTORS.
HOW DARE YOU! WHY, I RESENT THE IMPLICATION THAT I'M ANYTHING OTHER THAN A CHAMPION OF THE UNIVERSAL JUSTICE SYSTEM!
THAT I'M SOMEHOW MOTIVATED BY GREED, INSTEAD OF RIGHTEOUSNESS!
...
WHY DO YOU ASK?
DID YOU SAY YOU HAD A SPACESHIP?

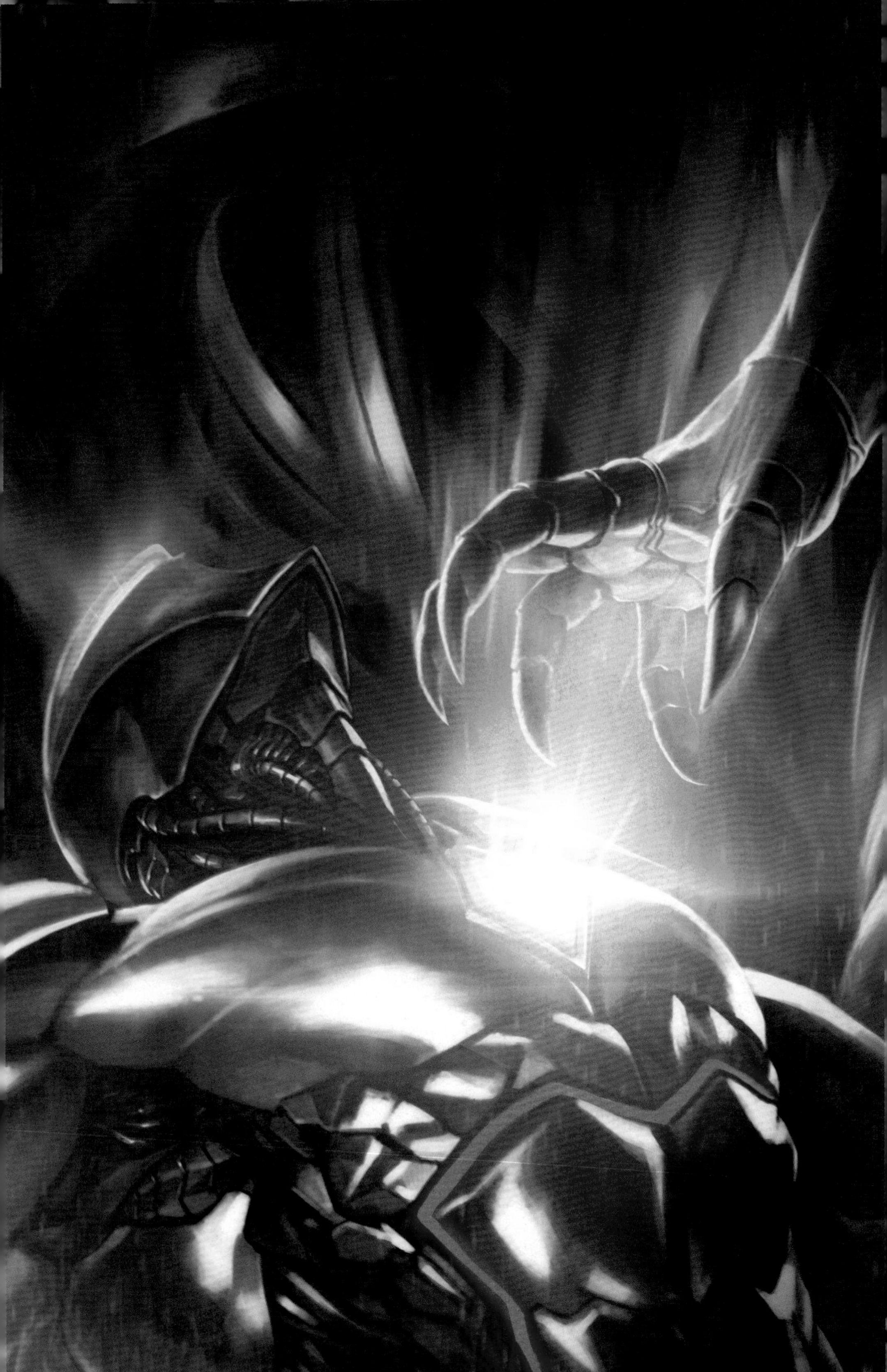

INFINITY COUNTDOWN: DARKHAWK 2

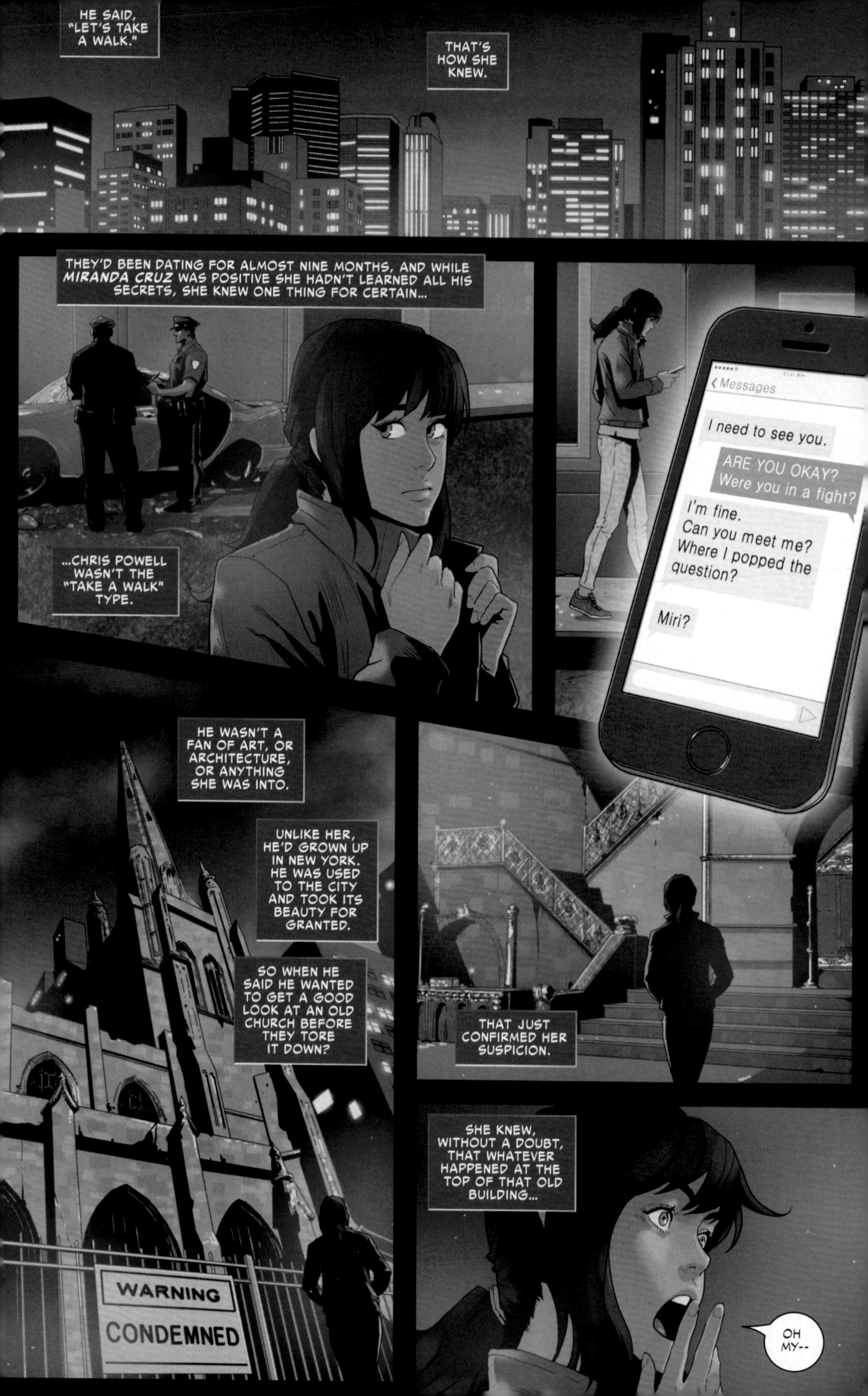

HE SAID, "LET'S TAKE A WALK."
THAT'S HOW SHE KNEW.
THEY'D BEEN DATING FOR ALMOST NINE MONTHS, AND WHILE *MIRANDA CRUZ* WAS POSITIVE SHE HADN'T LEARNED ALL HIS SECRETS, SHE KNEW ONE THING FOR CERTAIN...
...CHRIS POWELL WASN'T THE "TAKE A WALK" TYPE.
Messages
I need to see you.
ARE YOU OKAY? Were you in a fight?
I'm fine. Can you meet me? Where I popped the question?
Miri?
HE WASN'T A FAN OF ART, OR ARCHITECTURE, OR ANYTHING SHE WAS INTO.
UNLIKE HER, HE'D GROWN UP IN NEW YORK. HE WAS USED TO THE CITY AND TOOK ITS BEAUTY FOR GRANTED.
SO WHEN HE SAID HE WANTED TO GET A GOOD LOOK AT AN OLD CHURCH BEFORE THEY TORE IT DOWN?
WARNING
CONDEMNED
THAT JUST CONFIRMED HER SUSPICION.
SHE KNEW, WITHOUT A DOUBT, THAT WHATEVER HAPPENED AT THE TOP OF THAT OLD BUILDING...
OH MY--

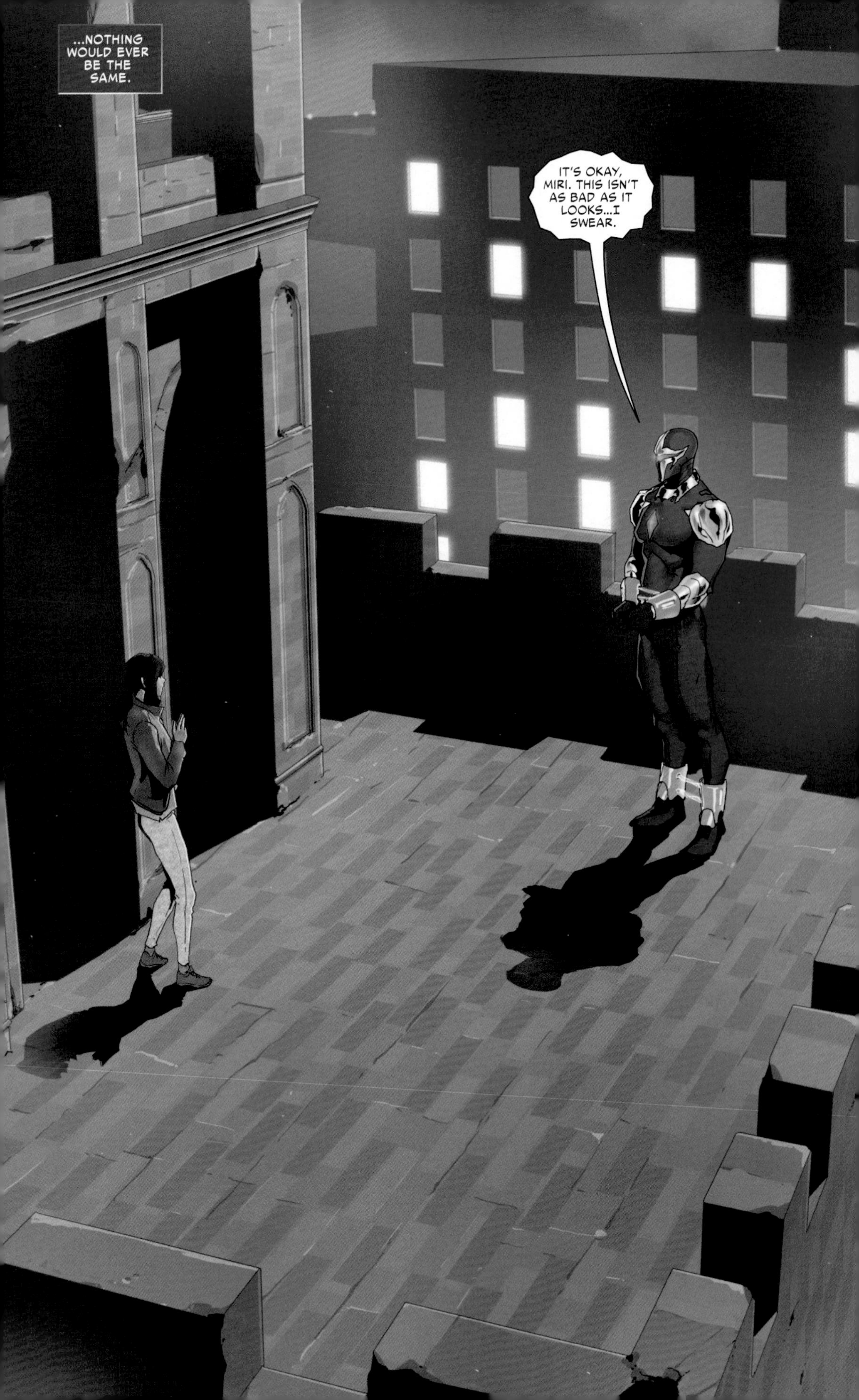
...NOTHING WOULD EVER BE THE SAME.
IT'S OKAY, MIRI. THIS ISN'T AS BAD AS IT LOOKS...I SWEAR.

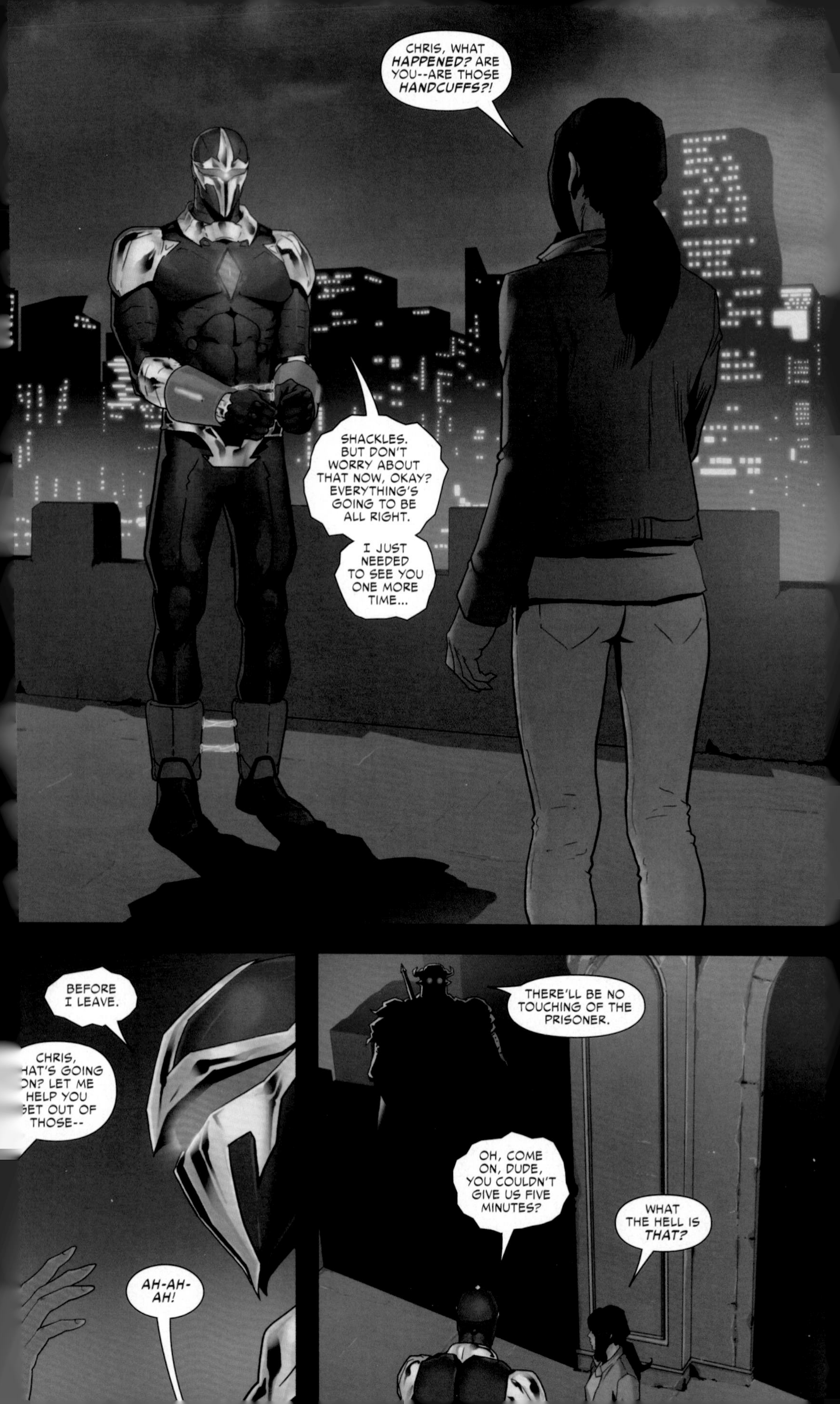
CHRIS, WHAT HAPPENED? ARE YOU--ARE THOSE HANDCUFFS?!
SHACKLES. BUT DON'T WORRY ABOUT THAT NOW, OKAY? EVERYTHING'S GOING TO BE ALL RIGHT.
I JUST NEEDED TO SEE YOU ONE MORE TIME...
BEFORE I LEAVE.
CHRIS, HAT'S GOING ON? LET ME HELP YOU GET OUT OF THOSE--
AH-AH-AH!
THERE'LL BE NO TOUCHING OF THE PRISONER.
OH, COME ON, DUDE, YOU COULDN'T GIVE US FIVE MINUTES?
WHAT THE HELL IS THAT?

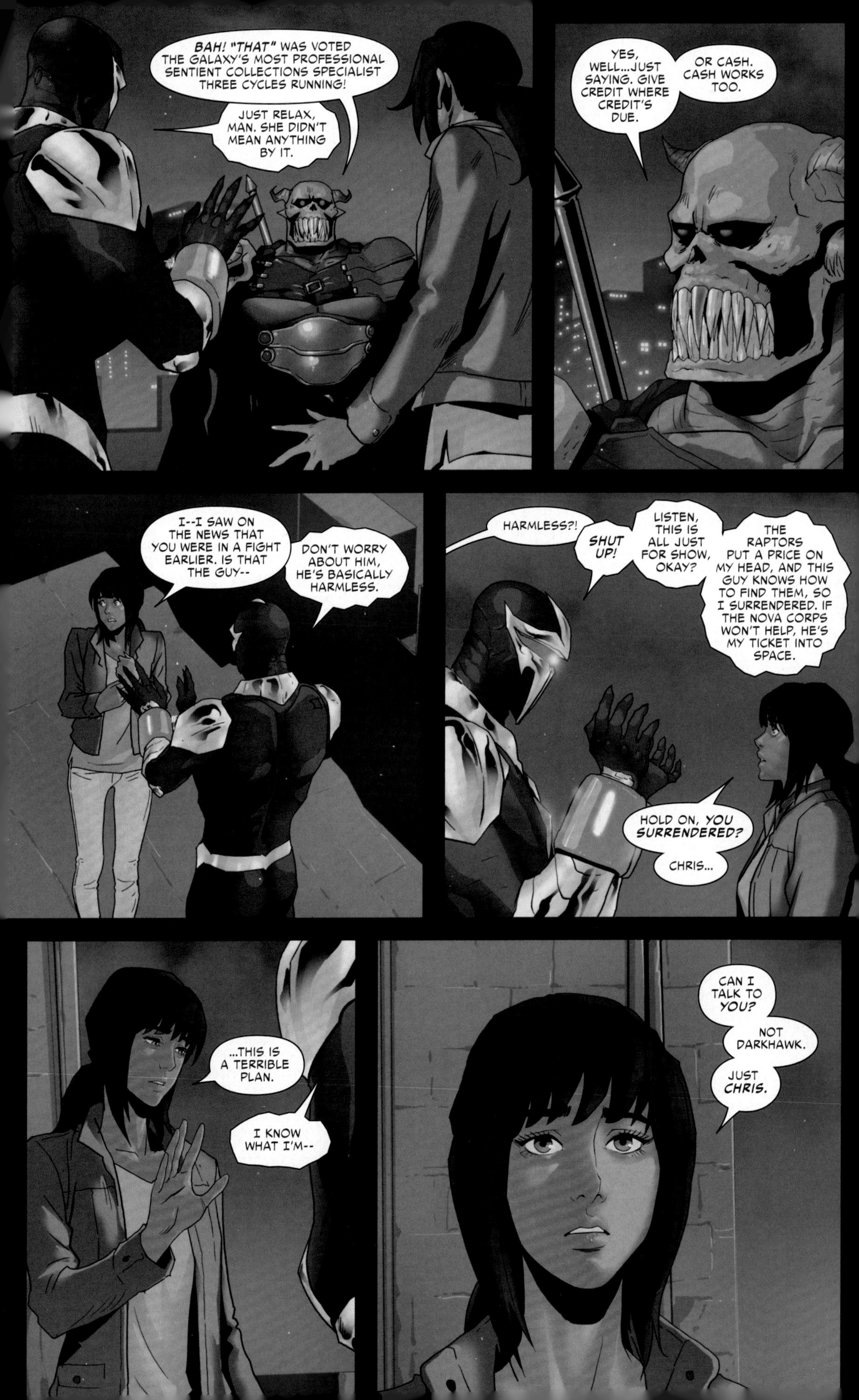
BAH! "THAT" WAS VOTED THE GALAXY'S MOST PROFESSIONAL SENTIENT COLLECTIONS SPECIALIST THREE CYCLES RUNNING!
JUST RELAX, MAN. SHE DIDN'T MEAN ANYTHING BY IT.
YES, WELL...JUST SAYING. GIVE CREDIT WHERE CREDIT'S DUE.
OR CASH. CASH WORKS TOO.
I--I SAW ON THE NEWS THAT YOU WERE IN A FIGHT EARLIER. IS THAT THE GUY--
DON'T WORRY ABOUT HIM, HE'S BASICALLY HARMLESS.
HARMLESS?!
SHUT UP!
LISTEN, THIS IS ALL JUST FOR SHOW, OKAY?
THE RAPTORS PUT A PRICE ON MY HEAD, AND THIS GUY KNOWS HOW TO FIND THEM, SO I SURRENDERED. IF THE NOVA CORPS WON'T HELP, HE'S MY TICKET INTO SPACE.
HOLD ON, YOU SURRENDERED?
CHRIS...
...THIS IS A TERRIBLE PLAN.
I KNOW WHAT I'M--
CAN I TALK TO YOU?
NOT DARKHAWK.
JUST CHRIS.

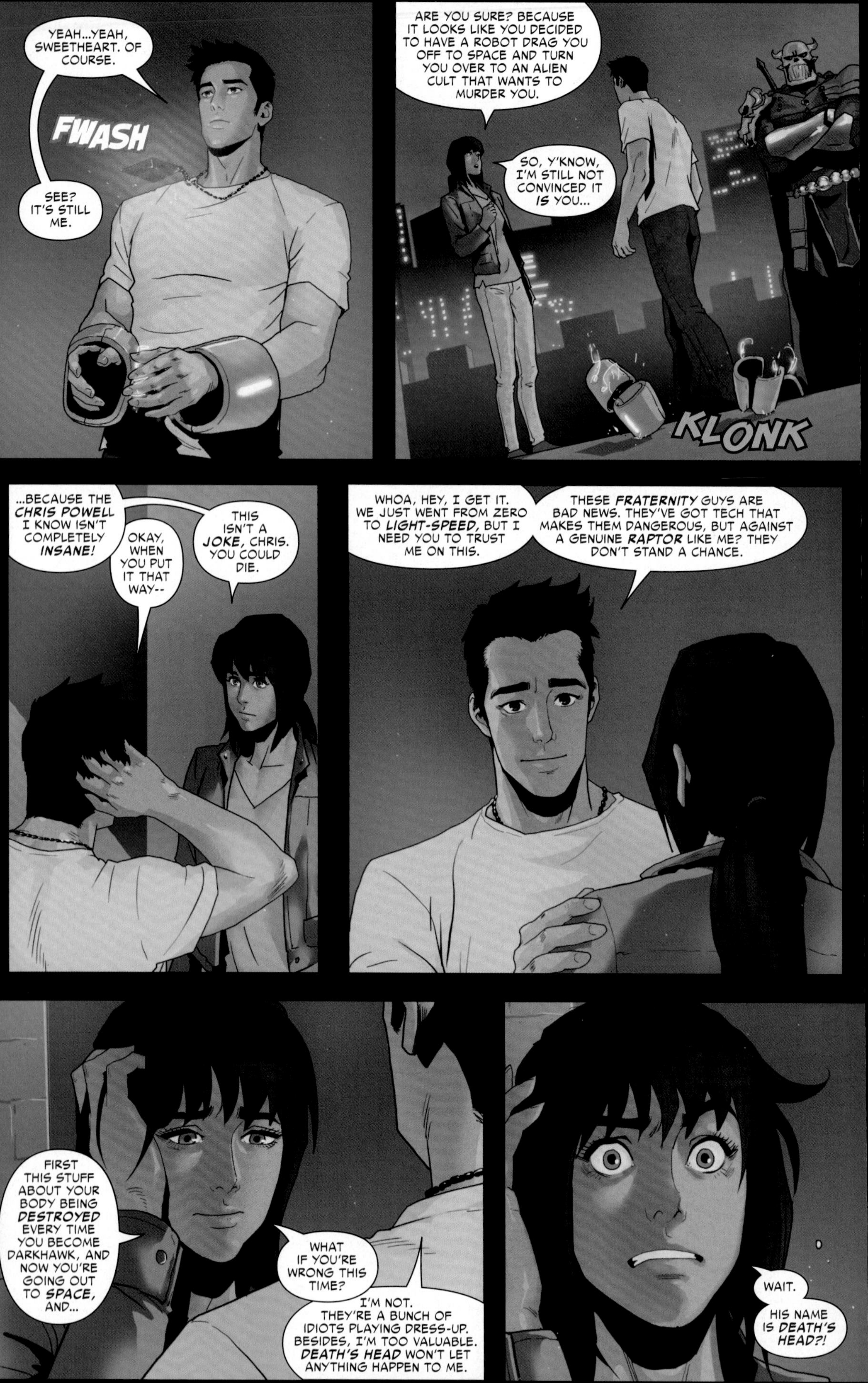
YEAH...YEAH, SWEETHEART. OF COURSE.
FWASH
SEE? IT'S STILL ME.
ARE YOU SURE? BECAUSE IT LOOKS LIKE YOU DECIDED TO HAVE A ROBOT DRAG YOU OFF TO SPACE AND TURN YOU OVER TO AN ALIEN CULT THAT WANTS TO MURDER YOU.
SO, Y'KNOW, I'M STILL NOT CONVINCED IT *IS* YOU...
KLONK
...BECAUSE THE ***CHRIS POWELL*** I KNOW ISN'T COMPLETELY ***INSANE!***
OKAY, WHEN YOU PUT IT THAT WAY--
THIS ISN'T A ***JOKE***, CHRIS. YOU COULD DIE.
WHOA, HEY, I GET IT. WE JUST WENT FROM ZERO TO ***LIGHT-SPEED,*** BUT I NEED YOU TO TRUST ME ON THIS.
THESE ***FRATERNITY*** GUYS ARE BAD NEWS. THEY'VE GOT TECH THAT MAKES THEM DANGEROUS, BUT AGAINST A GENUINE ***RAPTOR*** LIKE ME? THEY DON'T STAND A CHANCE.
FIRST THIS STUFF ABOUT YOUR BODY BEING ***DESTROYED*** EVERY TIME YOU BECOME DARKHAWK, AND NOW YOU'RE GOING OUT TO ***SPACE,*** AND...
WHAT IF YOU'RE WRONG THIS TIME?
I'M NOT. THEY'RE A BUNCH OF IDIOTS PLAYING DRESS-UP. BESIDES, I'M TOO VALUABLE. ***DEATH'S HEAD*** WON'T LET ANYTHING HAPPEN TO ME.
WAIT.
HIS NAME IS ***DEATH'S HEAD?!***

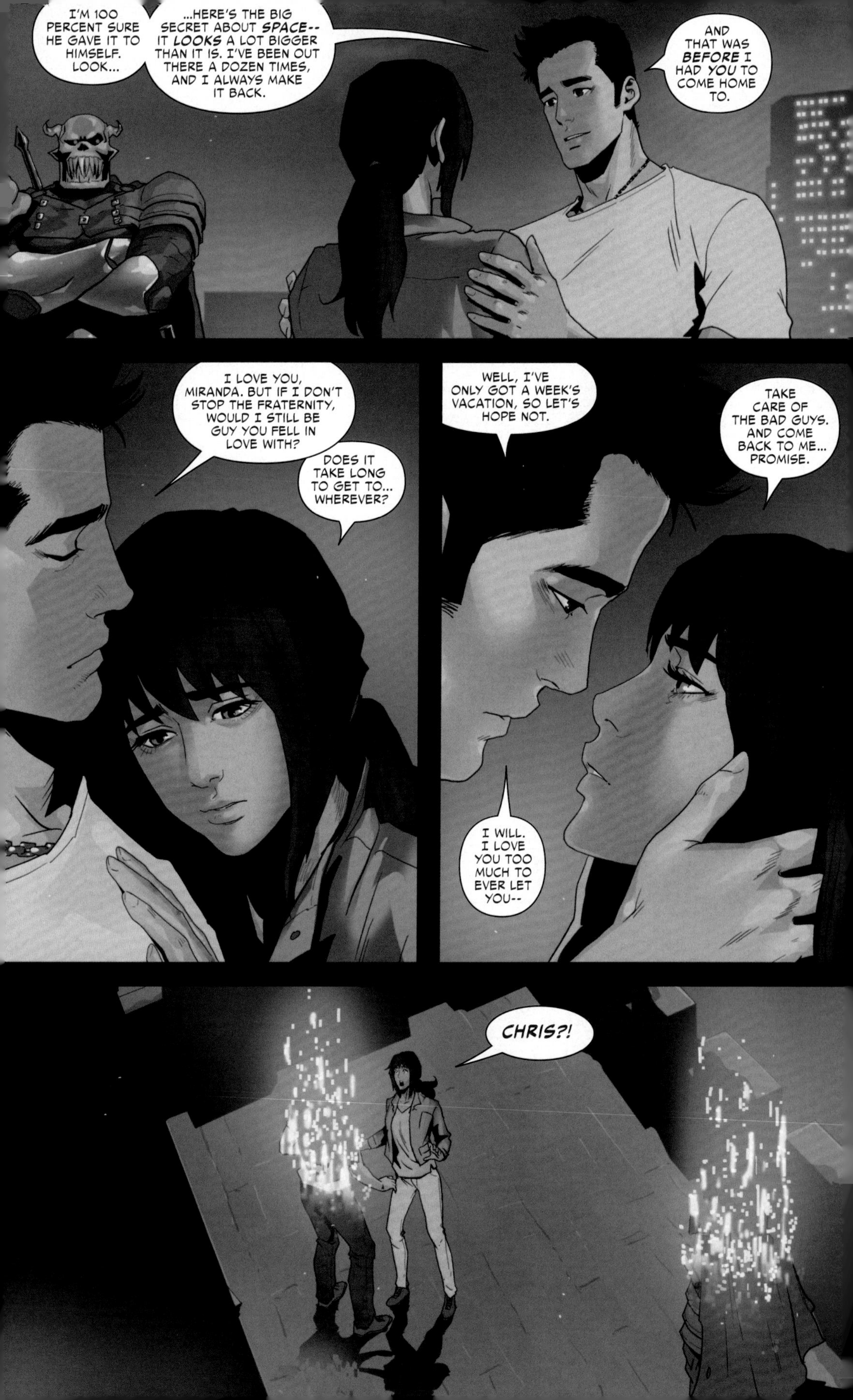
I'M 100 PERCENT SURE HE GAVE IT TO HIMSELF. LOOK...
...HERE'S THE BIG SECRET ABOUT SPACE-- IT LOOKS A LOT BIGGER THAN IT IS. I'VE BEEN OUT THERE A DOZEN TIMES, AND I ALWAYS MAKE IT BACK.
AND THAT WAS BEFORE I HAD YOU TO COME HOME TO.
I LOVE YOU, MIRANDA. BUT IF I DON'T STOP THE FRATERNITY, WOULD I STILL BE GUY YOU FELL IN LOVE WITH?
DOES IT TAKE LONG TO GET TO... WHEREVER?
WELL, I'VE ONLY GOT A WEEK'S VACATION, SO LET'S HOPE NOT.
TAKE CARE OF THE BAD GUYS. AND COME BACK TO ME... PROMISE.
I WILL. I LOVE YOU TOO MUCH TO EVER LET YOU--
CHRIS?!

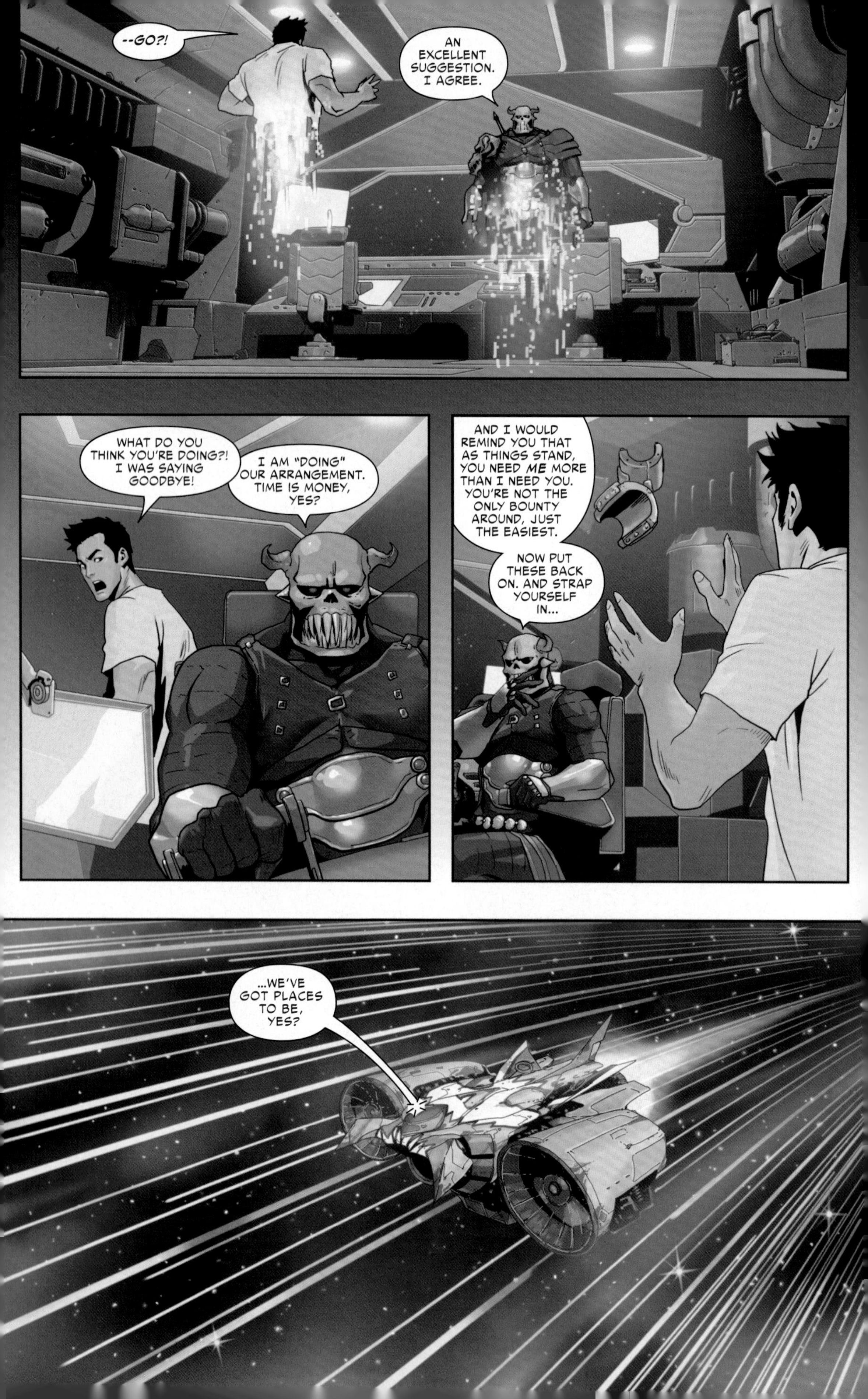
--GO?!
AN EXCELLENT SUGGESTION. I AGREE.
WHAT DO YOU THINK YOU'RE DOING?! I WAS SAYING GOODBYE!
I AM "DOING" OUR ARRANGEMENT. TIME IS MONEY, YES?
AND I WOULD REMIND YOU THAT AS THINGS STAND, YOU NEED *ME* MORE THAN I NEED YOU. YOU'RE NOT THE ONLY BOUNTY AROUND, JUST THE EASIEST.
NOW PUT THESE BACK ON. AND STRAP YOURSELF IN...
...WE'VE GOT PLACES TO BE, YES?

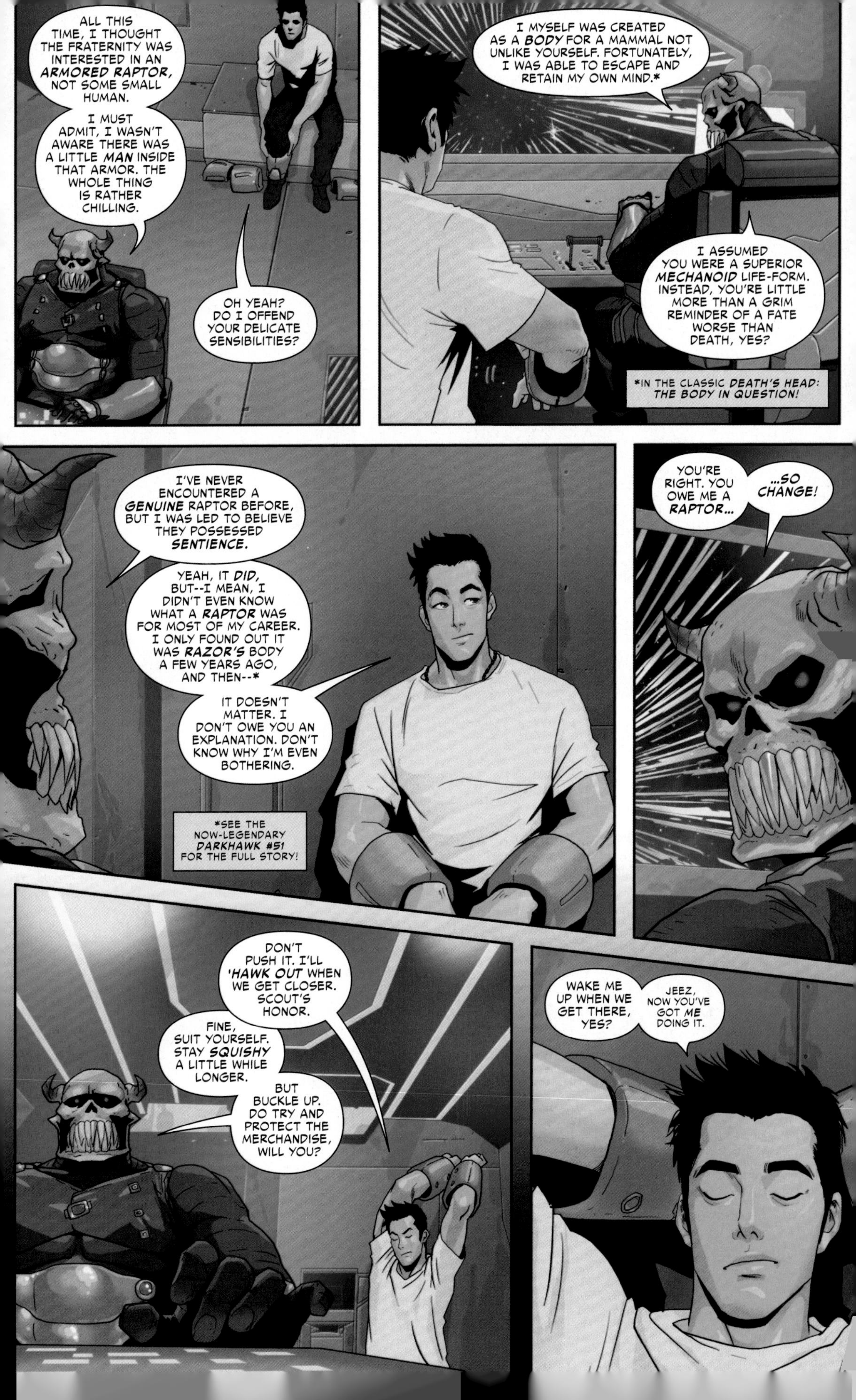
ALL THIS TIME, I THOUGHT THE FRATERNITY WAS INTERESTED IN AN ARMORED RAPTOR, NOT SOME SMALL HUMAN.
I MUST ADMIT, I WASN'T AWARE THERE WAS A LITTLE MAN INSIDE THAT ARMOR. THE WHOLE THING IS RATHER CHILLING.
OH YEAH? DO I OFFEND YOUR DELICATE SENSIBILITIES?
I MYSELF WAS CREATED AS A BODY FOR A MAMMAL NOT UNLIKE YOURSELF. FORTUNATELY, I WAS ABLE TO ESCAPE AND RETAIN MY OWN MIND.*
I ASSUMED YOU WERE A SUPERIOR MECHANOID LIFE-FORM. INSTEAD, YOU'RE LITTLE MORE THAN A GRIM REMINDER OF A FATE WORSE THAN DEATH, YES?
*IN THE CLASSIC DEATH'S HEAD: THE BODY IN QUESTION!
I'VE NEVER ENCOUNTERED A GENUINE RAPTOR BEFORE, BUT I WAS LED TO BELIEVE THEY POSSESSED SENTIENCE.
YEAH, IT DID, BUT--I MEAN, I DIDN'T EVEN KNOW WHAT A RAPTOR WAS FOR MOST OF MY CAREER. I ONLY FOUND OUT IT WAS RAZOR'S BODY A FEW YEARS AGO, AND THEN--*
IT DOESN'T MATTER. I DON'T OWE YOU AN EXPLANATION. DON'T KNOW WHY I'M EVEN BOTHERING.
*SEE THE NOW-LEGENDARY DARKHAWK #51 FOR THE FULL STORY!
YOU'RE RIGHT. YOU OWE ME A RAPTOR...
...SO CHANGE!
DON'T PUSH IT. I'LL 'HAWK OUT WHEN WE GET CLOSER. SCOUT'S HONOR.
FINE, SUIT YOURSELF. STAY SQUISHY A LITTLE WHILE LONGER.
BUT BUCKLE UP. DO TRY AND PROTECT THE MERCHANDISE, WILL YOU?
WAKE ME UP WHEN WE GET THERE, YES?
JEEZ, NOW YOU'VE GOT ME DOING IT.

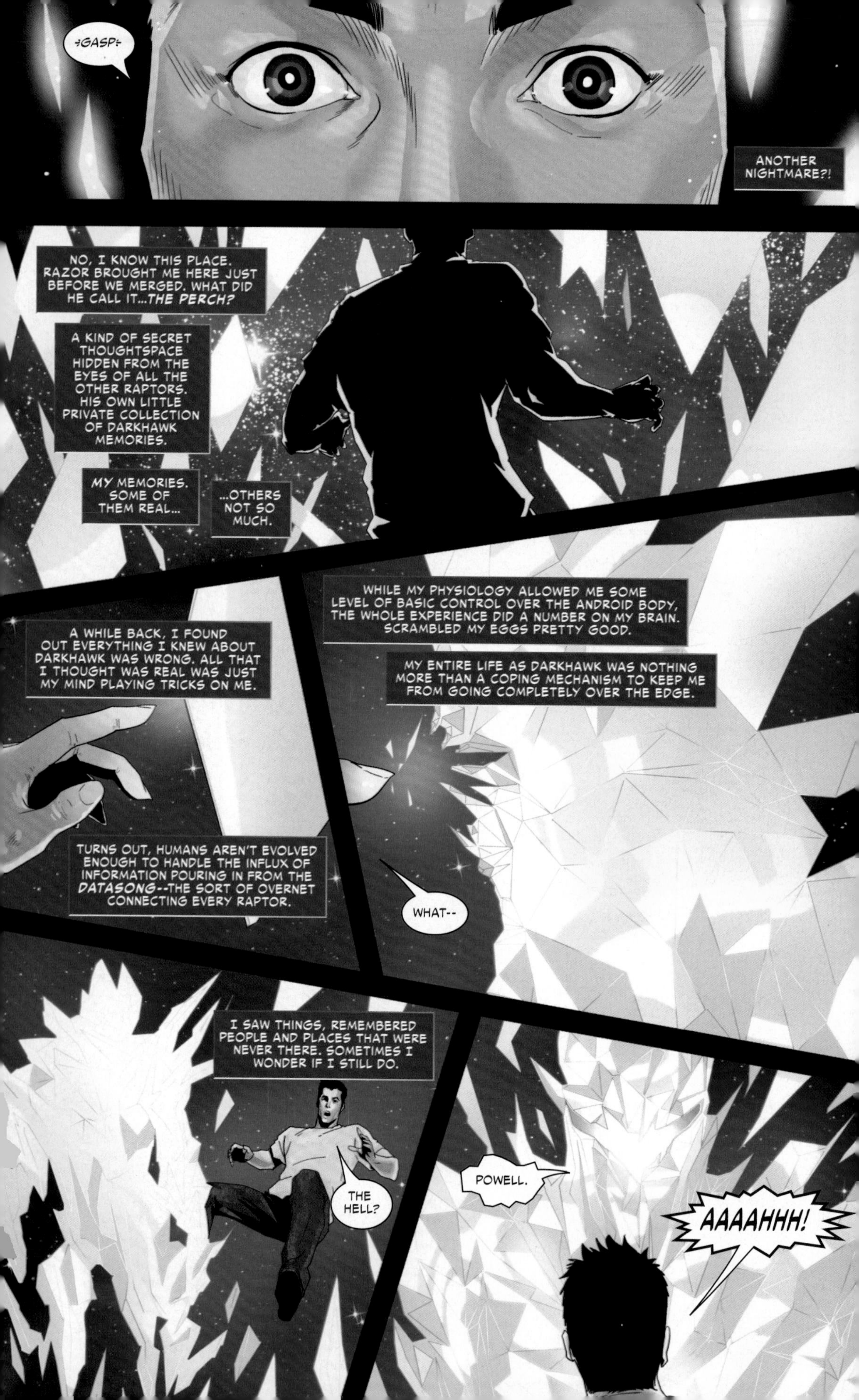

GASP
ANOTHER NIGHTMARE?!
NO, I KNOW THIS PLACE. RAZOR BROUGHT ME HERE JUST BEFORE WE MERGED. WHAT DID HE CALL IT...*THE PERCH?*
A KIND OF SECRET THOUGHTSPACE HIDDEN FROM THE EYES OF ALL THE OTHER RAPTORS. HIS OWN LITTLE PRIVATE COLLECTION OF DARKHAWK MEMORIES.
MY MEMORIES. SOME OF THEM REAL...
...OTHERS NOT SO MUCH.
A WHILE BACK, I FOUND OUT EVERYTHING I KNEW ABOUT DARKHAWK WAS WRONG. ALL THAT I THOUGHT WAS REAL WAS JUST MY MIND PLAYING TRICKS ON ME.
TURNS OUT, HUMANS AREN'T EVOLVED ENOUGH TO HANDLE THE INFLUX OF INFORMATION POURING IN FROM THE *DATASONG*--THE SORT OF OVERNET CONNECTING EVERY RAPTOR.
WHILE MY PHYSIOLOGY ALLOWED ME SOME LEVEL OF BASIC CONTROL OVER THE ANDROID BODY, THE WHOLE EXPERIENCE DID A NUMBER ON MY BRAIN. SCRAMBLED MY EGGS PRETTY GOOD.
MY ENTIRE LIFE AS DARKHAWK WAS NOTHING MORE THAN A COPING MECHANISM TO KEEP ME FROM GOING COMPLETELY OVER THE EDGE.
WHAT--
I SAW THINGS, REMEMBERED PEOPLE AND PLACES THAT WERE NEVER THERE. SOMETIMES I WONDER IF I STILL DO.
THE HELL?
POWELL.
AAAAHHH!

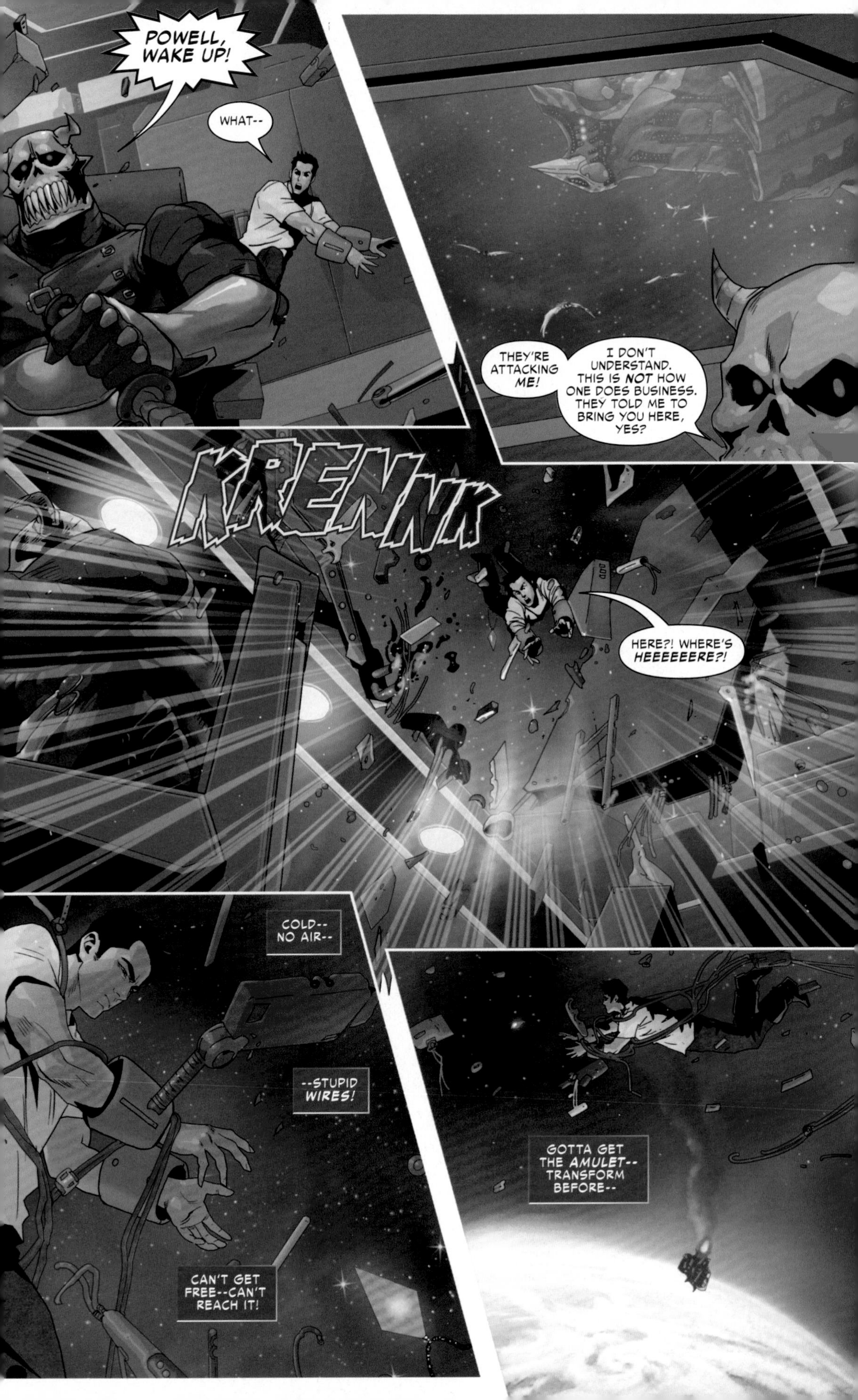
POWELL, WAKE UP!
WHAT--
THEY'RE ATTACKING ME!
I DON'T UNDERSTAND. THIS IS NOT HOW ONE DOES BUSINESS. THEY TOLD ME TO BRING YOU HERE, YES?
KRENNNK
HERE?! WHERE'S HEEEEEERE?!
COLD-- NO AIR--
--STUPID WIRES!
CAN'T GET FREE--CAN'T REACH IT!
GOTTA GET THE AMULET-- TRANSFORM BEFORE--

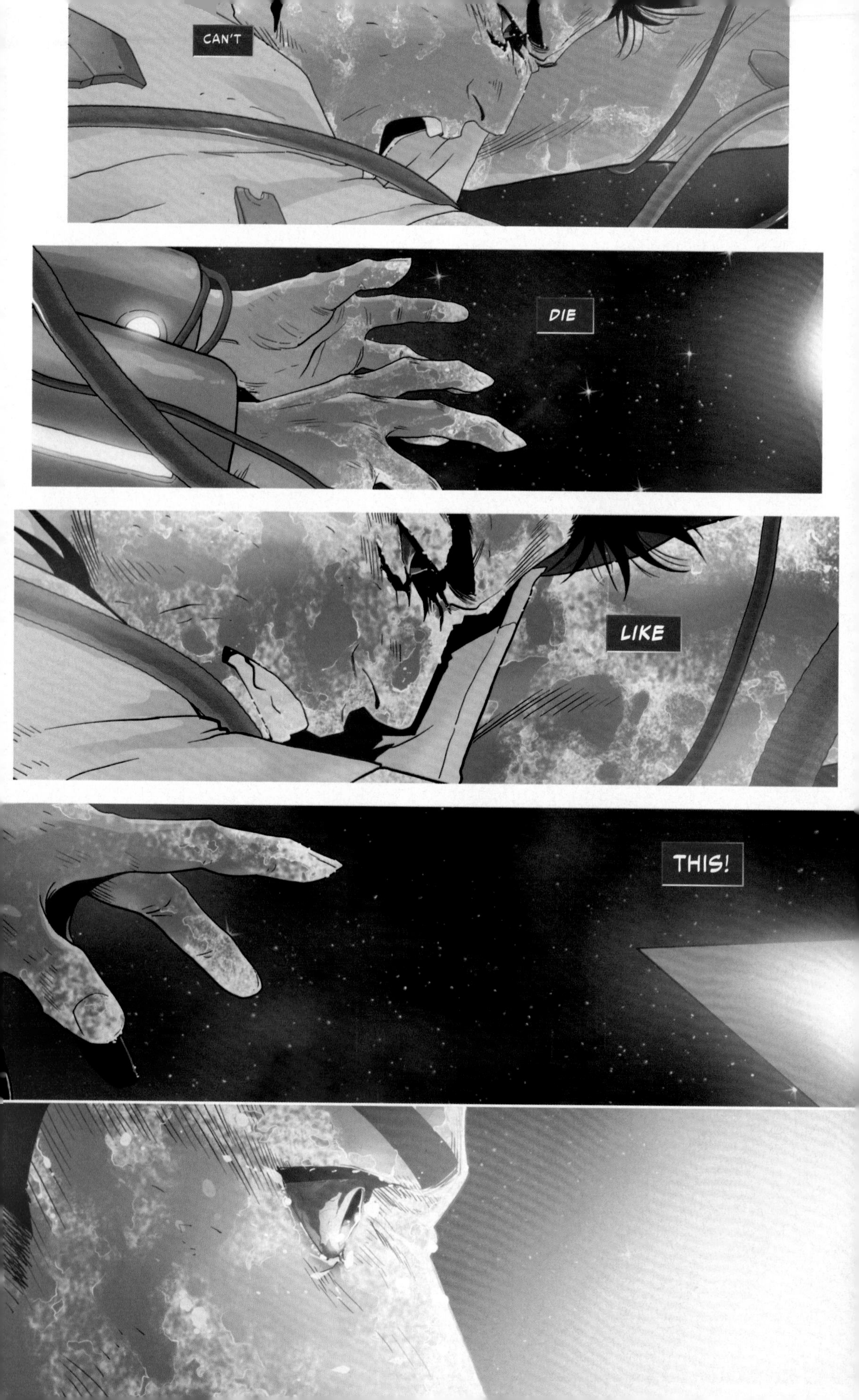
CAN'T
DIE
LIKE
THIS!

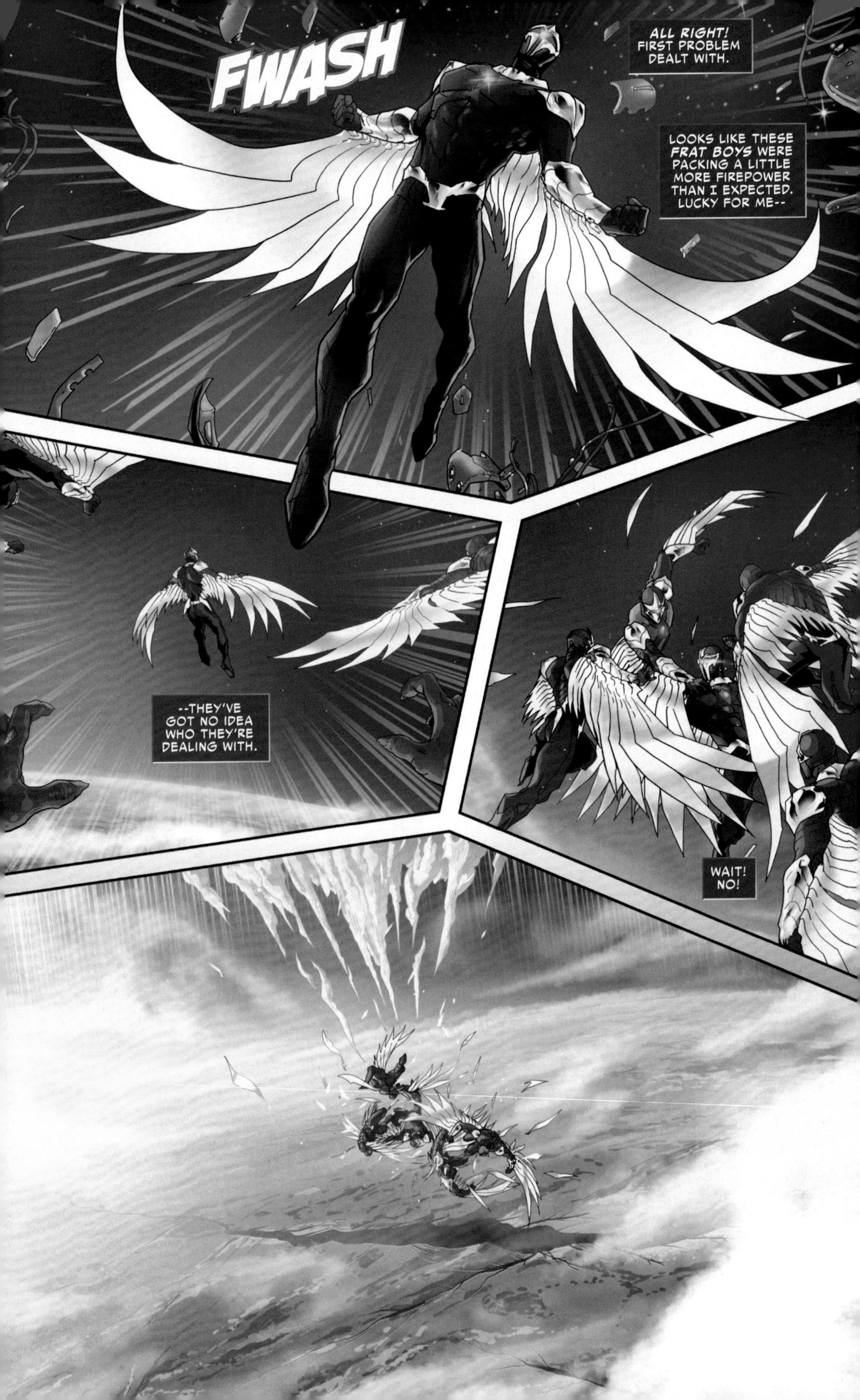
FWASH
ALL RIGHT! FIRST PROBLEM DEALT WITH.
LOOKS LIKE THESE FRAT BOYS WERE PACKING A LITTLE MORE FIREPOWER THAN I EXPECTED. LUCKY FOR ME--
--THEY'VE GOT NO IDEA WHO THEY'RE DEALING WITH.
WAIT! NO!

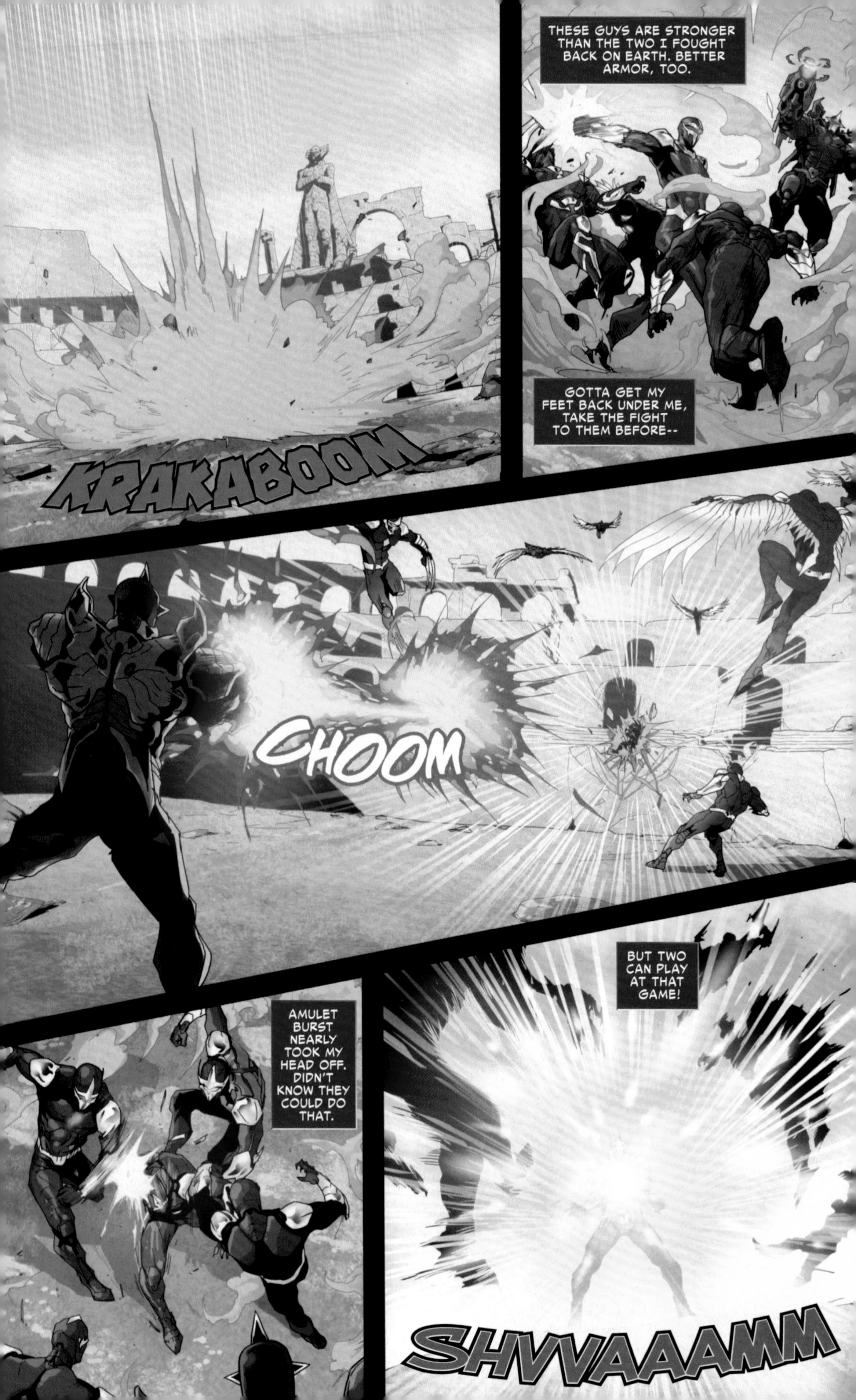
KRAKABOOM
THESE GUYS ARE STRONGER THAN THE TWO I FOUGHT BACK ON EARTH. BETTER ARMOR, TOO.
GOTTA GET MY FEET BACK UNDER ME, TAKE THE FIGHT TO THEM BEFORE--
CHOOM
AMULET BURST NEARLY TOOK MY HEAD OFF. DIDN'T KNOW THEY COULD DO THAT.
BUT TWO CAN PLAY AT THAT GAME!
SHVVAAAMM

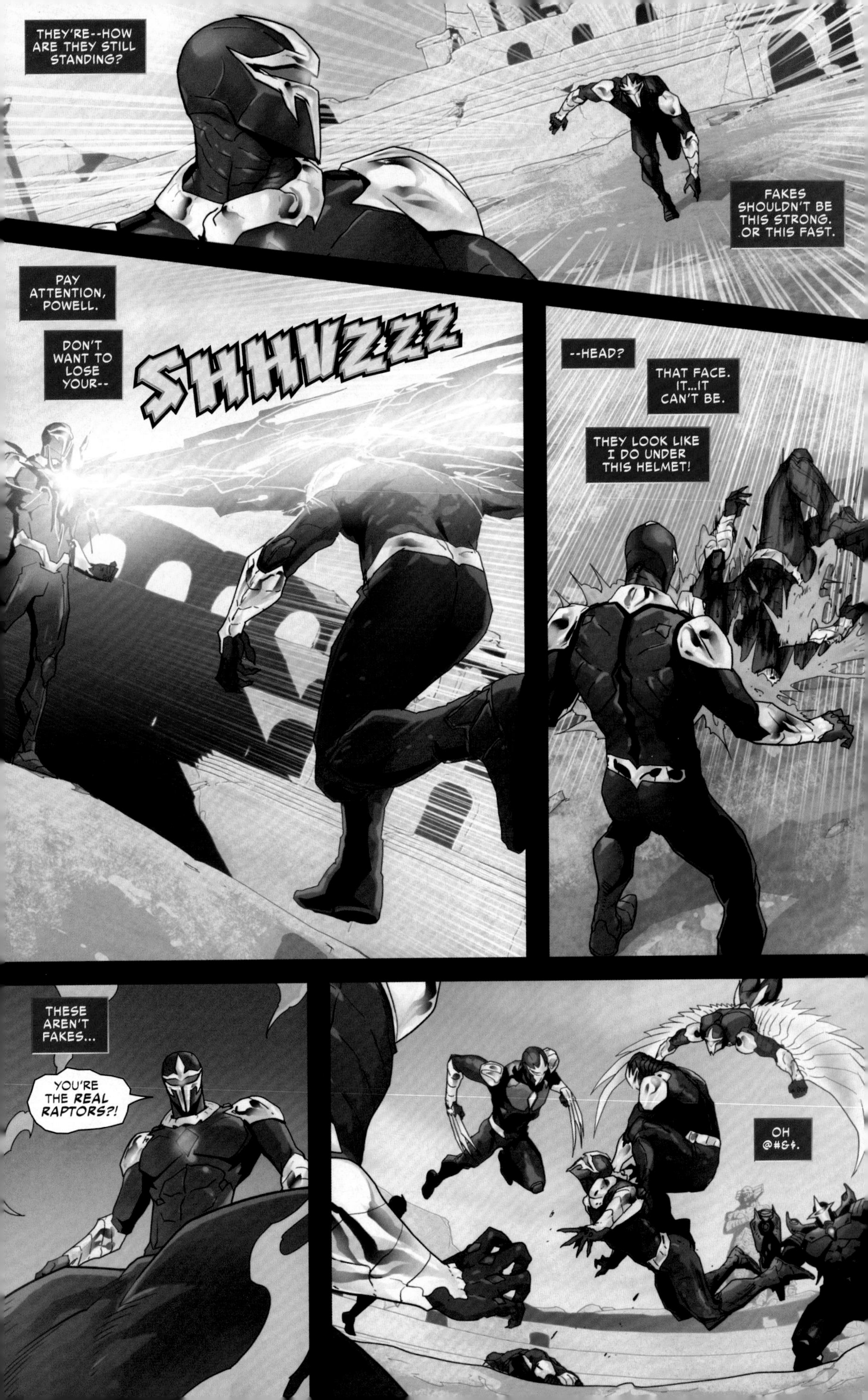
THEY'RE--HOW ARE THEY STILL STANDING?
FAKES SHOULDN'T BE THIS STRONG. OR THIS FAST.
PAY ATTENTION, POWELL.
DON'T WANT TO LOSE YOUR--
SHHVZZZ
--HEAD?
THAT FACE. IT...IT CAN'T BE.
THEY LOOK LIKE I DO UNDER THIS HELMET!
THESE AREN'T FAKES...
YOU'RE THE *REAL RAPTORS?!*
OH @#&$.

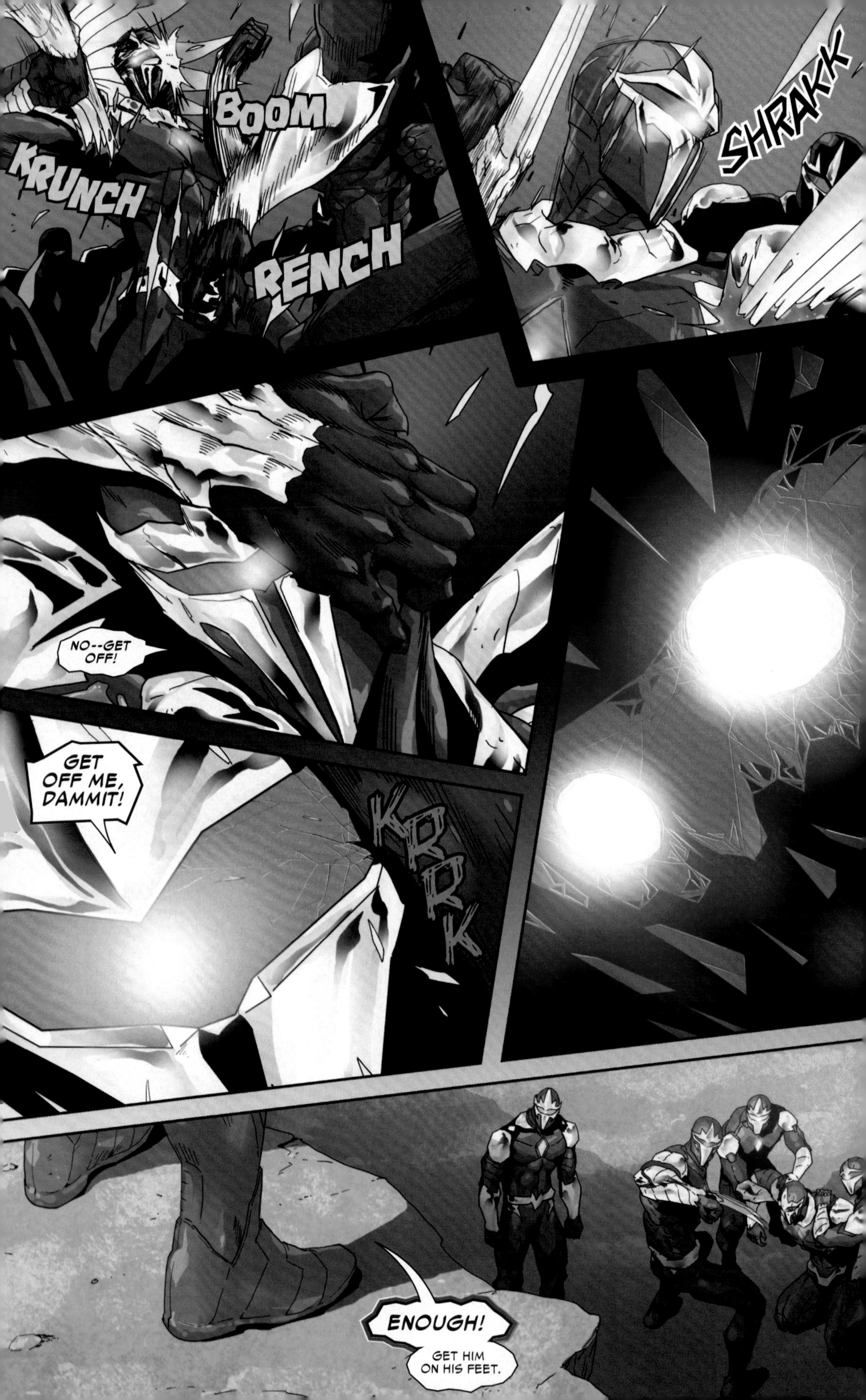
BOOM
KRUNCH
RENCH
SHRAKK
NO--GET OFF!
GET OFF ME, DAMMIT!
KRRRK
ENOUGH!
GET HIM ON HIS FEET.

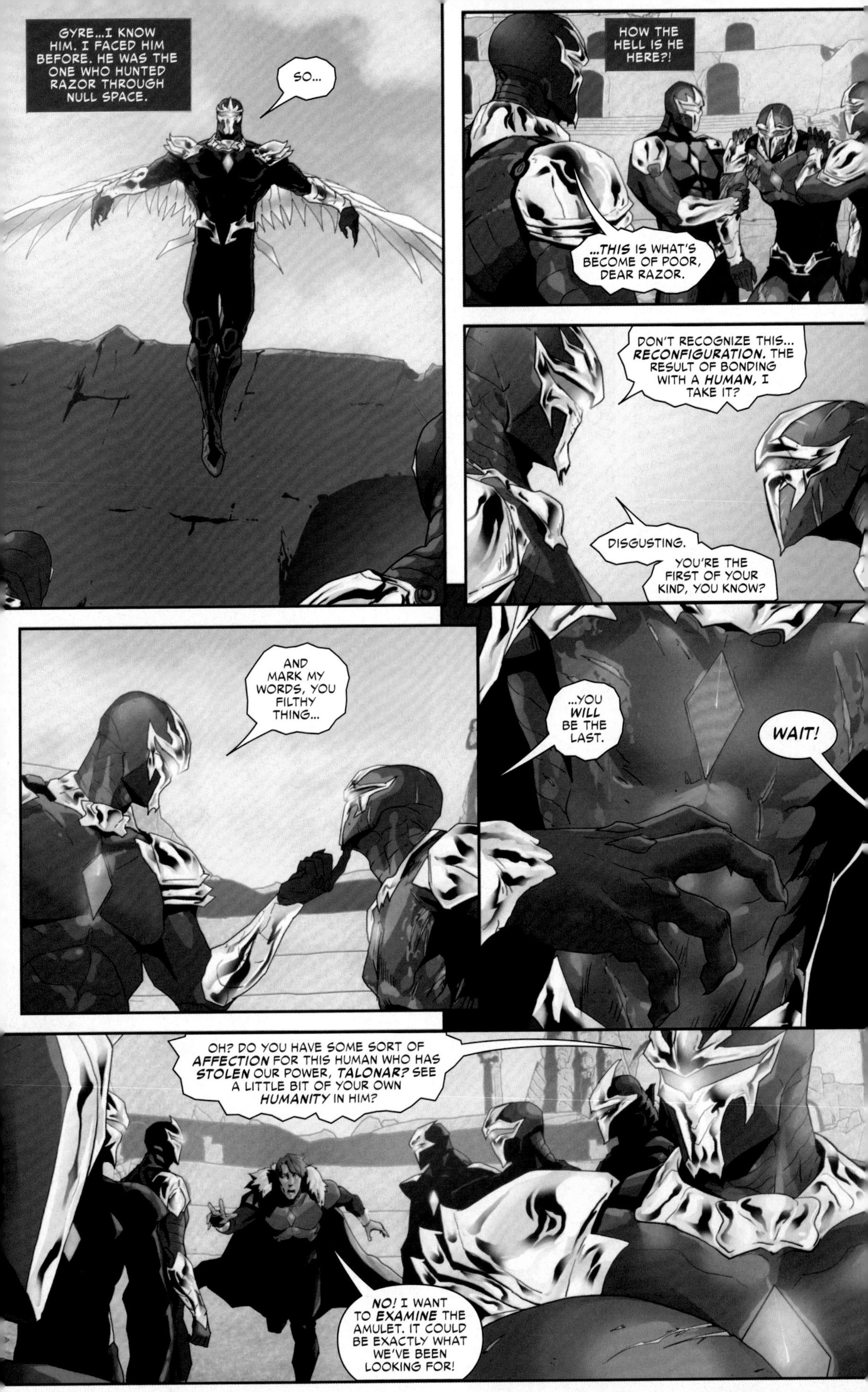
GYRE...I KNOW HIM. I FACED HIM BEFORE. HE WAS THE ONE WHO HUNTED RAZOR THROUGH NULL SPACE.
SO...
HOW THE HELL IS HE HERE?!
...THIS IS WHAT'S BECOME OF POOR, DEAR RAZOR.
DON'T RECOGNIZE THIS... RECONFIGURATION. THE RESULT OF BONDING WITH A HUMAN, I TAKE IT?
DISGUSTING.
YOU'RE THE FIRST OF YOUR KIND, YOU KNOW?
AND MARK MY WORDS, YOU FILTHY THING...
...YOU WILL BE THE LAST.
WAIT!
OH? DO YOU HAVE SOME SORT OF AFFECTION FOR THIS HUMAN WHO HAS STOLEN OUR POWER, TALONAR? SEE A LITTLE BIT OF YOUR OWN HUMANITY IN HIM?
NO! I WANT TO EXAMINE THE AMULET. IT COULD BE EXACTLY WHAT WE'VE BEEN LOOKING FOR!

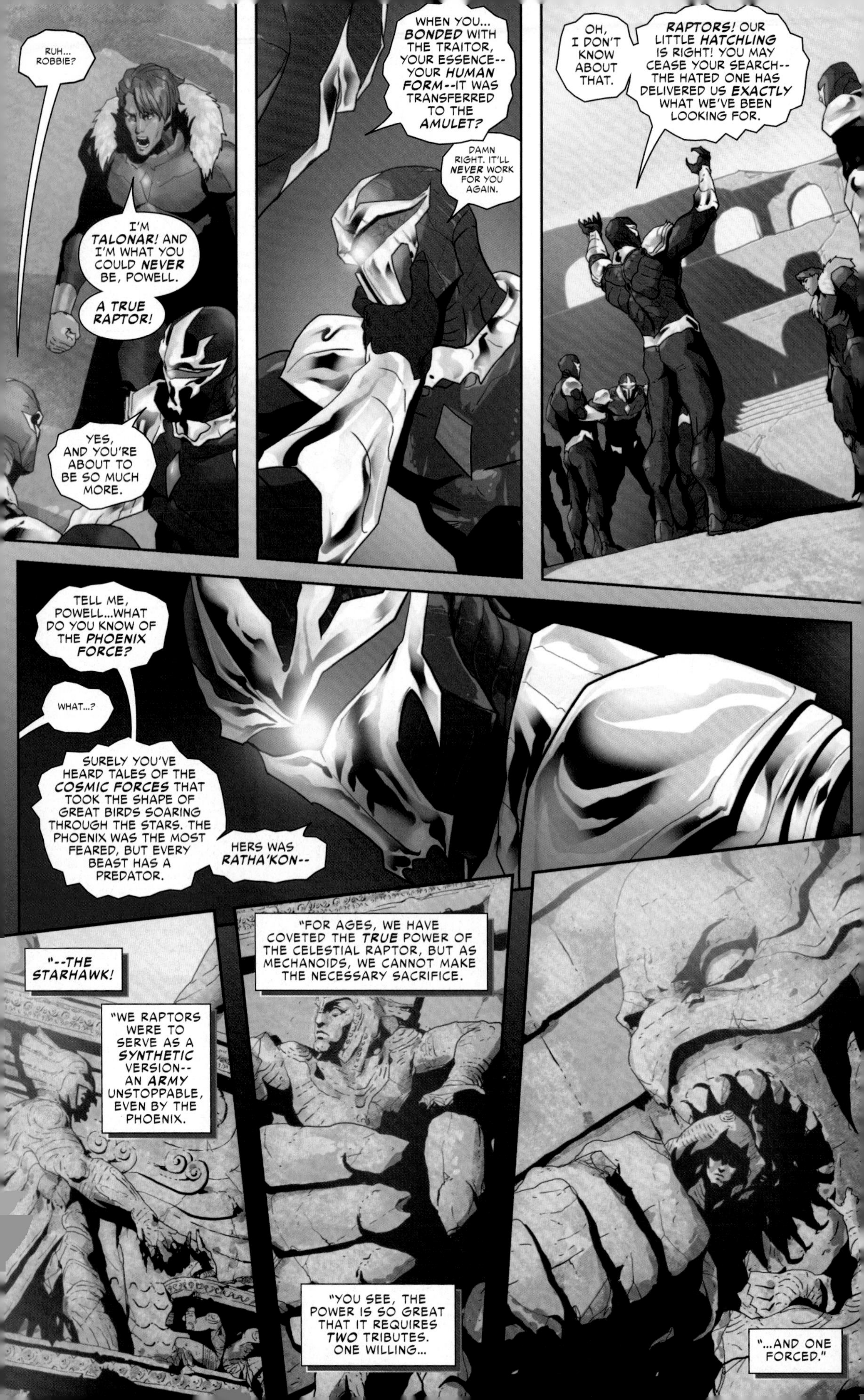
RUH... ROBBIE?
I'M TALONAR! AND I'M WHAT YOU COULD NEVER BE, POWELL.
A TRUE RAPTOR!
YES, AND YOU'RE ABOUT TO BE SO MUCH MORE.
WHEN YOU... BONDED WITH THE TRAITOR, YOUR ESSENCE--YOUR HUMAN FORM--IT WAS TRANSFERRED TO THE AMULET?
DAMN RIGHT. IT'LL NEVER WORK FOR YOU AGAIN.
OH, I DON'T KNOW ABOUT THAT.
RAPTORS! OUR LITTLE HATCHLING IS RIGHT! YOU MAY CEASE YOUR SEARCH--THE HATED ONE HAS DELIVERED US EXACTLY WHAT WE'VE BEEN LOOKING FOR.
TELL ME, POWELL...WHAT DO YOU KNOW OF THE PHOENIX FORCE?
WHAT...?
SURELY YOU'VE HEARD TALES OF THE COSMIC FORCES THAT TOOK THE SHAPE OF GREAT BIRDS SOARING THROUGH THE STARS. THE PHOENIX WAS THE MOST FEARED, BUT EVERY BEAST HAS A PREDATOR.
HERS WAS RATHA'KON--
"--THE STARHAWK!
"WE RAPTORS WERE TO SERVE AS A SYNTHETIC VERSION--AN ARMY UNSTOPPABLE, EVEN BY THE PHOENIX.
"FOR AGES, WE HAVE COVETED THE TRUE POWER OF THE CELESTIAL RAPTOR, BUT AS MECHANOIDS, WE CANNOT MAKE THE NECESSARY SACRIFICE.
"YOU SEE, THE POWER IS SO GREAT THAT IT REQUIRES TWO TRIBUTES. ONE WILLING...
"...AND ONE FORCED."

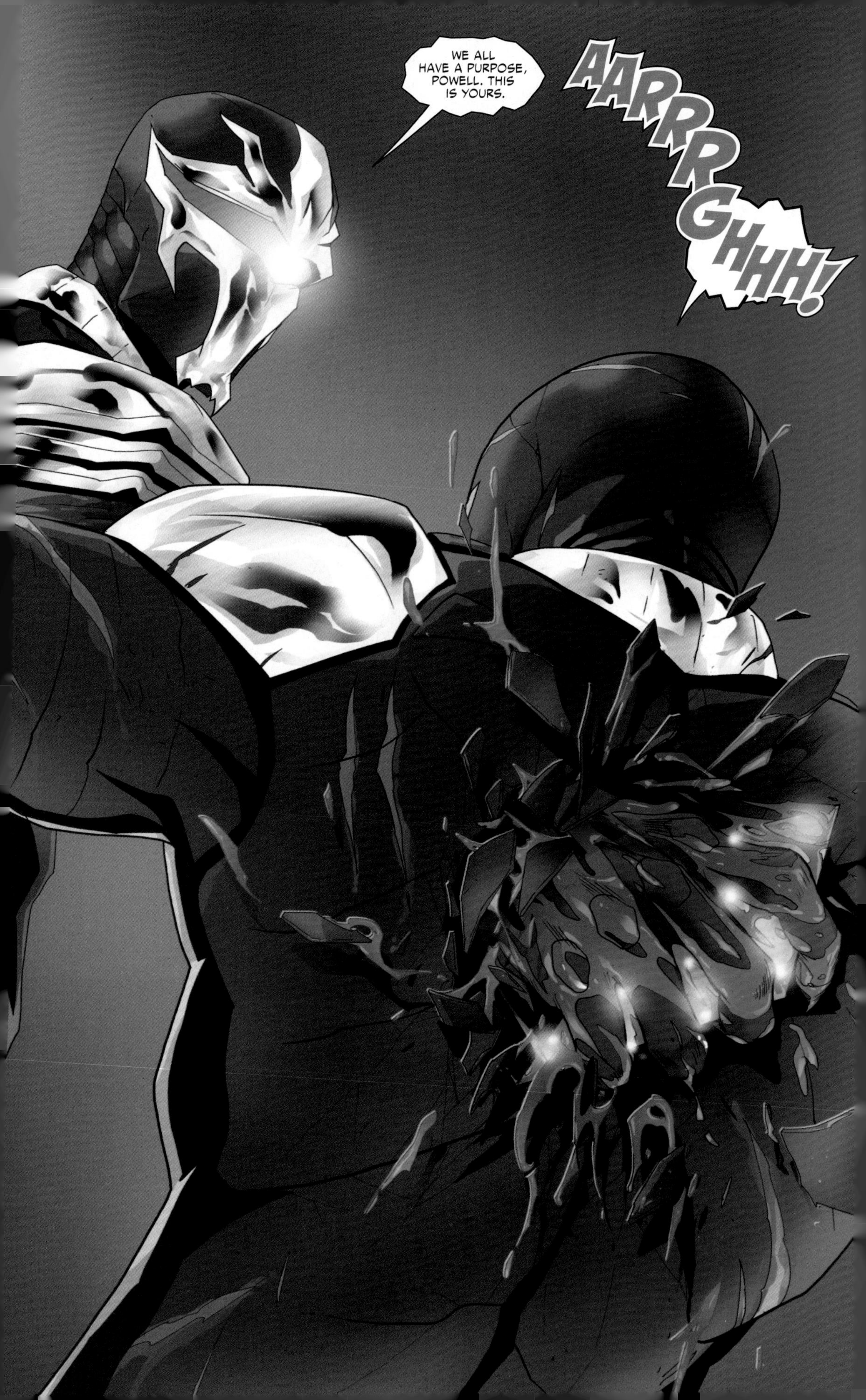
WE ALL HAVE A PURPOSE, POWELL. THIS IS YOURS.
AARRRGHHH!

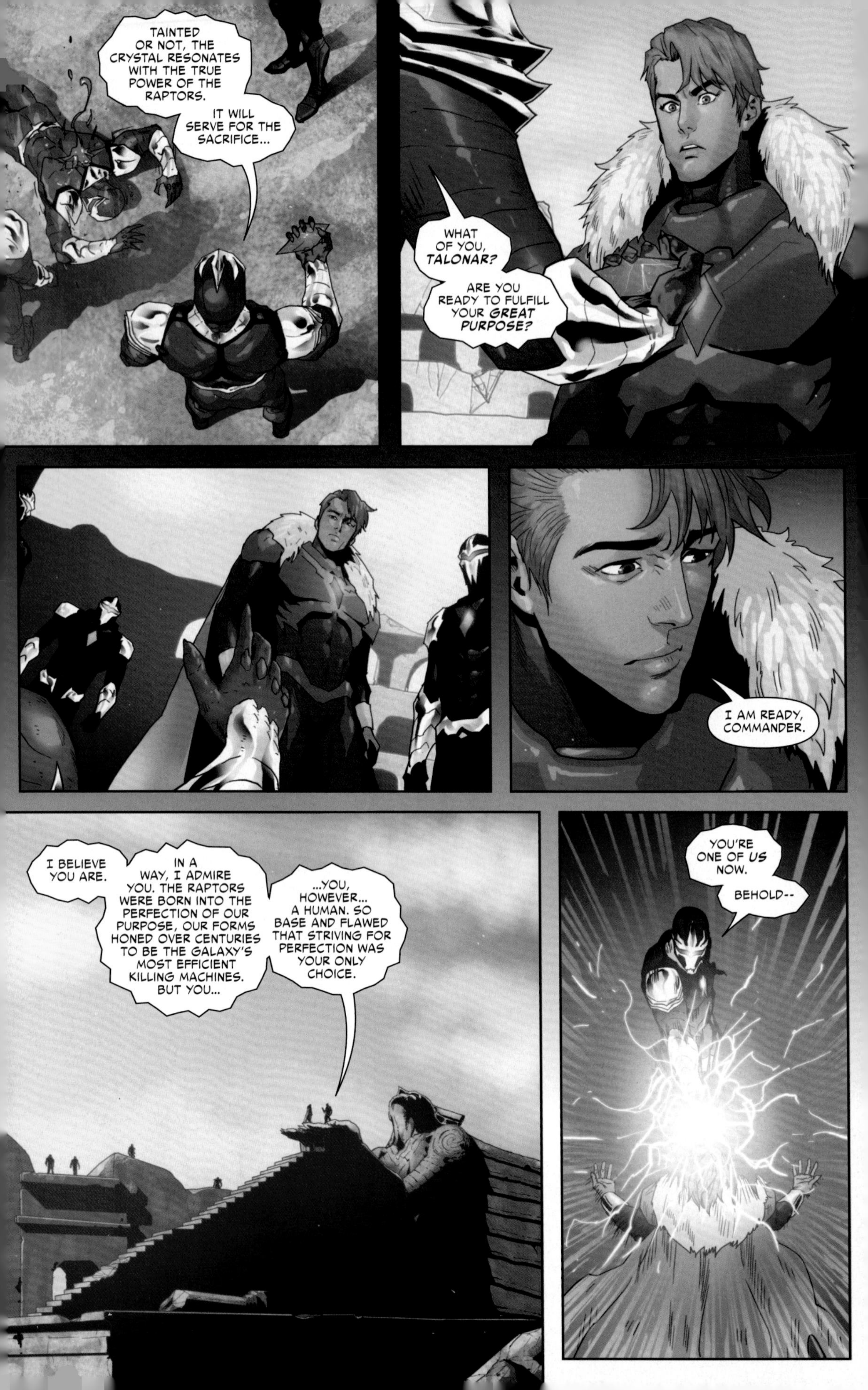
TAINTED OR NOT, THE CRYSTAL RESONATES WITH THE TRUE POWER OF THE RAPTORS.
IT WILL SERVE FOR THE SACRIFICE...
WHAT OF YOU, *TALONAR?*
ARE YOU READY TO FULFILL YOUR *GREAT PURPOSE?*
I AM READY, COMMANDER.
I BELIEVE YOU ARE.
IN A WAY, I ADMIRE YOU. THE RAPTORS WERE BORN INTO THE PERFECTION OF OUR PURPOSE, OUR FORMS HONED OVER CENTURIES TO BE THE GALAXY'S MOST EFFICIENT KILLING MACHINES. BUT YOU...
...YOU, HOWEVER... A HUMAN. SO BASE AND FLAWED THAT STRIVING FOR PERFECTION WAS YOUR ONLY CHOICE.
YOU'RE ONE OF *US* NOW.
BEHOLD--

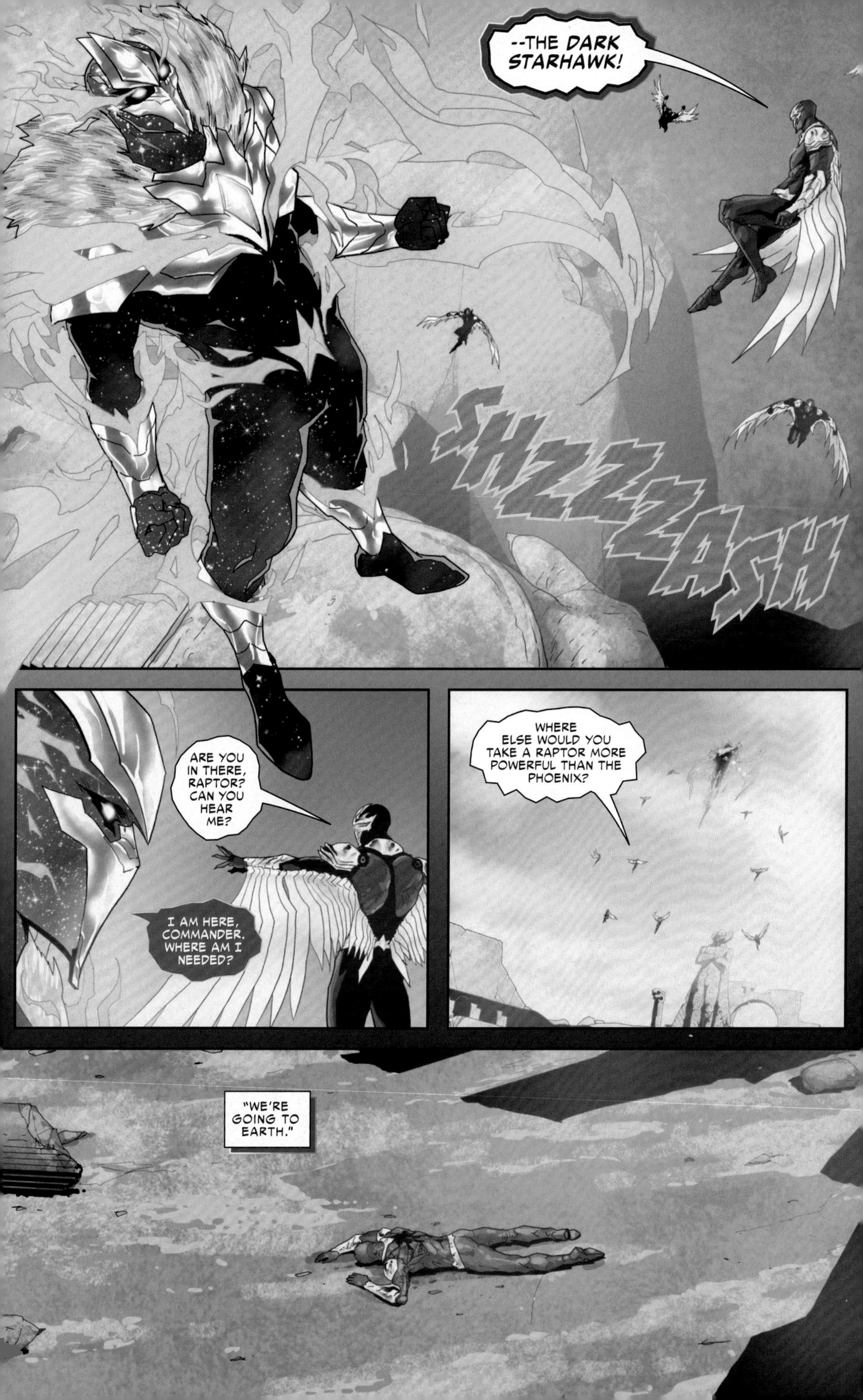
--THE DARK STARHAWK!
SHZZZASH
ARE YOU IN THERE, RAPTOR? CAN YOU HEAR ME?
I AM HERE, COMMANDER. WHERE AM I NEEDED?
WHERE ELSE WOULD YOU TAKE A RAPTOR MORE POWERFUL THAN THE PHOENIX?
"WE'RE GOING TO EARTH."

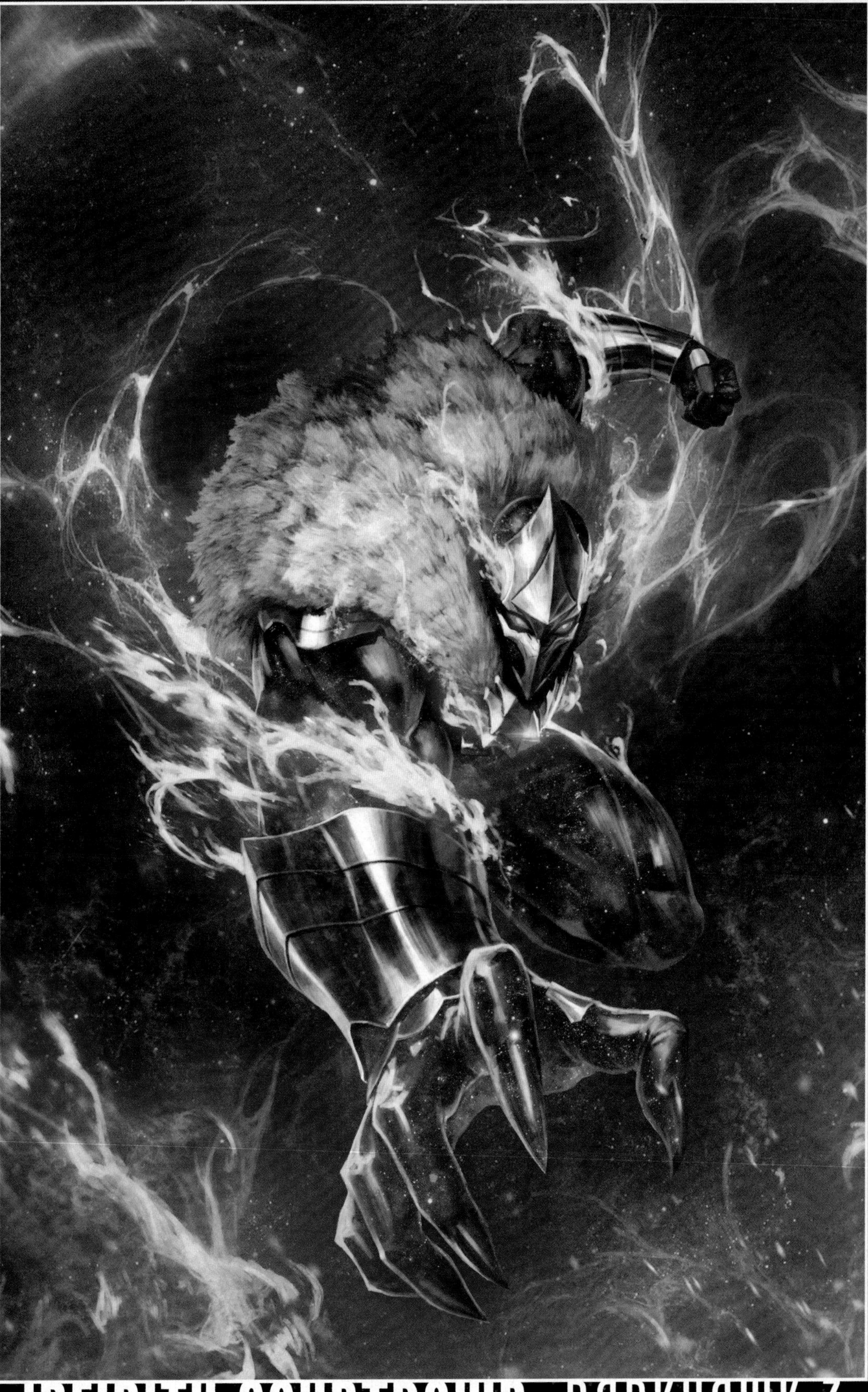

INFINITY COUNTDOWN: DARKHAWK 3

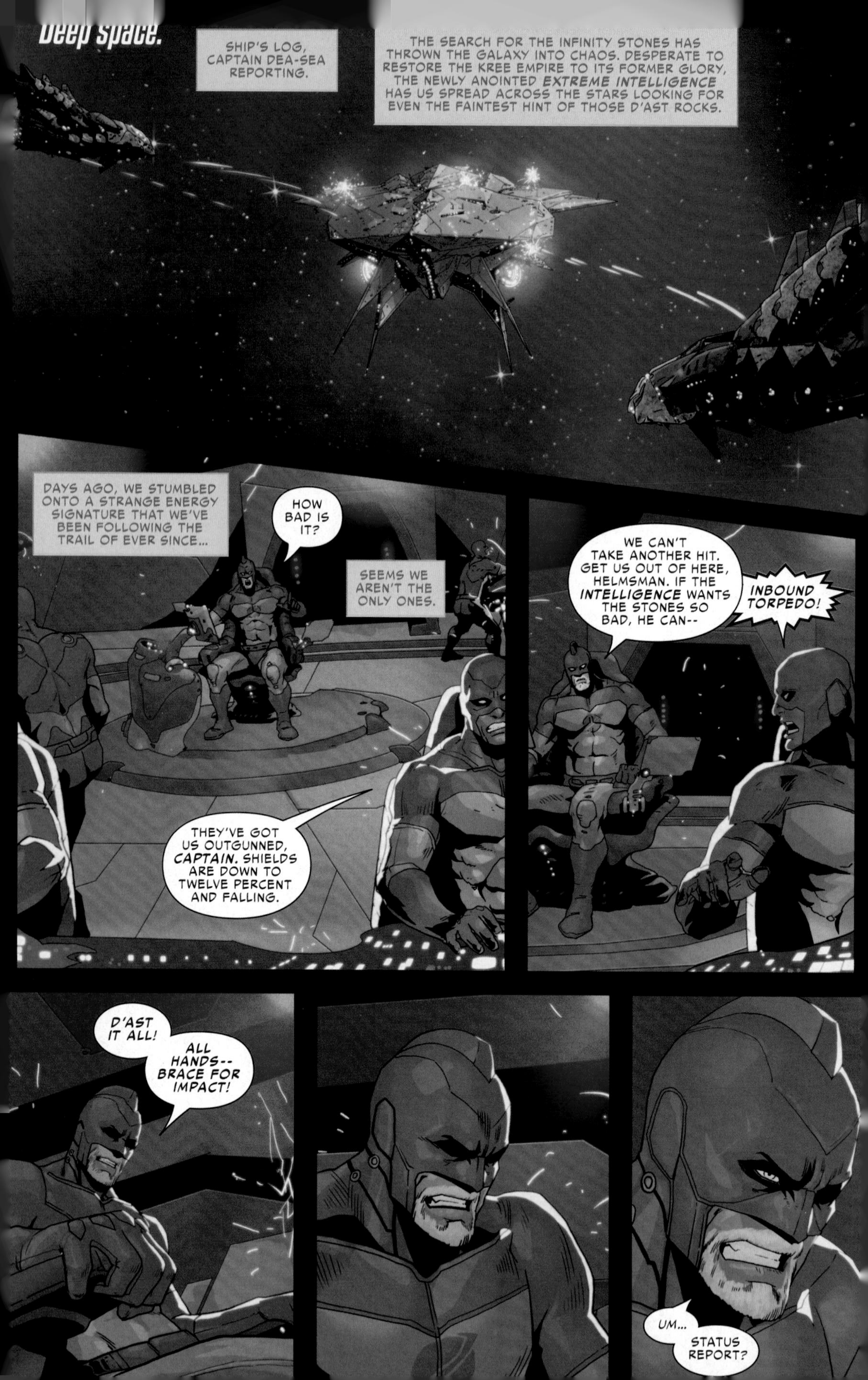
Deep Space.
SHIP'S LOG, CAPTAIN DEA-SEA REPORTING.
THE SEARCH FOR THE INFINITY STONES HAS THROWN THE GALAXY INTO CHAOS. DESPERATE TO RESTORE THE KREE EMPIRE TO ITS FORMER GLORY, THE NEWLY ANOINTED EXTREME INTELLIGENCE HAS US SPREAD ACROSS THE STARS LOOKING FOR EVEN THE FAINTEST HINT OF THOSE D'AST ROCKS.
DAYS AGO, WE STUMBLED ONTO A STRANGE ENERGY SIGNATURE THAT WE'VE BEEN FOLLOWING THE TRAIL OF EVER SINCE...
HOW BAD IS IT?
SEEMS WE AREN'T THE ONLY ONES.
THEY'VE GOT US OUTGUNNED, CAPTAIN. SHIELDS ARE DOWN TO TWELVE PERCENT AND FALLING.
WE CAN'T TAKE ANOTHER HIT. GET US OUT OF HERE, HELMSMAN. IF THE INTELLIGENCE WANTS THE STONES SO BAD, HE CAN--
INBOUND TORPEDO!
D'AST IT ALL!
ALL HANDS-- BRACE FOR IMPACT!
UM...
STATUS REPORT?

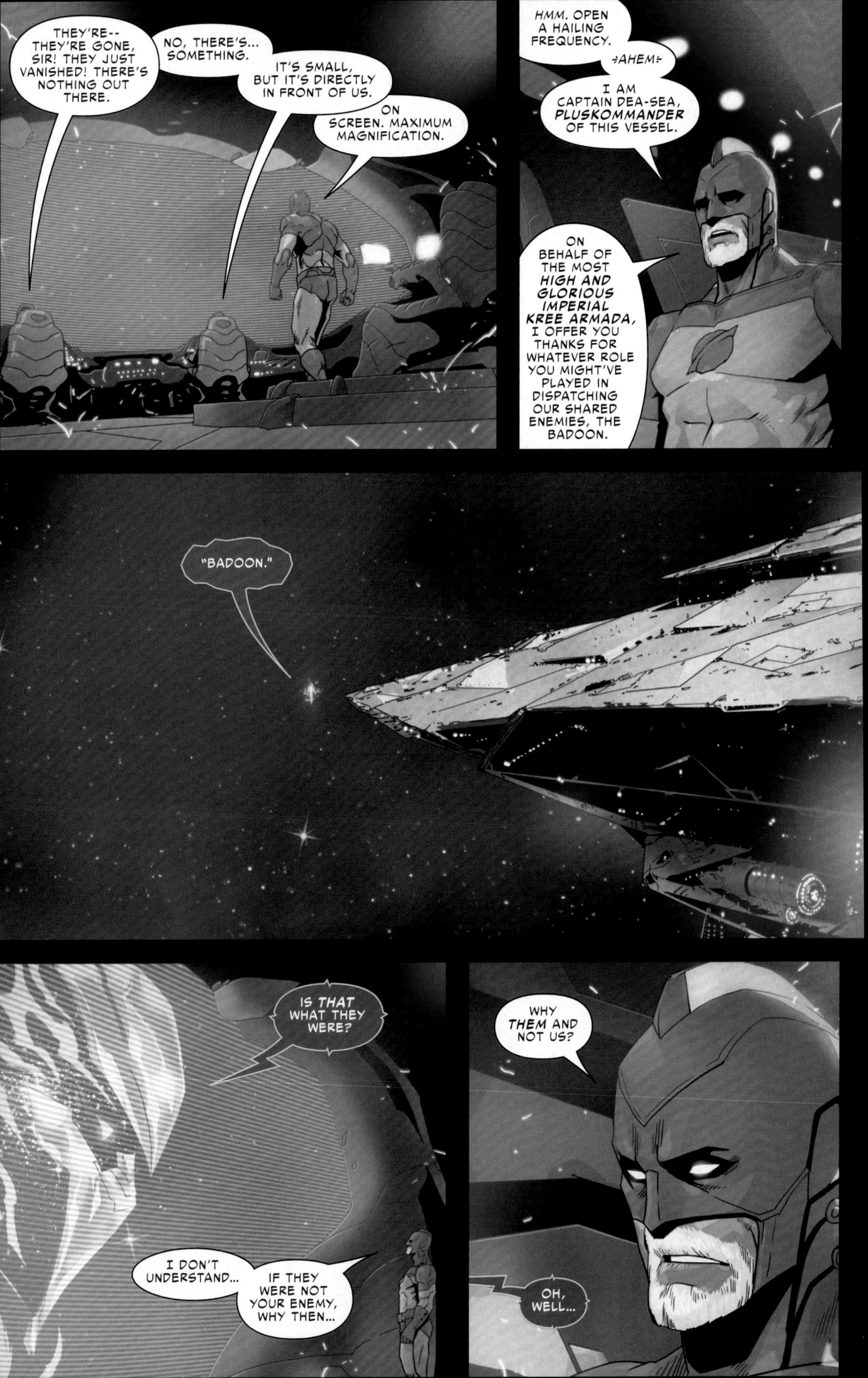
THEY'RE-- THEY'RE GONE, SIR! THEY JUST VANISHED! THERE'S NOTHING OUT THERE.
NO, THERE'S... SOMETHING.
IT'S SMALL, BUT IT'S DIRECTLY IN FRONT OF US.
ON SCREEN. MAXIMUM MAGNIFICATION.
HMM. OPEN A HAILING FREQUENCY.
AHEM
I AM CAPTAIN DEA-SEA, PLUSKOMMANDER OF THIS VESSEL.
ON BEHALF OF THE MOST HIGH AND GLORIOUS IMPERIAL KREE ARMADA, I OFFER YOU THANKS FOR WHATEVER ROLE YOU MIGHT'VE PLAYED IN DISPATCHING OUR SHARED ENEMIES, THE BADOON.
"BADOON."
IS THAT WHAT THEY WERE?
I DON'T UNDERSTAND...
IF THEY WERE NOT YOUR ENEMY, WHY THEN...
WHY THEM AND NOT US?
OH, WELL...

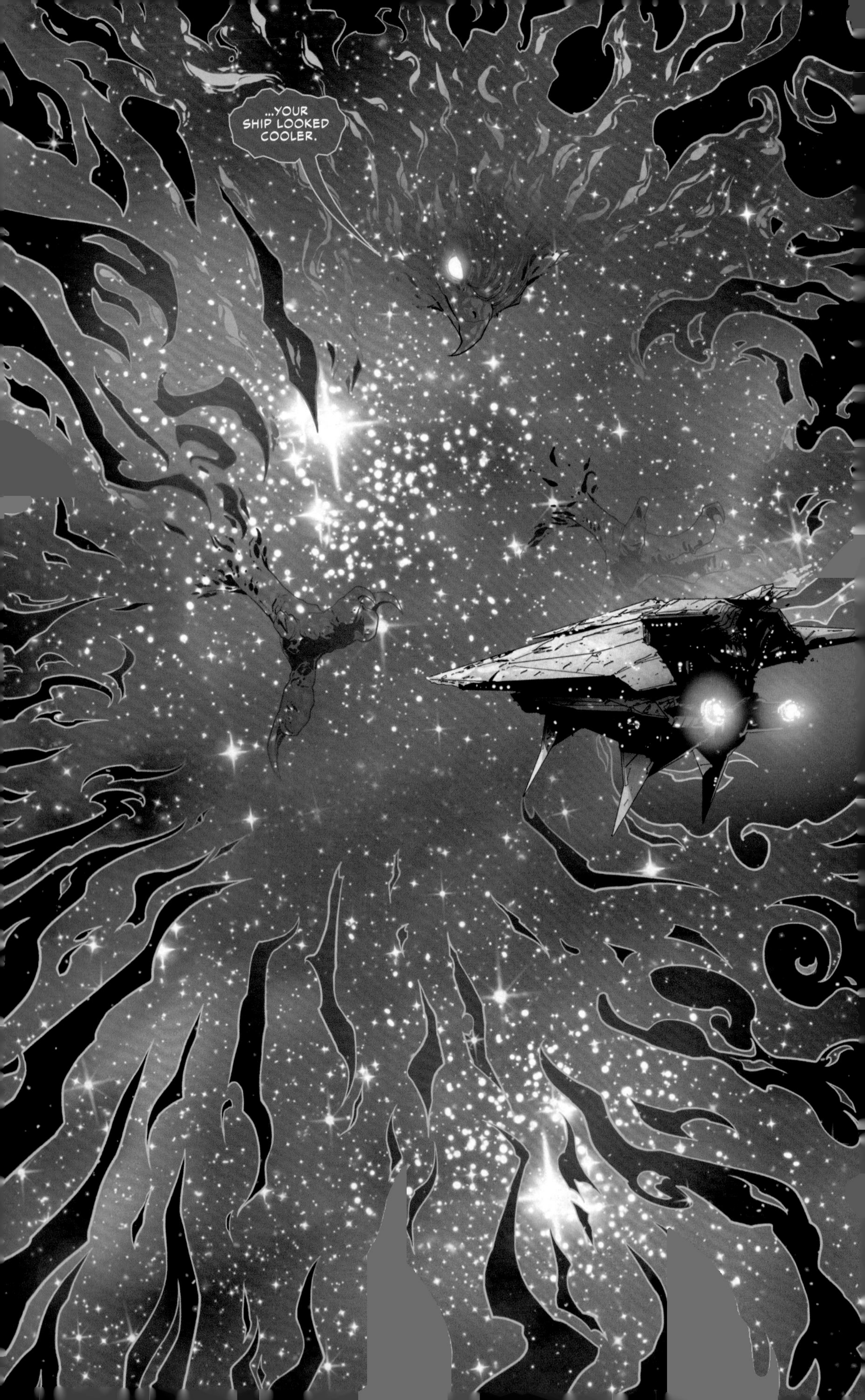
...YOUR SHIP LOOKED COOLER.

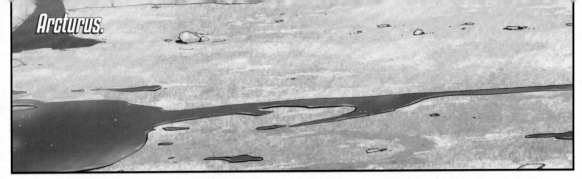

SEEMS LIKE THIS SHOULD HURT MORE.

I MEAN, DON'T GET ME WRONG...IT SUCKS REAL BAD. BUT COMPARED TO GETTING MY EARS GAUGED, THIS IS *NOTHING*.

THAT'S IT, CHRIS. KEEP MAKING JOKES.

ANYTHING TO TAKE MY MIND OFF THE GIANT, GAPING HOLE IN MY CHEST, AND THE BUCKETS OF WHATEVER THIS GREEN STUFF IS LEAKING OUT OF ME.

I REALLY SCREWED UP. CAME OUT HERE HALF-COCKED, AND GOT MY BUTT KICKED GOOD.

MIRANDA TRIED TO WARN ME. AND NOW I'M DYING ON SOME ALIEN WORLD I'VE NEVER EVEN HEARD OF...

...WHILE GYRE AND THE *RAPTORS* USE MY *SOUL* TO POWER A SPACE GOD READY TO DESTROY EARTH.

IF I DON'T STOP THEM, EVERYONE I KNOW WILL DIE.

CAN'T LET THEM, BUT...HOW CAN I FIGHT WHEN I CAN'T EVEN STAND? HOW--

NO...

WHO...

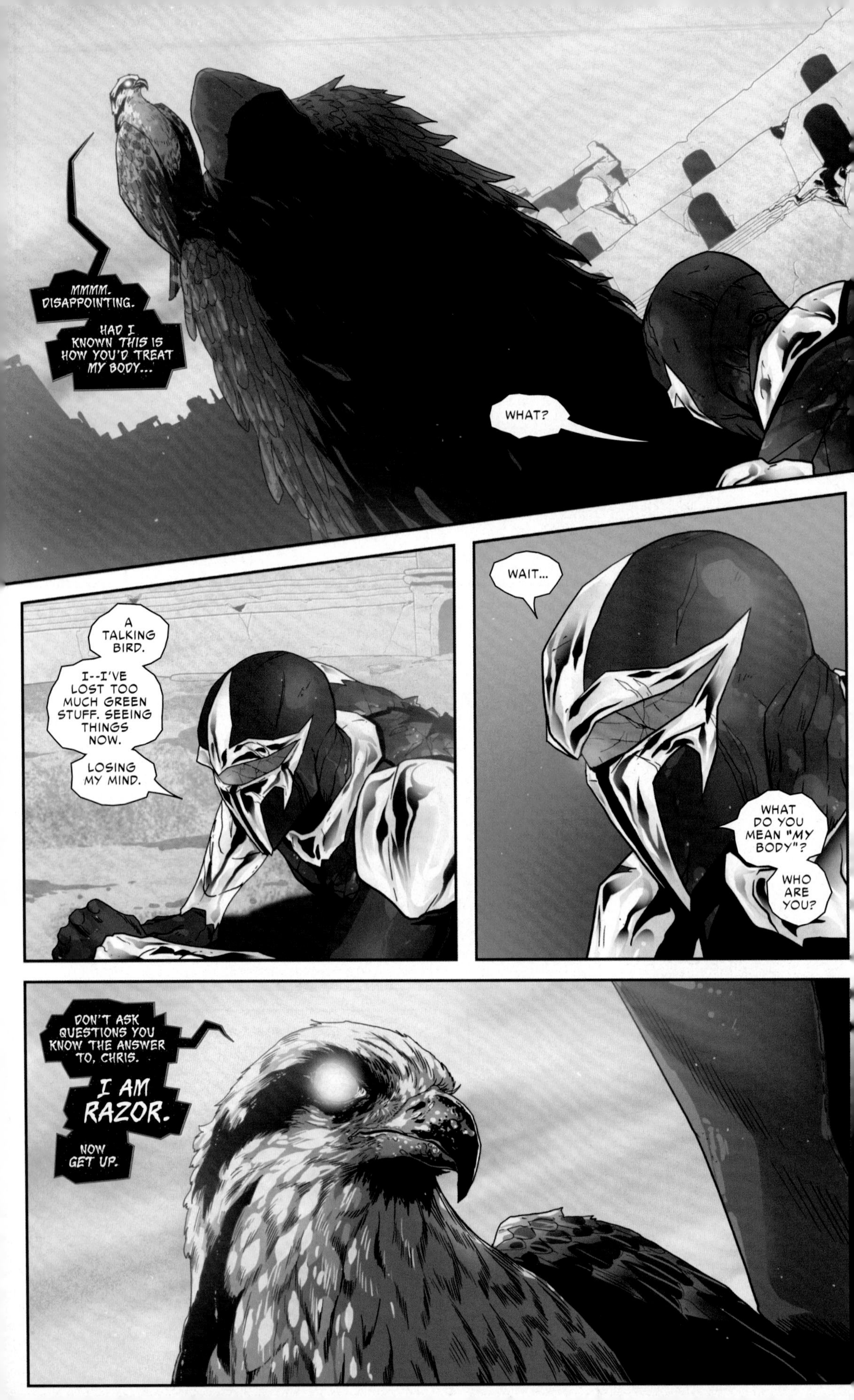
MMMM. DISAPPOINTING.
HAD I KNOWN THIS IS HOW YOU'D TREAT MY BODY...
WHAT?
A TALKING BIRD.
I--I'VE LOST TOO MUCH GREEN STUFF. SEEING THINGS NOW.
LOSING MY MIND.
WAIT...
WHAT DO YOU MEAN "MY BODY"?
WHO ARE YOU?
DON'T ASK QUESTIONS YOU KNOW THE ANSWER TO, CHRIS.
I AM RAZOR.
NOW GET UP.

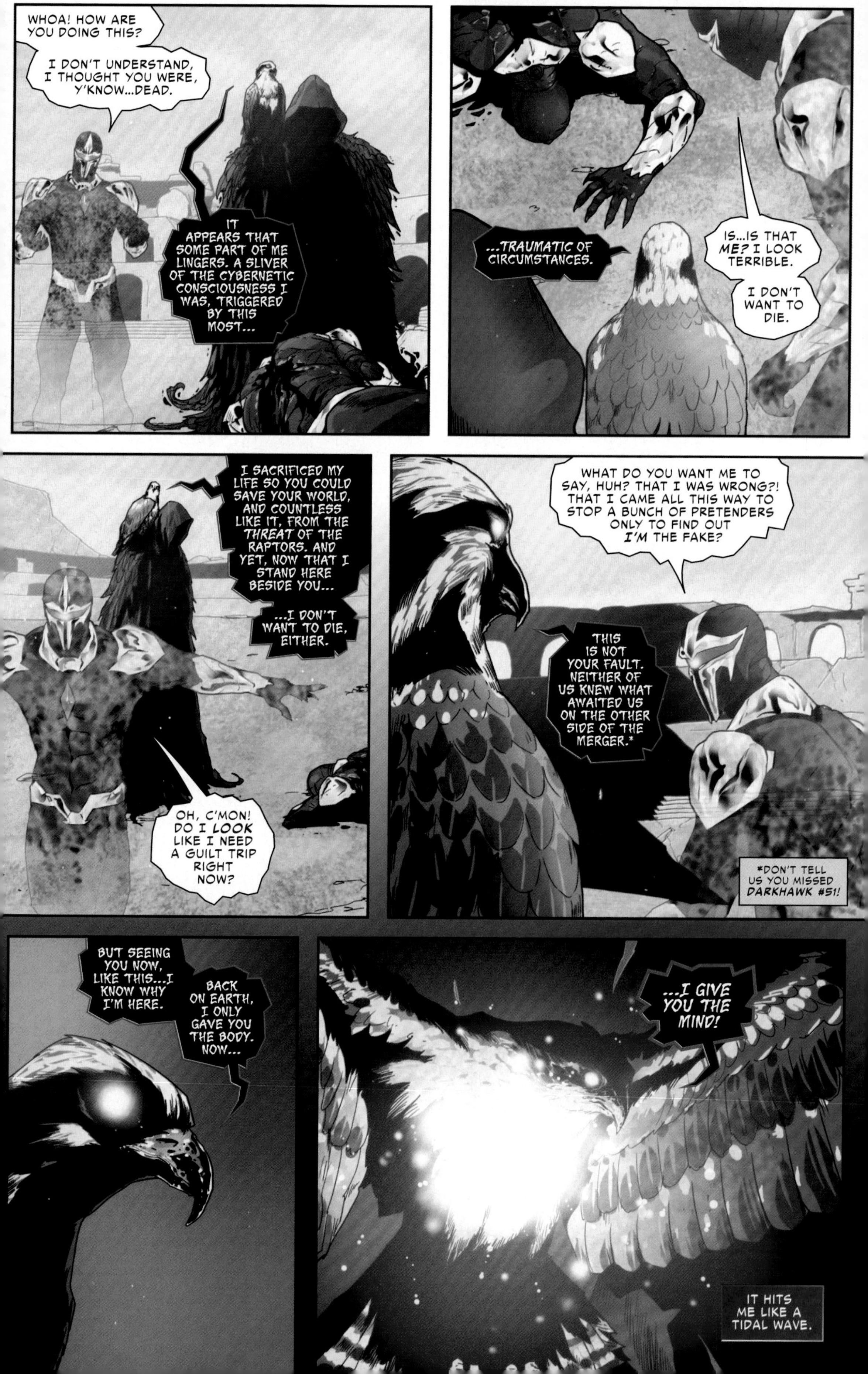
WHOA! HOW ARE YOU DOING THIS?
I DON'T UNDERSTAND, I THOUGHT YOU WERE, Y'KNOW...DEAD.
IT APPEARS THAT SOME PART OF ME LINGERS. A SLIVER OF THE CYBERNETIC CONSCIOUSNESS I WAS, TRIGGERED BY THIS MOST...
...TRAUMATIC OF CIRCUMSTANCES.
IS...IS THAT ME? I LOOK TERRIBLE.
I DON'T WANT TO DIE.
I SACRIFICED MY LIFE SO YOU COULD SAVE YOUR WORLD, AND COUNTLESS LIKE IT, FROM THE THREAT OF THE RAPTORS. AND YET, NOW THAT I STAND HERE BESIDE YOU...
...I DON'T WANT TO DIE, EITHER.
OH, C'MON! DO I LOOK LIKE I NEED A GUILT TRIP RIGHT NOW?
WHAT DO YOU WANT ME TO SAY, HUH? THAT I WAS WRONG?! THAT I CAME ALL THIS WAY TO STOP A BUNCH OF PRETENDERS ONLY TO FIND OUT I'M THE FAKE?
THIS IS NOT YOUR FAULT. NEITHER OF US KNEW WHAT AWAITED US ON THE OTHER SIDE OF THE MERGER.*
*DON'T TELL US YOU MISSED DARKHAWK #51!
BUT SEEING YOU NOW, LIKE THIS...I KNOW WHY I'M HERE.
BACK ON EARTH, I ONLY GAVE YOU THE BODY. NOW...
...I GIVE YOU THE MIND!
IT HITS ME LIKE A TIDAL WAVE.

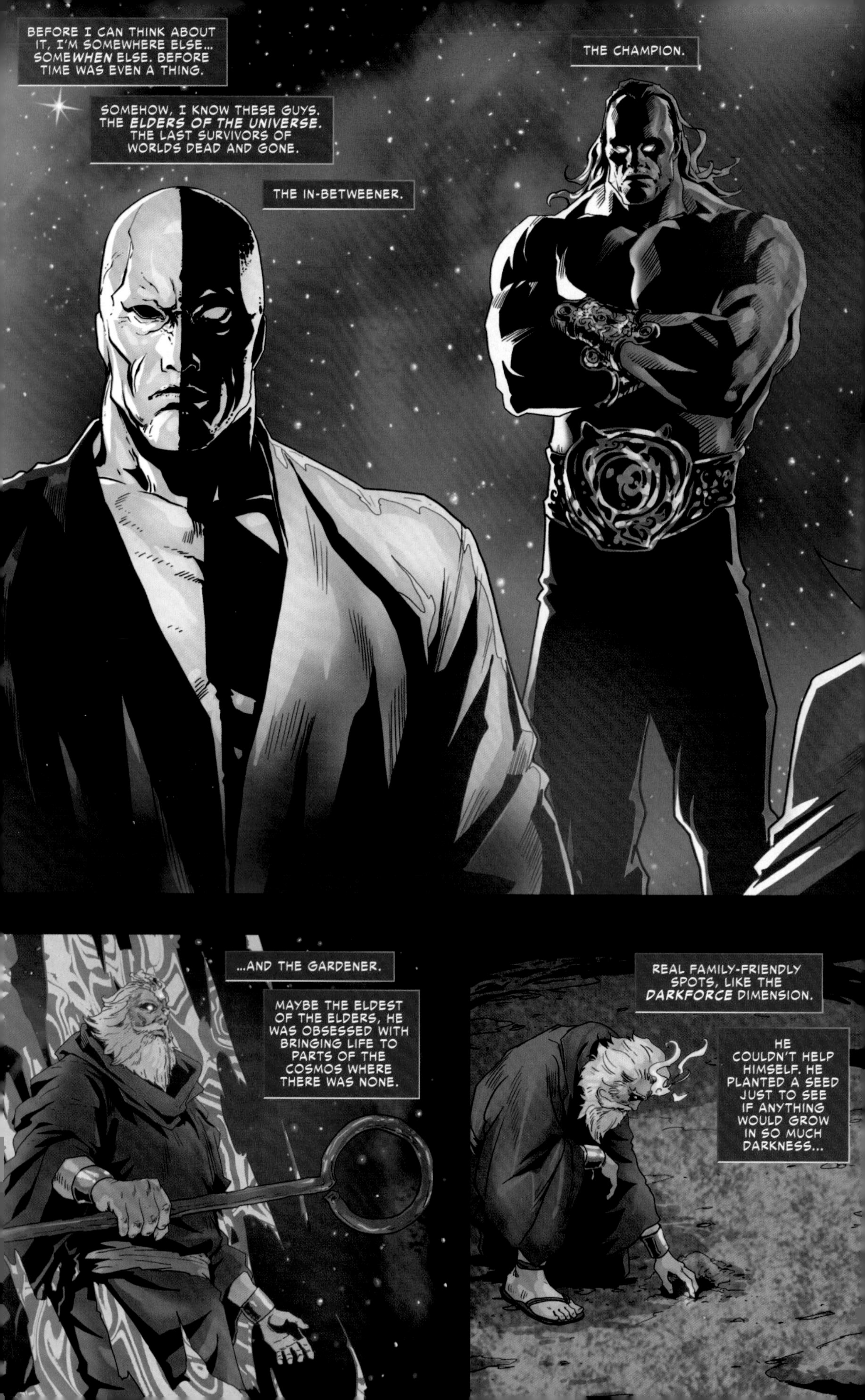
BEFORE I CAN THINK ABOUT IT, I'M SOMEWHERE ELSE... SOMEWHEN ELSE. BEFORE TIME WAS EVEN A THING.
SOMEHOW, I KNOW THESE GUYS. THE ELDERS OF THE UNIVERSE. THE LAST SURVIVORS OF WORLDS DEAD AND GONE.
THE IN-BETWEENER.
THE CHAMPION.
...AND THE GARDENER.
MAYBE THE ELDEST OF THE ELDERS, HE WAS OBSESSED WITH BRINGING LIFE TO PARTS OF THE COSMOS WHERE THERE WAS NONE.
REAL FAMILY-FRIENDLY SPOTS, LIKE THE DARKFORCE DIMENSION.
HE COULDN'T HELP HIMSELF. HE PLANTED A SEED JUST TO SEE IF ANYTHING WOULD GROW IN SO MUCH DARKNESS...

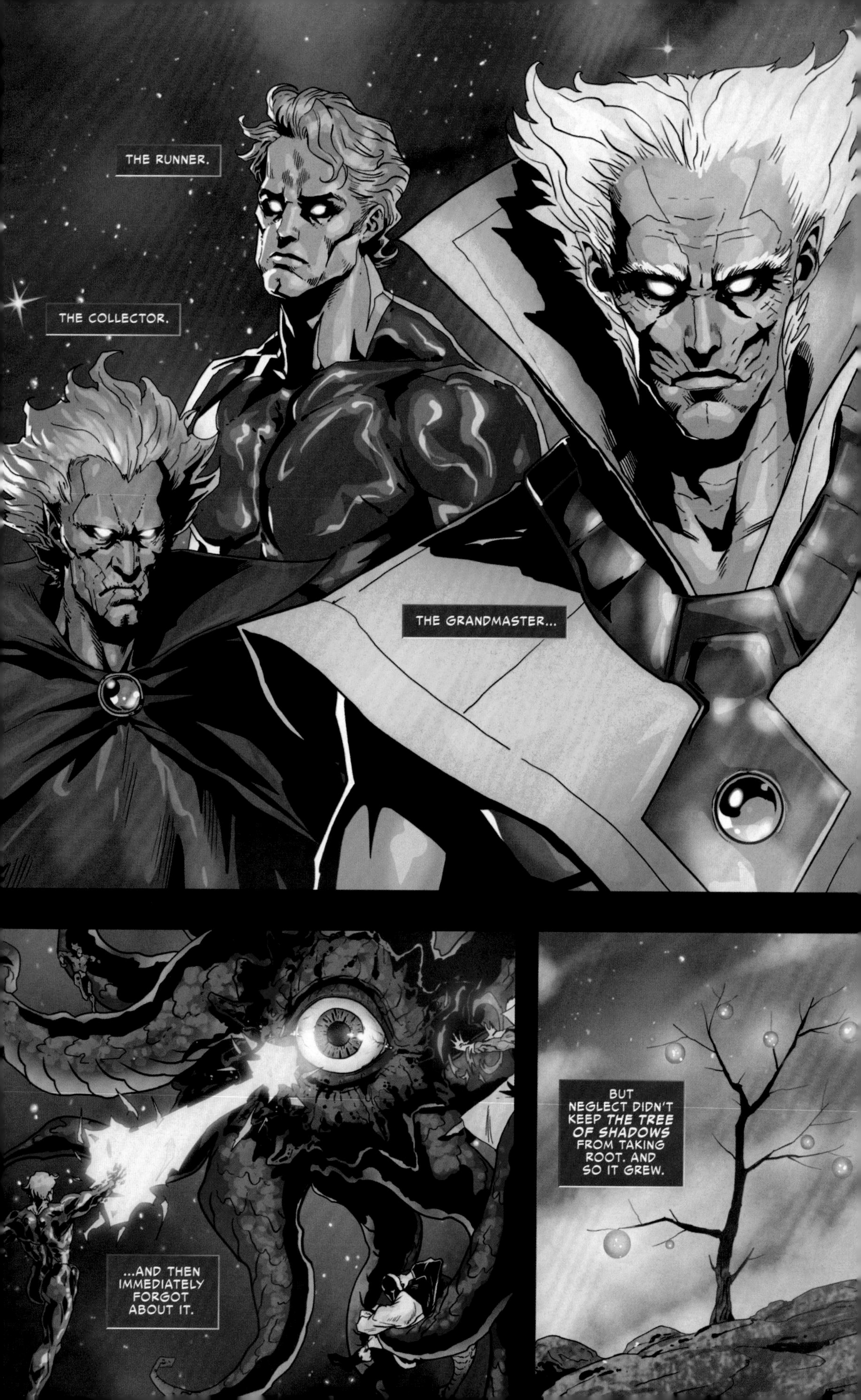
THE RUNNER.
THE COLLECTOR.
THE GRANDMASTER...
...AND THEN IMMEDIATELY FORGOT ABOUT IT.
BUT NEGLECT DIDN'T KEEP THE TREE OF SHADOWS FROM TAKING ROOT. AND SO IT GREW.

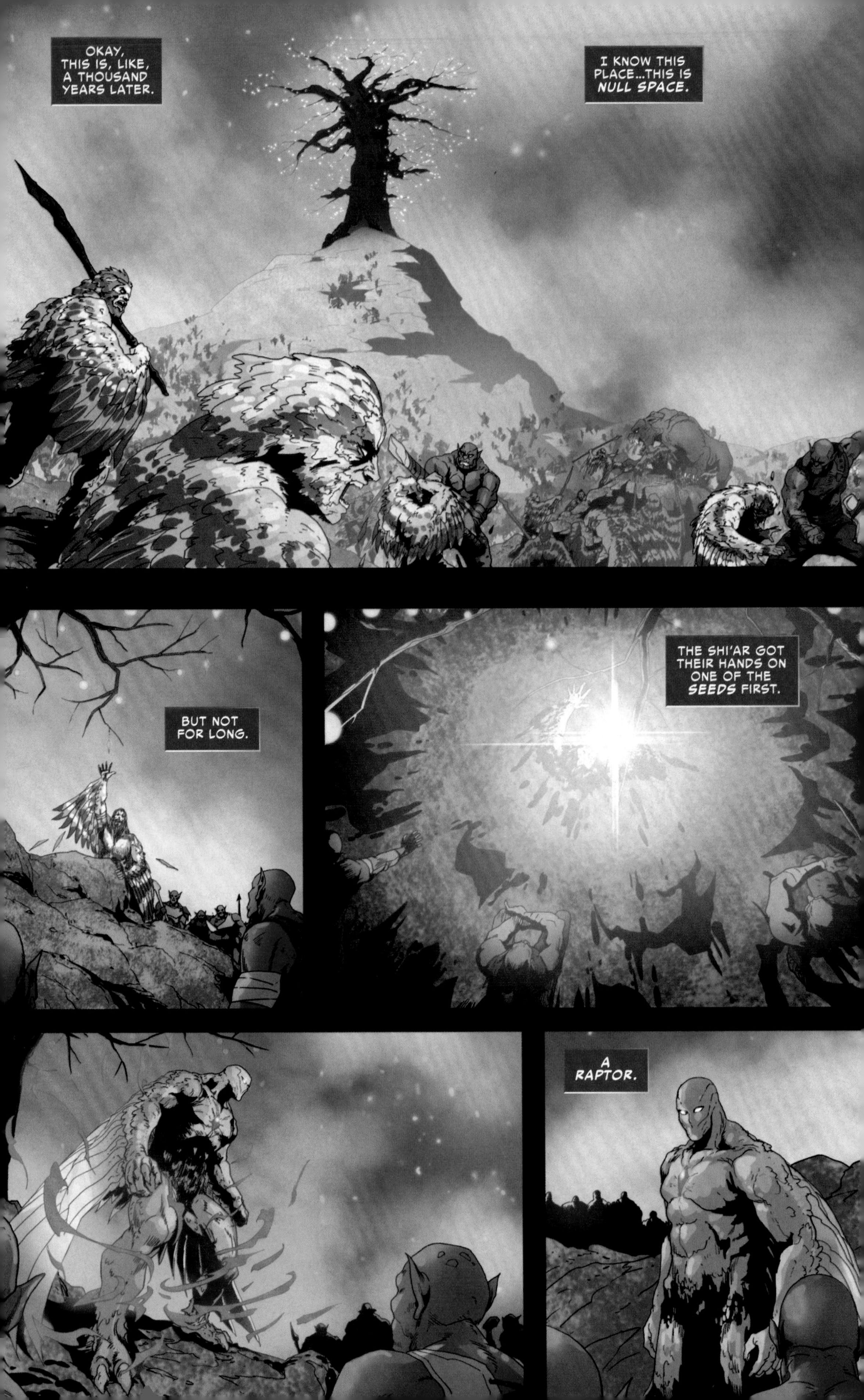
OKAY, THIS IS, LIKE, A THOUSAND YEARS LATER.
I KNOW THIS PLACE...THIS IS NULL SPACE.
BUT NOT FOR LONG.
THE SHI'AR GOT THEIR HANDS ON ONE OF THE SEEDS FIRST.
A RAPTOR.

THOSE GUYS WITH THE FEATHERS, THEY'RE SHI'AR, AND THE GREEN SHAPE-SHIFTERS, THOSE ARE SKRULLS.

THEY'RE FIGHTING OVER THE TREE.

THEIR PHYSIOLOGY, AND ALL THEIR FEARS AND BELIEFS, SHAPED WHAT WAS BORN THAT DAY.

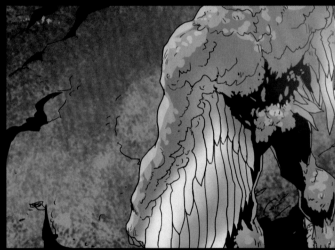

THE FIRST OF ITS KIND.

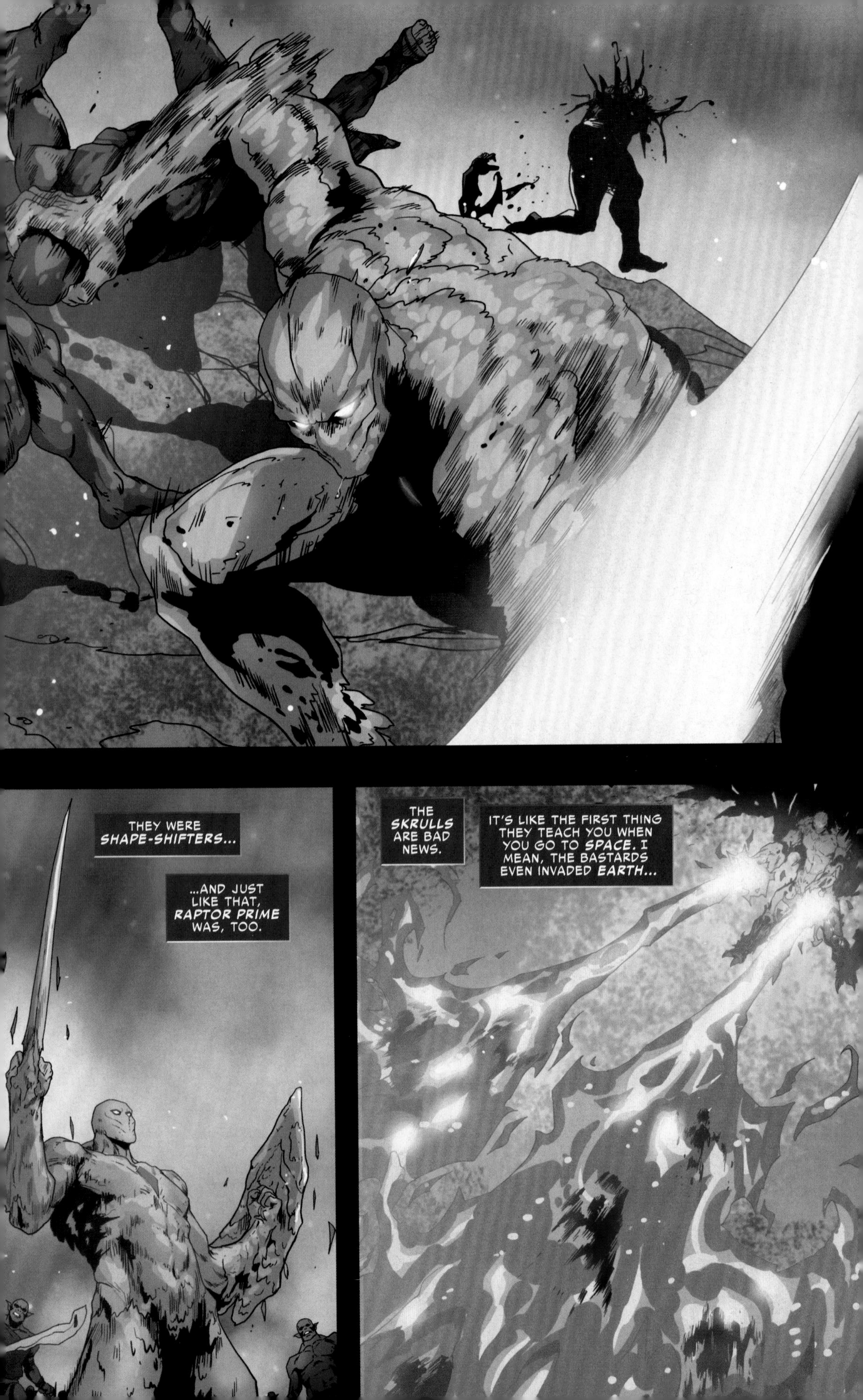
THEY WERE SHAPE-SHIFTERS...
...AND JUST LIKE THAT, RAPTOR PRIME WAS, TOO.
THE SKRULLS ARE BAD NEWS.
IT'S LIKE THE FIRST THING THEY TEACH YOU WHEN YOU GO TO SPACE. I MEAN, THE BASTARDS EVEN INVADED EARTH...

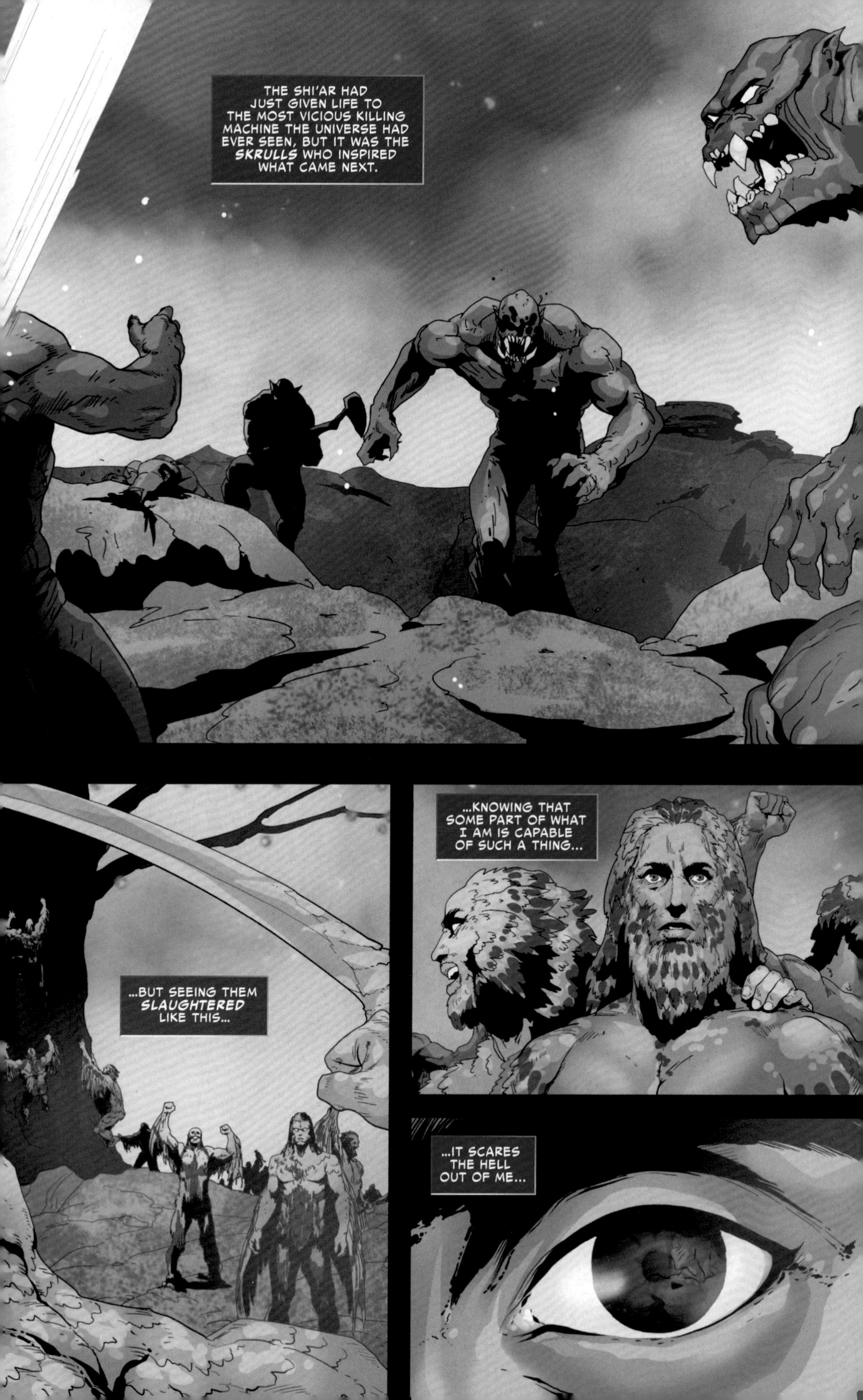
THE SHI'AR HAD JUST GIVEN LIFE TO THE MOST VICIOUS KILLING MACHINE THE UNIVERSE HAD EVER SEEN, BUT IT WAS THE SKRULLS WHO INSPIRED WHAT CAME NEXT.
...BUT SEEING THEM SLAUGHTERED LIKE THIS...
...KNOWING THAT SOME PART OF WHAT I AM IS CAPABLE OF SUCH A THING...
...IT SCARES THE HELL OUT OF ME...

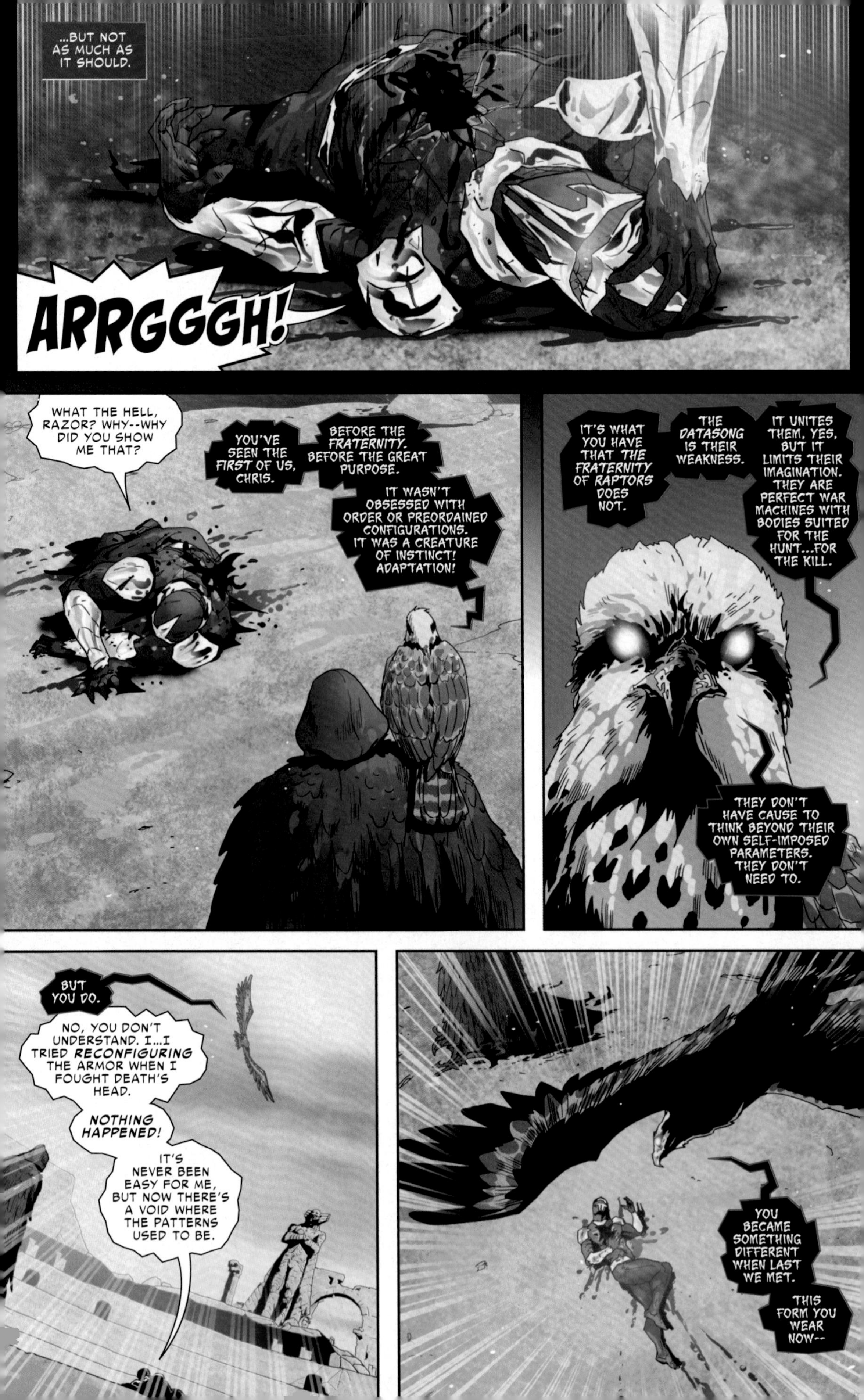
...BUT NOT AS MUCH AS IT SHOULD.
ARRGGGH!
WHAT THE HELL, RAZOR? WHY--WHY DID YOU SHOW ME THAT?
YOU'VE SEEN THE FIRST OF US, CHRIS.
BEFORE THE FRATERNITY. BEFORE THE GREAT PURPOSE.
IT WASN'T OBSESSED WITH ORDER OR PREORDAINED CONFIGURATIONS. IT WAS A CREATURE OF INSTINCT! ADAPTATION!
IT'S WHAT YOU HAVE THAT THE FRATERNITY OF RAPTORS DOES NOT.
THE DATASONG IS THEIR WEAKNESS.
IT UNITES THEM, YES, BUT IT LIMITS THEIR IMAGINATION. THEY ARE PERFECT WAR MACHINES WITH BODIES SUITED FOR THE HUNT...FOR THE KILL.
THEY DON'T HAVE CAUSE TO THINK BEYOND THEIR OWN SELF-IMPOSED PARAMETERS. THEY DON'T NEED TO.
BUT YOU DO.
NO, YOU DON'T UNDERSTAND. I...I TRIED RECONFIGURING THE ARMOR WHEN I FOUGHT DEATH'S HEAD.
NOTHING HAPPENED!
IT'S NEVER BEEN EASY FOR ME, BUT NOW THERE'S A VOID WHERE THE PATTERNS USED TO BE.
YOU BECAME SOMETHING DIFFERENT WHEN LAST WE MET.
THIS FORM YOU WEAR NOW--

--THIS IS RECONFIGURATION!

WHAT?

YOU TOOK THE BLUEPRINT OF WHAT WAS THERE, AND MODIFIED IT.

WHAT YOU WEAR AROUND YOUR SOUL NOW IS NOT A RAPTOR. IT IS SO MUCH MORE! AND YOU WILL FIGHT TO KEEP IT ALIVE!

REACH WITHIN YOURSELF, POWELL! FIND YOUR TRUEST FORM!

STOP. I CAN'T--

FINE! THEN DIE HERE AS YOUR GHOST DESTROYS EVERYTHING YOU'VE EVER LOVED.

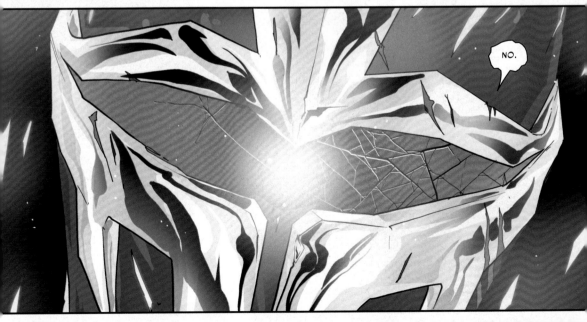

NO.

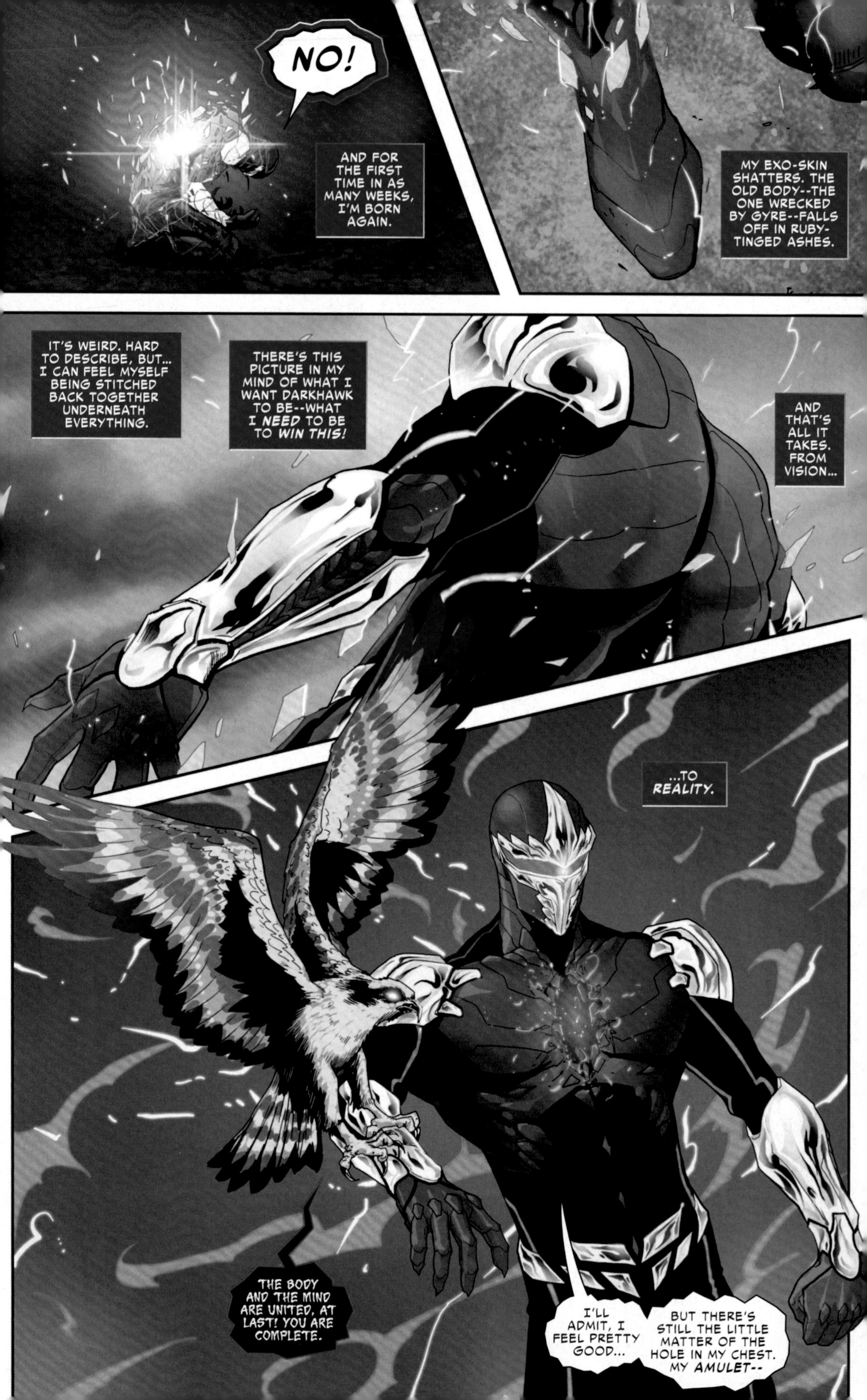
NO!
AND FOR THE FIRST TIME IN AS MANY WEEKS, I'M BORN AGAIN.
MY EXO-SKIN SHATTERS. THE OLD BODY--THE ONE WRECKED BY GYRE--FALLS OFF IN RUBY-TINGED ASHES.
IT'S WEIRD. HARD TO DESCRIBE, BUT... I CAN FEEL MYSELF BEING STITCHED BACK TOGETHER UNDERNEATH EVERYTHING.
THERE'S THIS PICTURE IN MY MIND OF WHAT I WANT DARKHAWK TO BE--WHAT I NEED TO BE TO WIN THIS!
AND THAT'S ALL IT TAKES. FROM VISION...
...TO REALITY.
THE BODY AND THE MIND ARE UNITED, AT LAST! YOU ARE COMPLETE.
I'LL ADMIT, I FEEL PRETTY GOOD...
BUT THERE'S STILL THE LITTLE MATTER OF THE HOLE IN MY CHEST. MY AMULET--

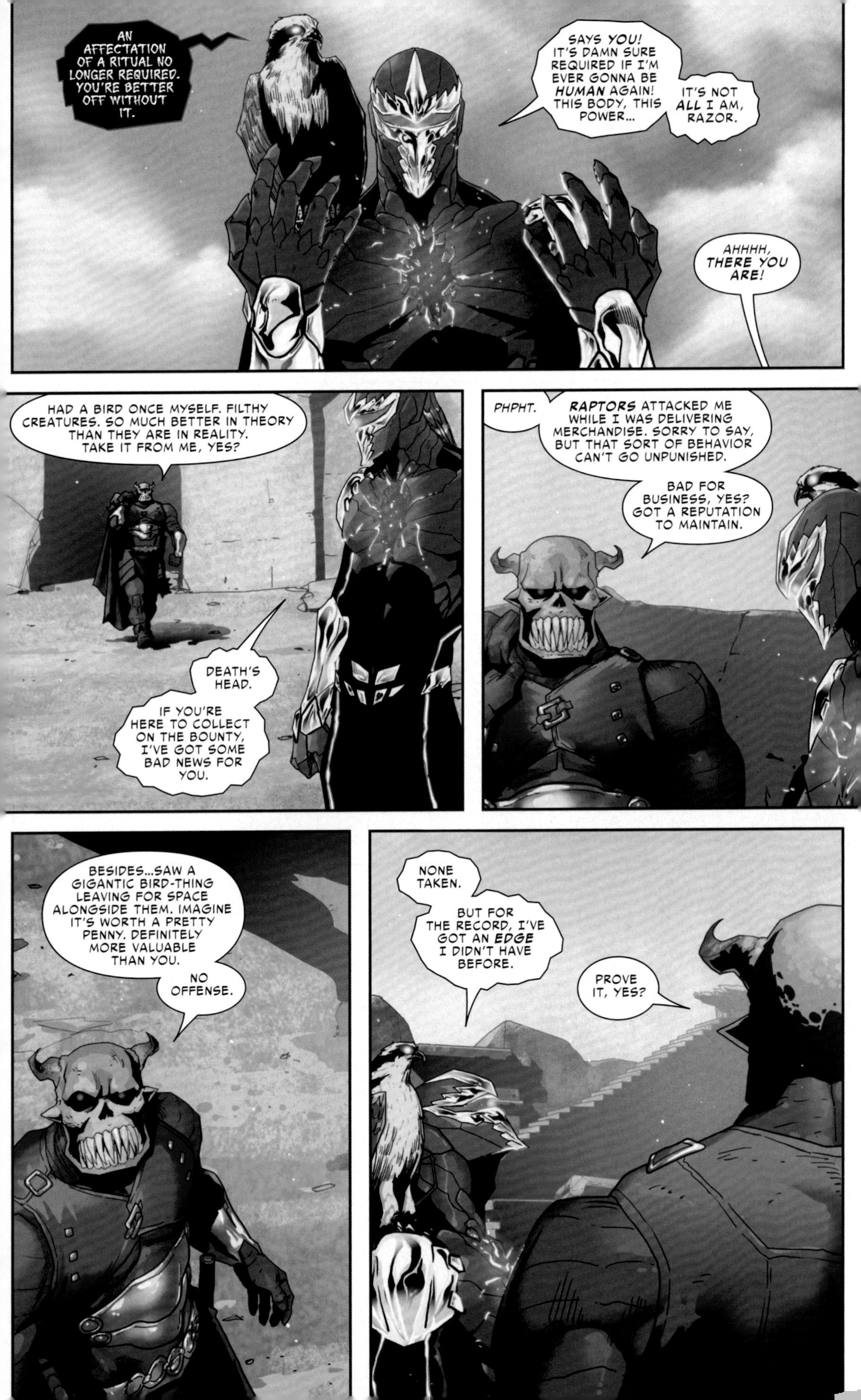
AN AFFECTATION OF A RITUAL NO LONGER REQUIRED. YOU'RE BETTER OFF WITHOUT IT.
SAYS YOU! IT'S DAMN SURE REQUIRED IF I'M EVER GONNA BE HUMAN AGAIN! THIS BODY, THIS POWER...
IT'S NOT ALL I AM, RAZOR.
AHHHH, THERE YOU ARE!
HAD A BIRD ONCE MYSELF. FILTHY CREATURES. SO MUCH BETTER IN THEORY THAN THEY ARE IN REALITY. TAKE IT FROM ME, YES?
DEATH'S HEAD.
IF YOU'RE HERE TO COLLECT ON THE BOUNTY, I'VE GOT SOME BAD NEWS FOR YOU.
PHPHT.
RAPTORS ATTACKED ME WHILE I WAS DELIVERING MERCHANDISE. SORRY TO SAY, BUT THAT SORT OF BEHAVIOR CAN'T GO UNPUNISHED.
BAD FOR BUSINESS, YES? GOT A REPUTATION TO MAINTAIN.
BESIDES...SAW A GIGANTIC BIRD-THING LEAVING FOR SPACE ALONGSIDE THEM. IMAGINE IT'S WORTH A PRETTY PENNY. DEFINITELY MORE VALUABLE THAN YOU.
NO OFFENSE.
NONE TAKEN.
BUT FOR THE RECORD, I'VE GOT AN EDGE I DIDN'T HAVE BEFORE.
PROVE IT, YES?

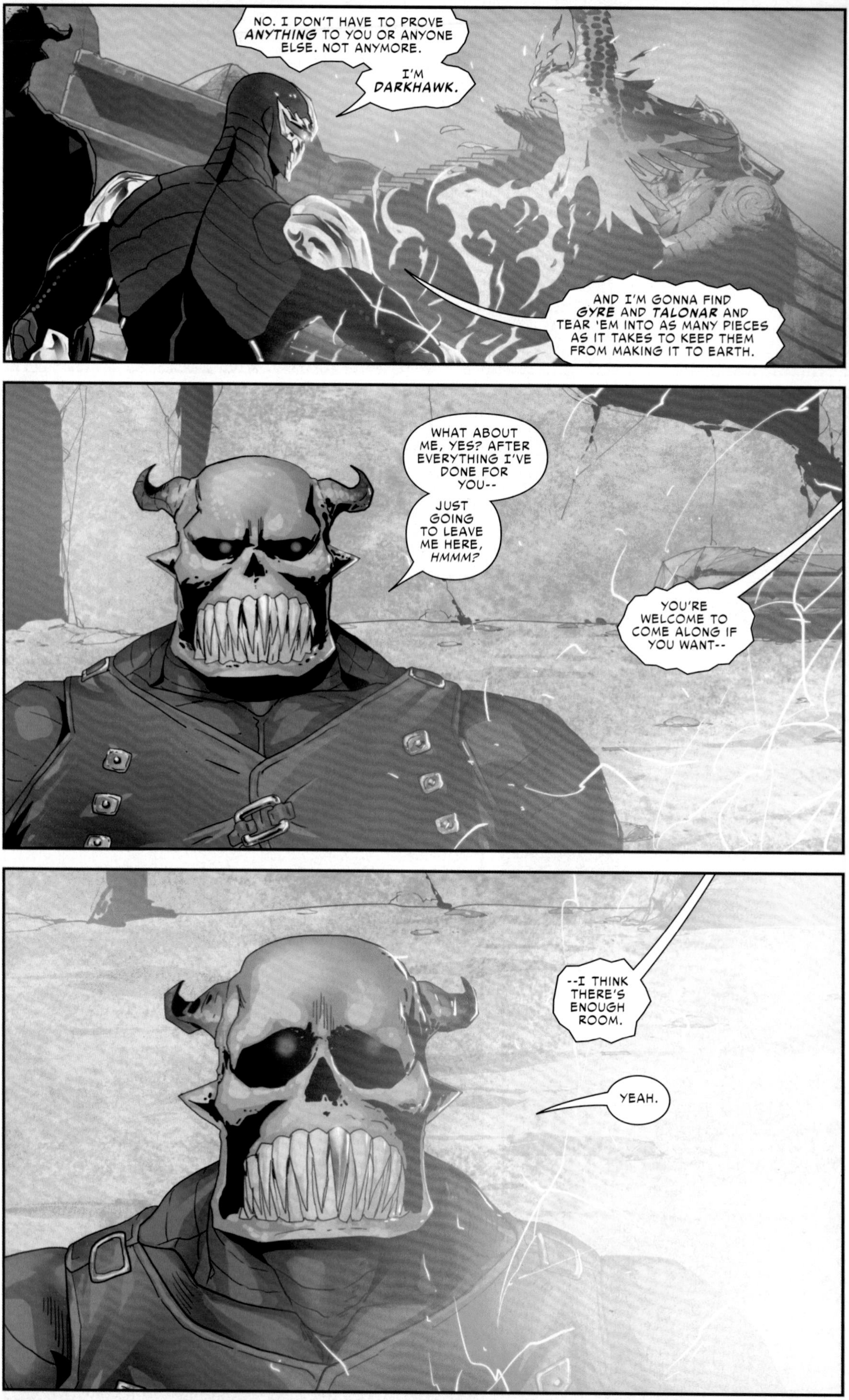
NO. I DON'T HAVE TO PROVE *ANYTHING* TO YOU OR ANYONE ELSE. NOT ANYMORE.
I'M *DARKHAWK.*
AND I'M GONNA FIND *GYRE* AND *TALONAR* AND TEAR 'EM INTO AS MANY PIECES AS IT TAKES TO KEEP THEM FROM MAKING IT TO EARTH.
WHAT ABOUT ME, YES? AFTER EVERYTHING I'VE DONE FOR YOU--
JUST GOING TO LEAVE ME HERE, *HMMM?*
YOU'RE WELCOME TO COME ALONG IF YOU WANT--
--I THINK THERE'S ENOUGH ROOM.
YEAH.

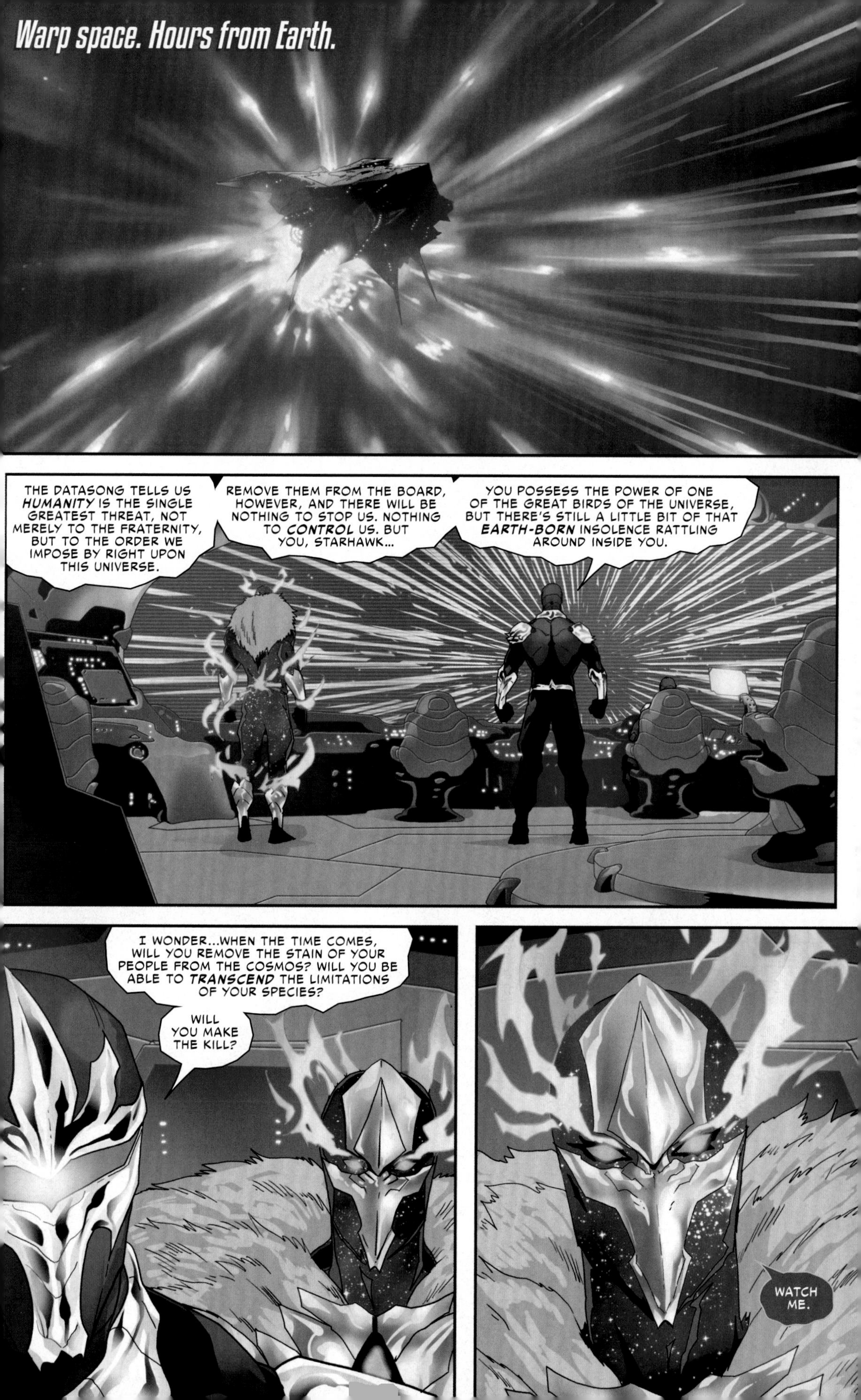
Warp space. Hours from Earth.
THE DATASONG TELLS US HUMANITY IS THE SINGLE GREATEST THREAT, NOT MERELY TO THE FRATERNITY, BUT TO THE ORDER WE IMPOSE BY RIGHT UPON THIS UNIVERSE.
REMOVE THEM FROM THE BOARD, HOWEVER, AND THERE WILL BE NOTHING TO STOP US. NOTHING TO CONTROL US. BUT YOU, STARHAWK...
YOU POSSESS THE POWER OF ONE OF THE GREAT BIRDS OF THE UNIVERSE, BUT THERE'S STILL A LITTLE BIT OF THAT EARTH-BORN INSOLENCE RATTLING AROUND INSIDE YOU.
I WONDER...WHEN THE TIME COMES, WILL YOU REMOVE THE STAIN OF YOUR PEOPLE FROM THE COSMOS? WILL YOU BE ABLE TO TRANSCEND THE LIMITATIONS OF YOUR SPECIES?
WILL YOU MAKE THE KILL?
WATCH ME.

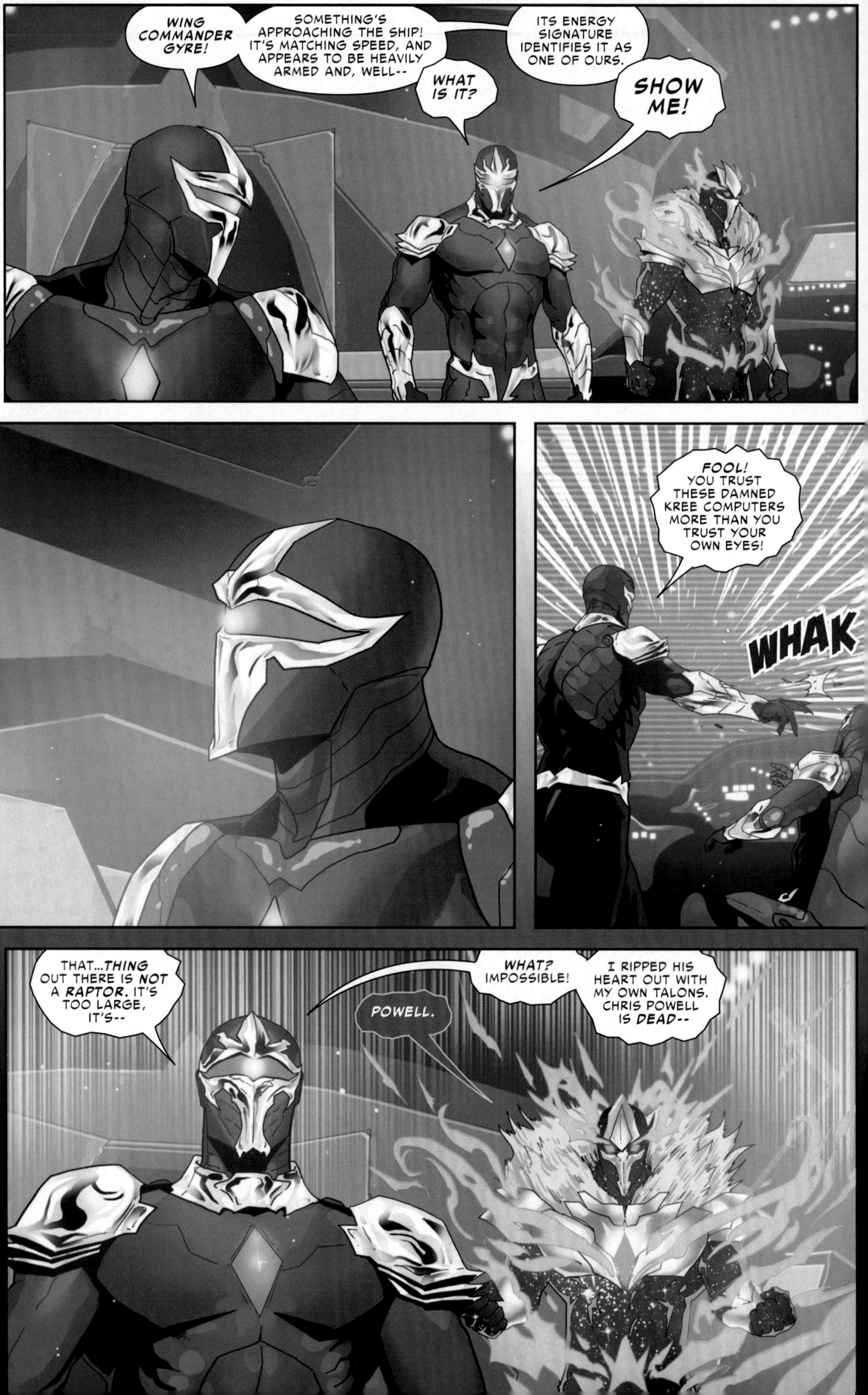
WING COMMANDER GYRE!
SOMETHING'S APPROACHING THE SHIP! IT'S MATCHING SPEED, AND APPEARS TO BE HEAVILY ARMED AND, WELL--
WHAT IS IT?
ITS ENERGY SIGNATURE IDENTIFIES IT AS ONE OF OURS.
SHOW ME!
FOOL! YOU TRUST THESE DAMNED KREE COMPUTERS MORE THAN YOU TRUST YOUR OWN EYES!
WHAK
THAT...THING OUT THERE IS NOT A RAPTOR. IT'S TOO LARGE, IT'S--
POWELL.
WHAT? IMPOSSIBLE!
I RIPPED HIS HEART OUT WITH MY OWN TALONS. CHRIS POWELL IS DEAD--

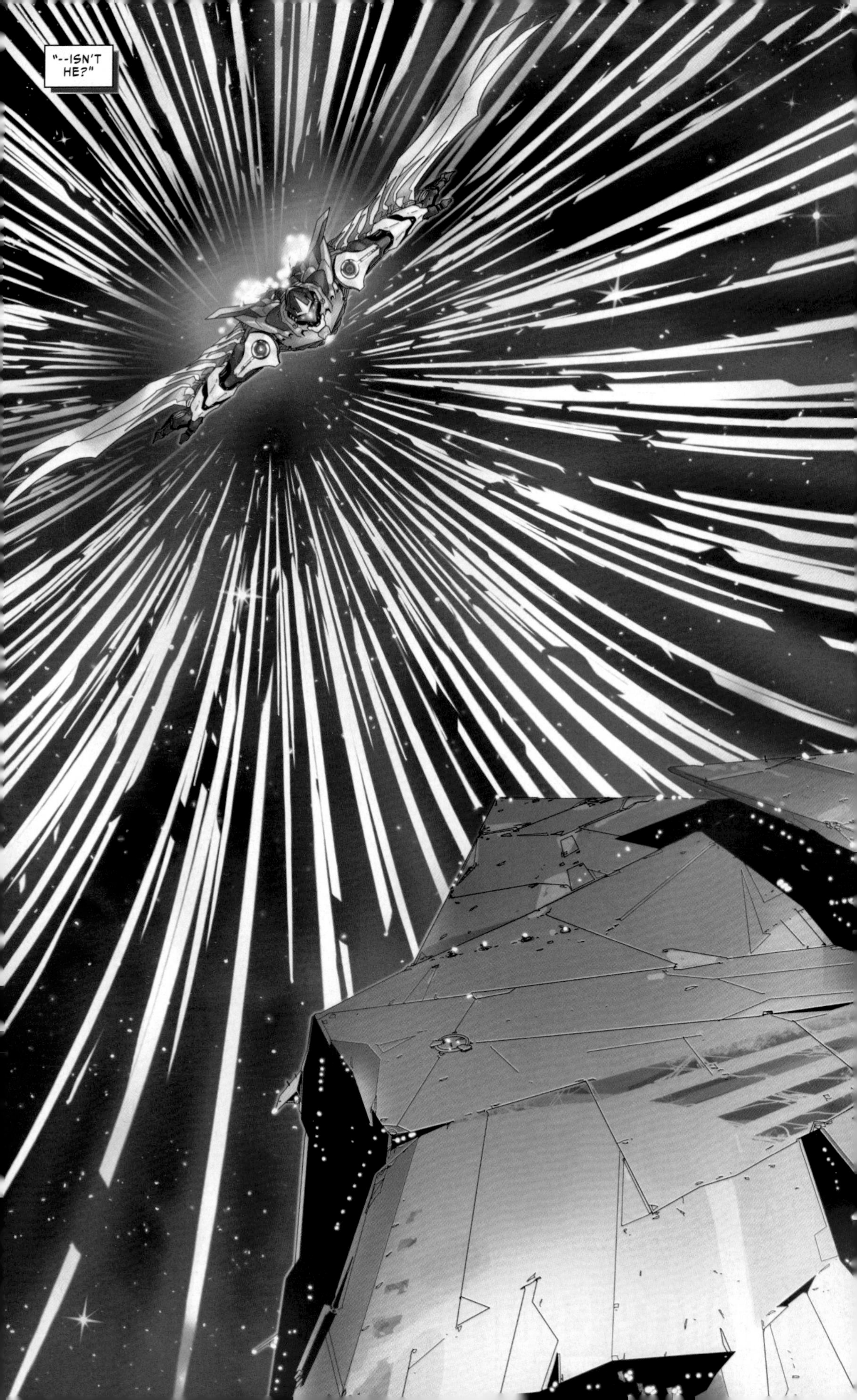
"--ISN'T HE?"

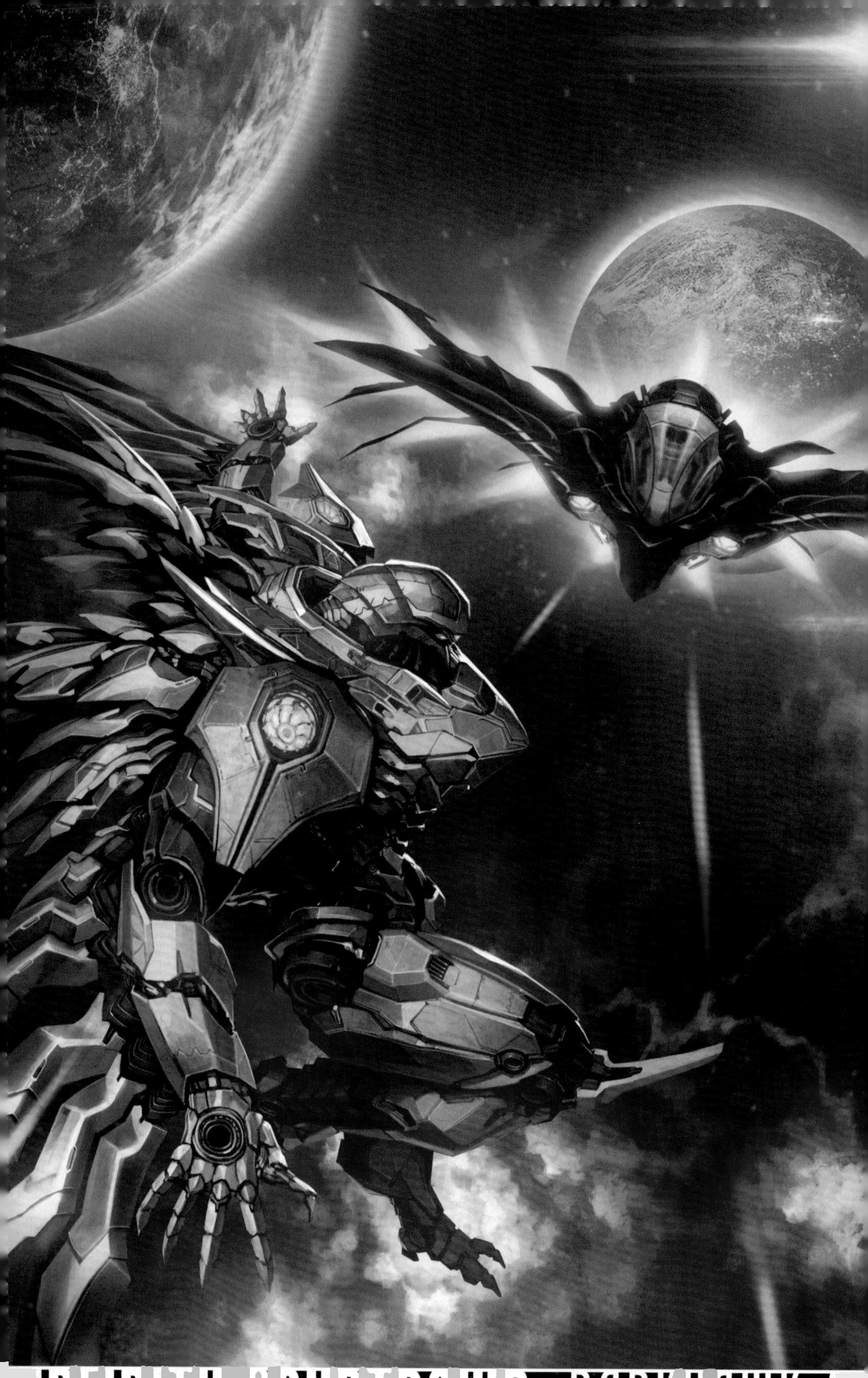

INFINITY COUNTDOWN: DARKHAWK 4

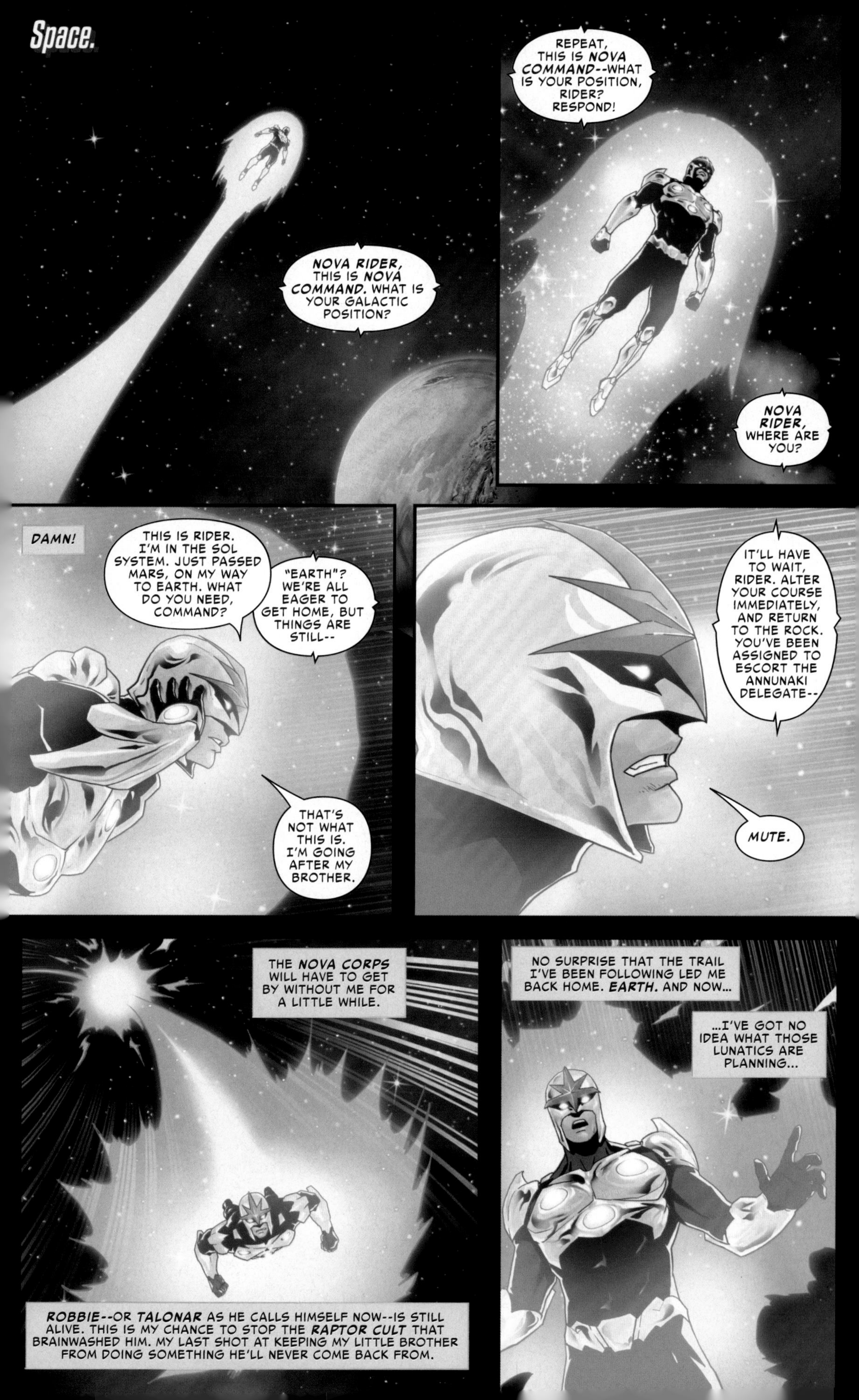

Space.
NOVA RIDER, THIS IS NOVA COMMAND. WHAT IS YOUR GALACTIC POSITION?
REPEAT, THIS IS NOVA COMMAND--WHAT IS YOUR POSITION, RIDER? RESPOND!
NOVA RIDER, WHERE ARE YOU?
DAMN!
THIS IS RIDER. I'M IN THE SOL SYSTEM. JUST PASSED MARS, ON MY WAY TO EARTH. WHAT DO YOU NEED, COMMAND?
"EARTH"? WE'RE ALL EAGER TO GET HOME, BUT THINGS ARE STILL--
THAT'S NOT WHAT THIS IS. I'M GOING AFTER MY BROTHER.
IT'LL HAVE TO WAIT, RIDER. ALTER YOUR COURSE IMMEDIATELY, AND RETURN TO THE ROCK. YOU'VE BEEN ASSIGNED TO ESCORT THE ANNUNAKI DELEGATE--
MUTE.
THE NOVA CORPS WILL HAVE TO GET BY WITHOUT ME FOR A LITTLE WHILE.
ROBBIE--OR TALONAR AS HE CALLS HIMSELF NOW--IS STILL ALIVE. THIS IS MY CHANCE TO STOP THE RAPTOR CULT THAT BRAINWASHED HIM. MY LAST SHOT AT KEEPING MY LITTLE BROTHER FROM DOING SOMETHING HE'LL NEVER COME BACK FROM.
NO SURPRISE THAT THE TRAIL I'VE BEEN FOLLOWING LED ME BACK HOME. EARTH. AND NOW...
...I'VE GOT NO IDEA WHAT THOSE LUNATICS ARE PLANNING...

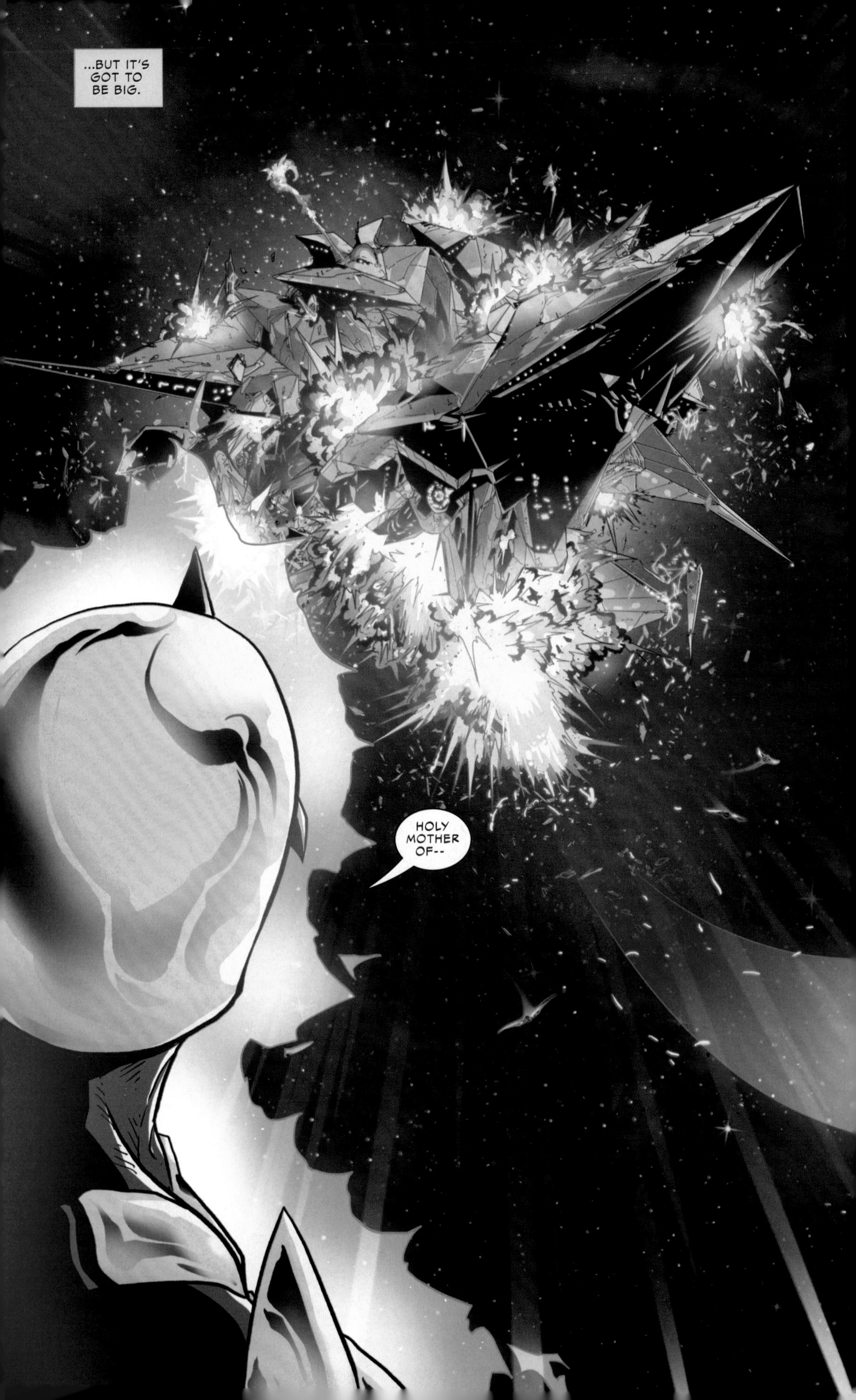
...BUT IT'S GOT TO BE BIG.
HOLY MOTHER OF--

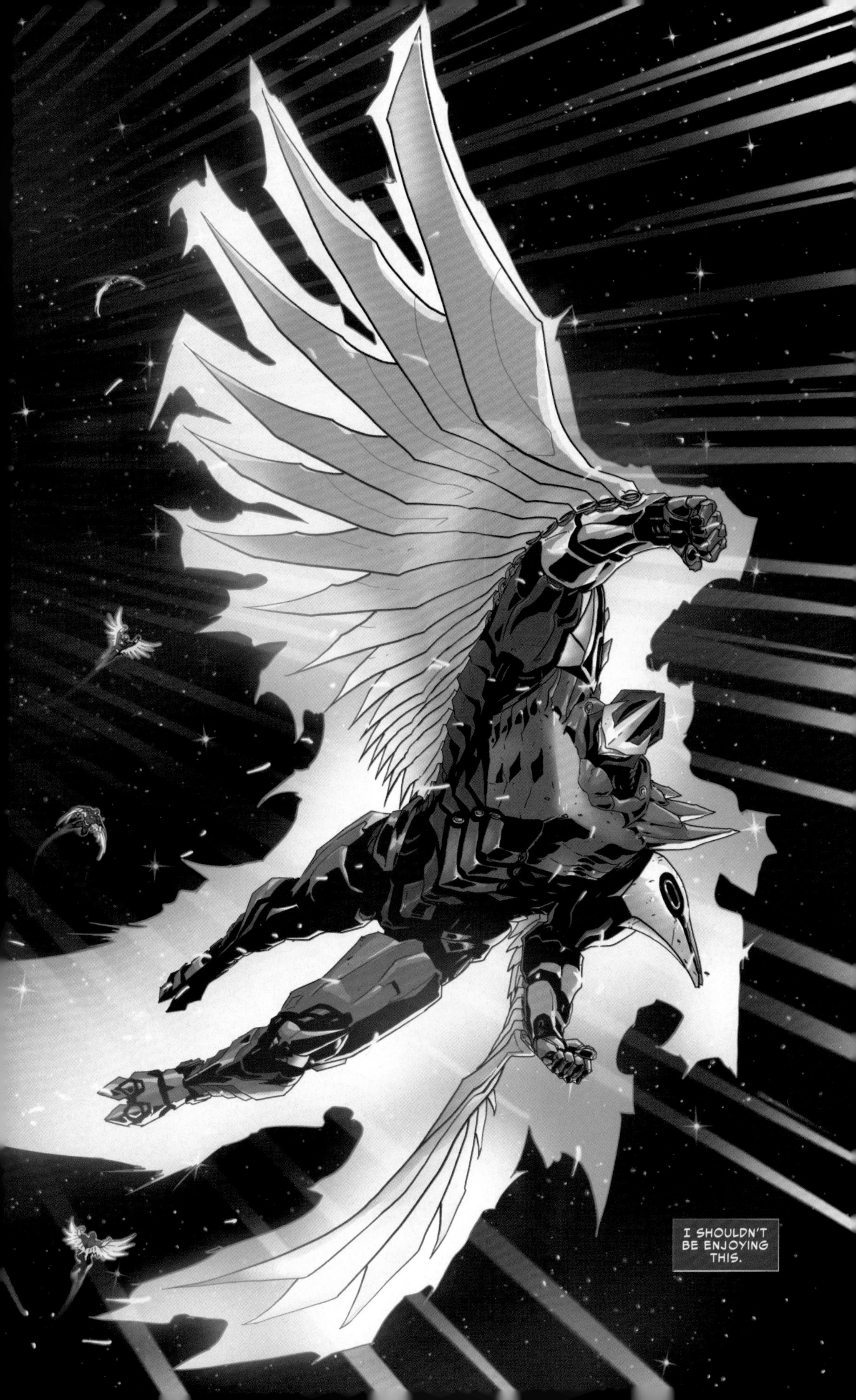
I SHOULDN'T BE ENJOYING THIS.

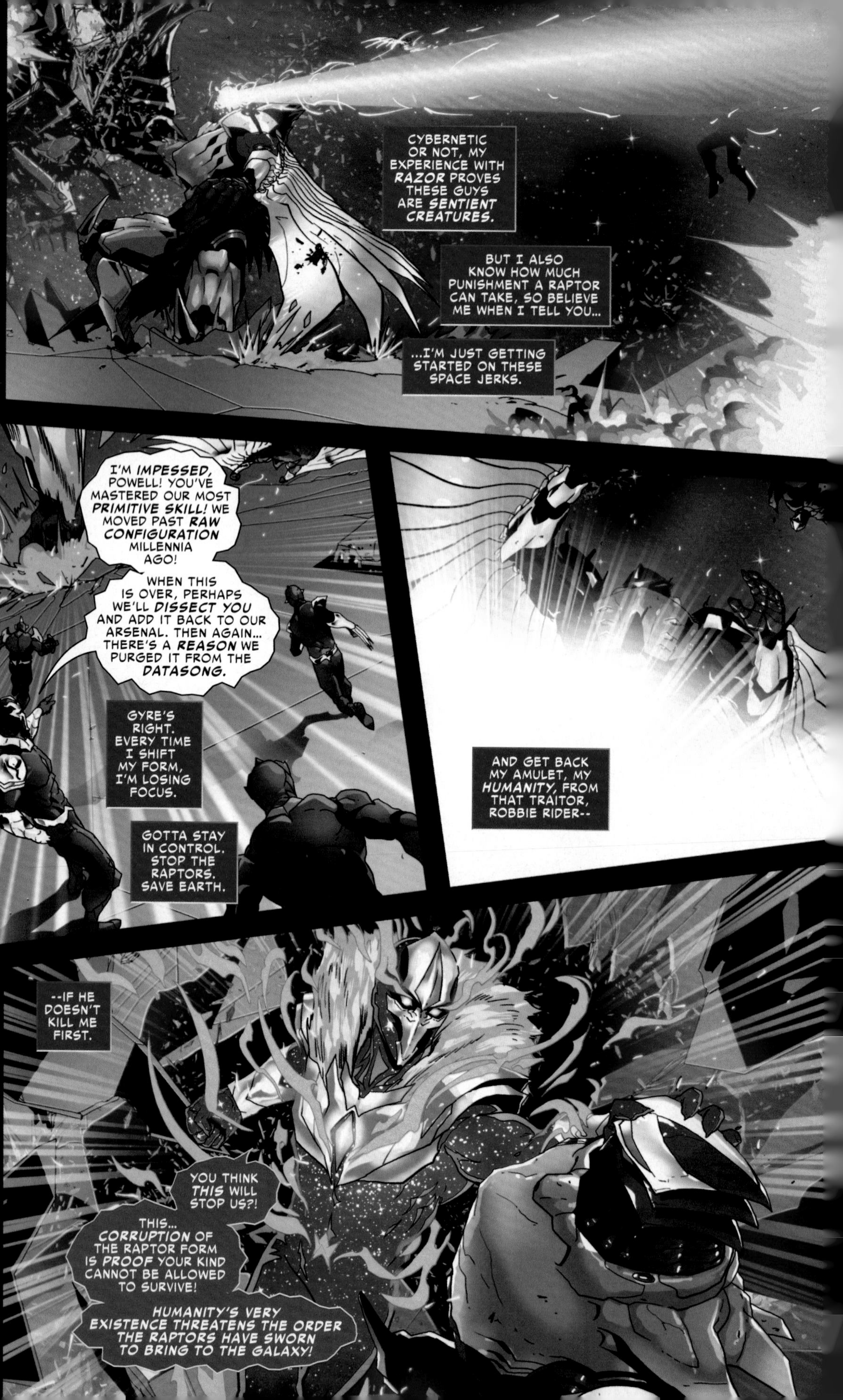
CYBERNETIC OR NOT, MY EXPERIENCE WITH RAZOR PROVES THESE GUYS ARE SENTIENT CREATURES.
BUT I ALSO KNOW HOW MUCH PUNISHMENT A RAPTOR CAN TAKE, SO BELIEVE ME WHEN I TELL YOU...
...I'M JUST GETTING STARTED ON THESE SPACE JERKS.
I'M IMPRESSED, POWELL! YOU'VE MASTERED OUR MOST PRIMITIVE SKILL! WE MOVED PAST RAW CONFIGURATION MILLENNIA AGO!
WHEN THIS IS OVER, PERHAPS WE'LL DISSECT YOU AND ADD IT BACK TO OUR ARSENAL. THEN AGAIN... THERE'S A REASON WE PURGED IT FROM THE DATASONG.
GYRE'S RIGHT. EVERY TIME I SHIFT MY FORM, I'M LOSING FOCUS.
GOTTA STAY IN CONTROL. STOP THE RAPTORS. SAVE EARTH.
AND GET BACK MY AMULET, MY HUMANITY, FROM THAT TRAITOR, ROBBIE RIDER--
--IF HE DOESN'T KILL ME FIRST.
YOU THINK THIS WILL STOP US?!
THIS... CORRUPTION OF THE RAPTOR FORM IS PROOF YOUR KIND CANNOT BE ALLOWED TO SURVIVE!
HUMANITY'S VERY EXISTENCE THREATENS THE ORDER THE RAPTORS HAVE SWORN TO BRING TO THE GALAXY!

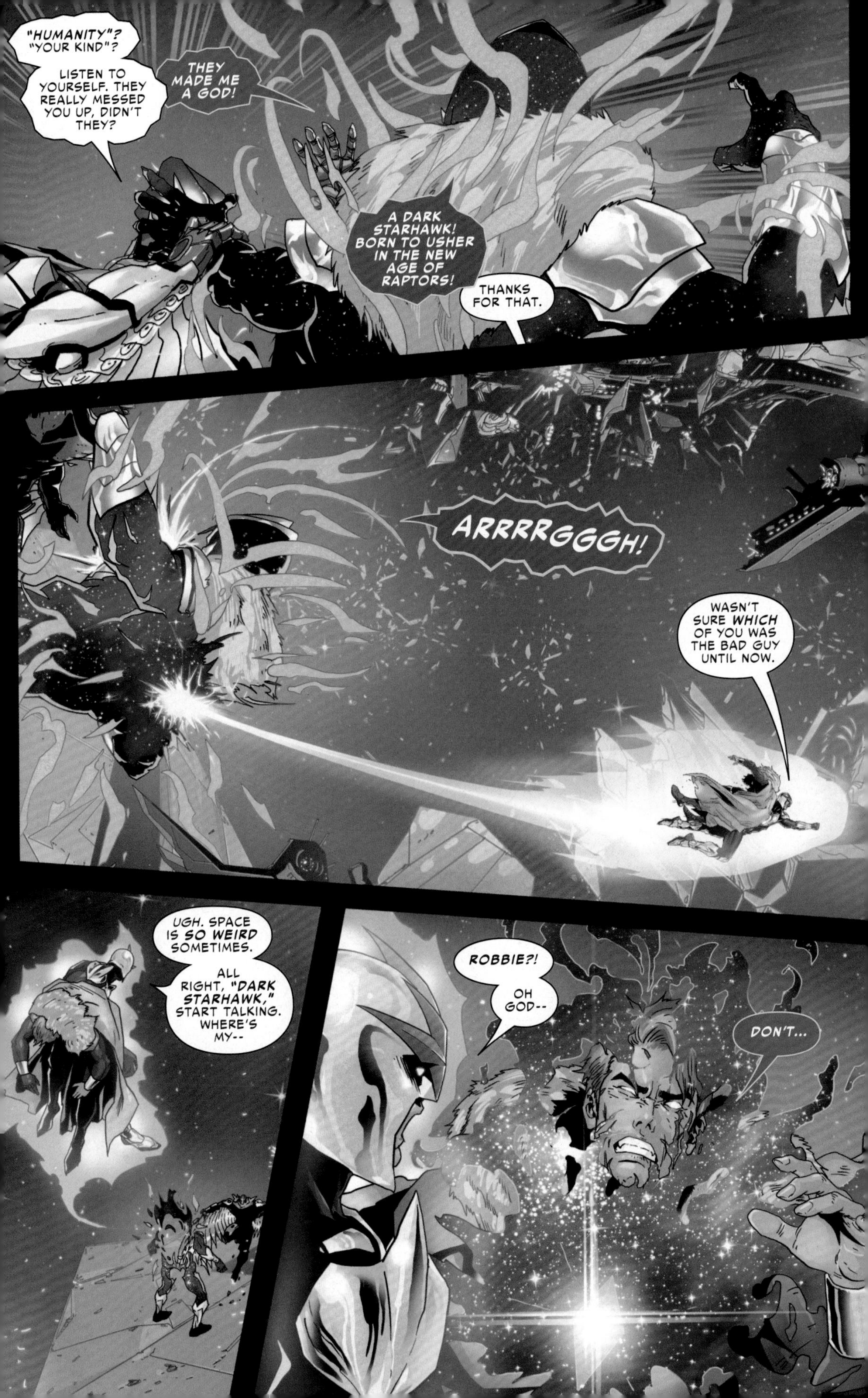
"HUMANITY"? "YOUR KIND"?
LISTEN TO YOURSELF. THEY REALLY MESSED YOU UP, DIDN'T THEY?
THEY MADE ME A GOD!
A DARK STARHAWK! BORN TO USHER IN THE NEW AGE OF RAPTORS!
THANKS FOR THAT.
ARRRRGGGH!
WASN'T SURE WHICH OF YOU WAS THE BAD GUY UNTIL NOW.
UGH. SPACE IS SO WEIRD SOMETIMES.
ALL RIGHT, "DARK STARHAWK," START TALKING. WHERE'S MY--
ROBBIE?!
OH GOD--
DON'T...

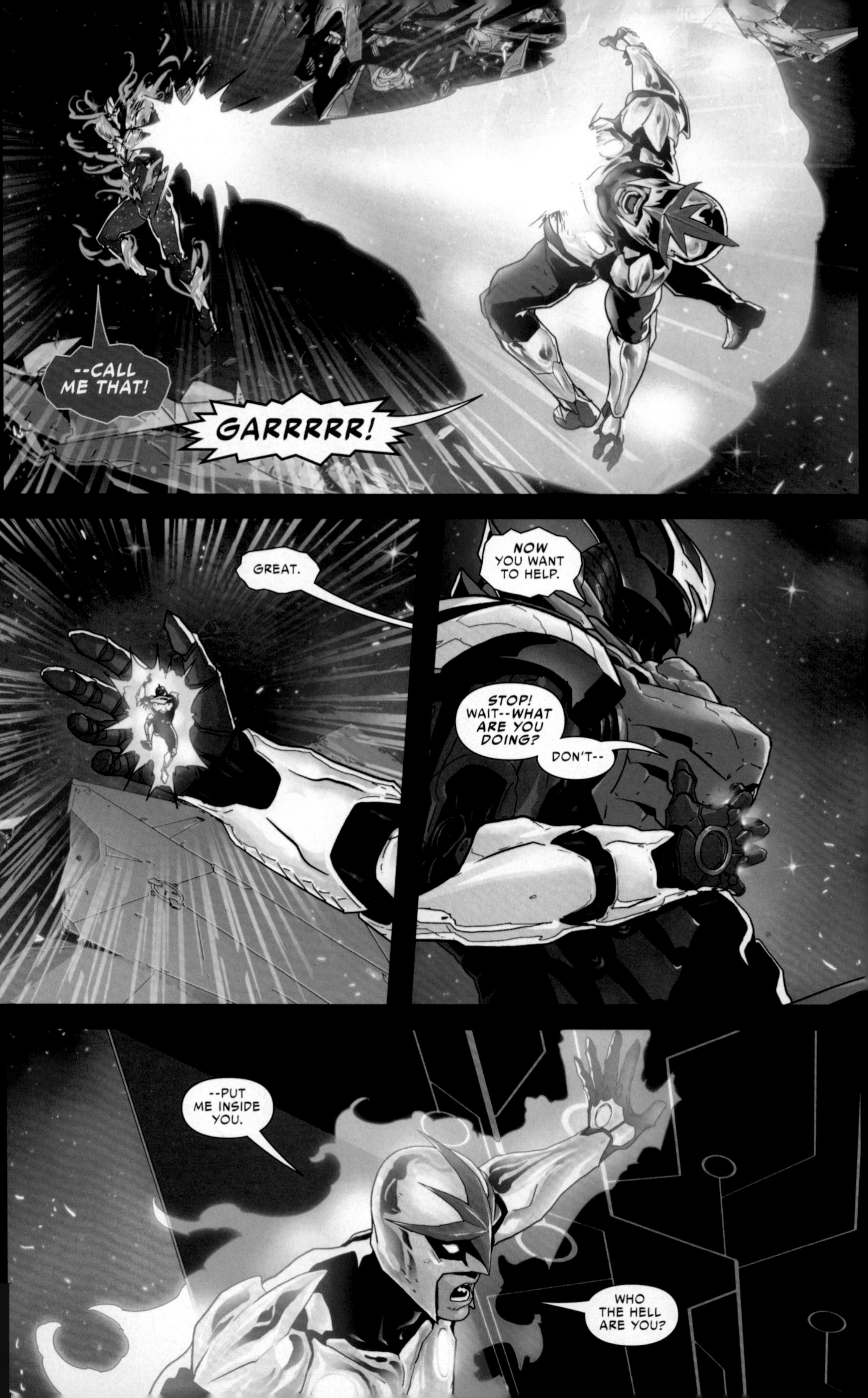
--CALL ME THAT!
GARRRRR!
GREAT.
NOW YOU WANT TO HELP.
STOP! WAIT--WHAT ARE YOU DOING?
DON'T--
--PUT ME INSIDE YOU.
WHO THE HELL ARE YOU?

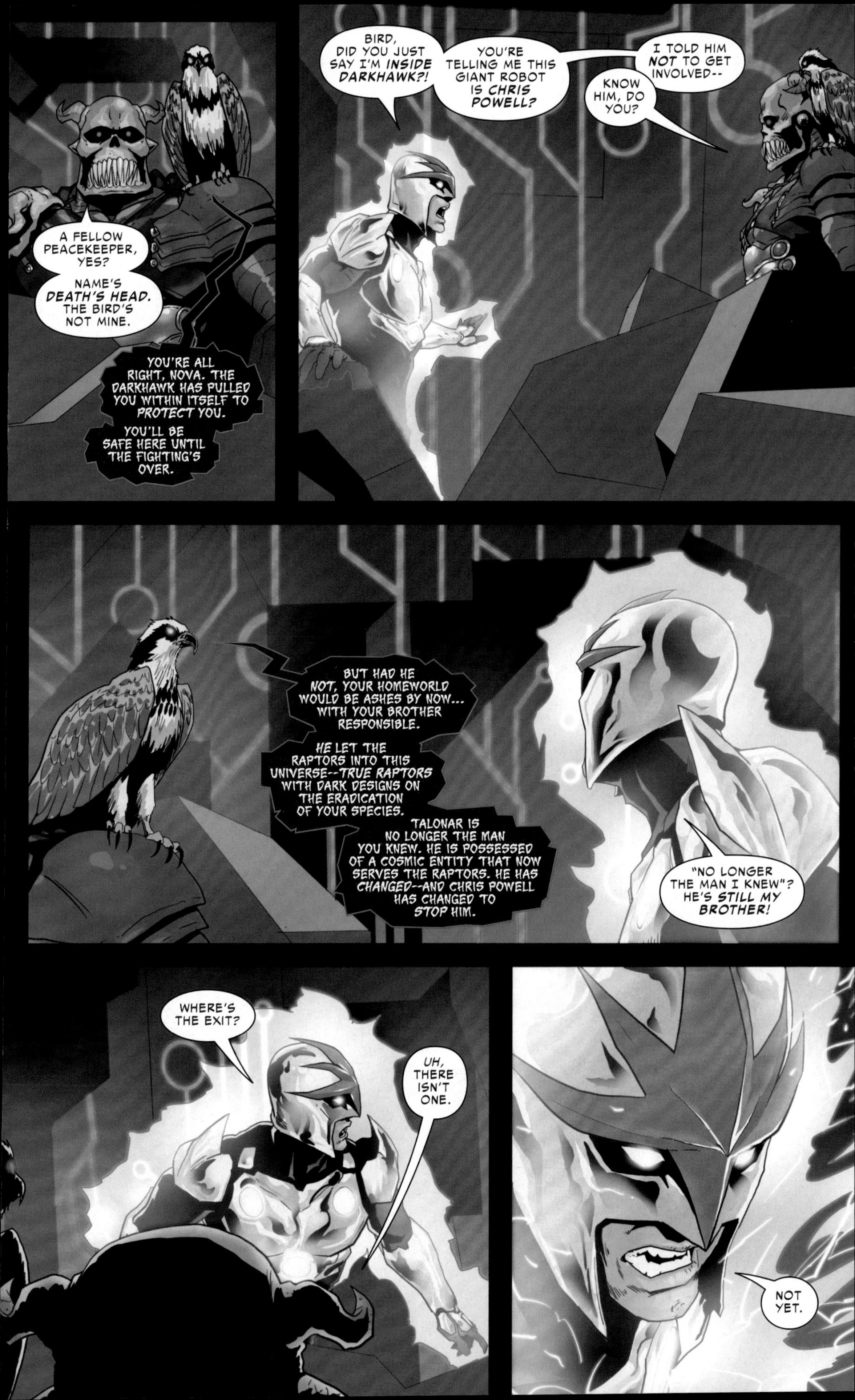
A FELLOW PEACEKEEPER, YES?
NAME'S *DEATH'S HEAD.* THE BIRD'S NOT MINE.
YOU'RE ALL RIGHT, NOVA. THE DARKHAWK HAS PULLED YOU WITHIN ITSELF TO *PROTECT* YOU.
YOU'LL BE SAFE HERE UNTIL THE FIGHTING'S OVER.
BIRD, DID YOU JUST SAY I'M *INSIDE DARKHAWK?!*
YOU'RE TELLING ME THIS GIANT ROBOT IS *CHRIS POWELL?*
I TOLD HIM *NOT* TO GET INVOLVED--
KNOW HIM, DO YOU?
BUT HAD HE *NOT,* YOUR HOMEWORLD WOULD BE ASHES BY NOW... WITH YOUR BROTHER RESPONSIBLE.
HE LET THE RAPTORS INTO THIS UNIVERSE--*TRUE RAPTORS* WITH DARK DESIGNS ON THE ERADICATION OF YOUR SPECIES.
TALONAR IS NO LONGER THE MAN YOU KNEW. HE IS POSSESSED OF A COSMIC ENTITY THAT NOW SERVES THE RAPTORS. HE HAS *CHANGED*--AND CHRIS POWELL HAS CHANGED TO *STOP* HIM.
"NO LONGER THE MAN I KNEW"? HE'S *STILL* MY *BROTHER!*
WHERE'S THE EXIT?
UH, THERE ISN'T ONE.
NOT YET.

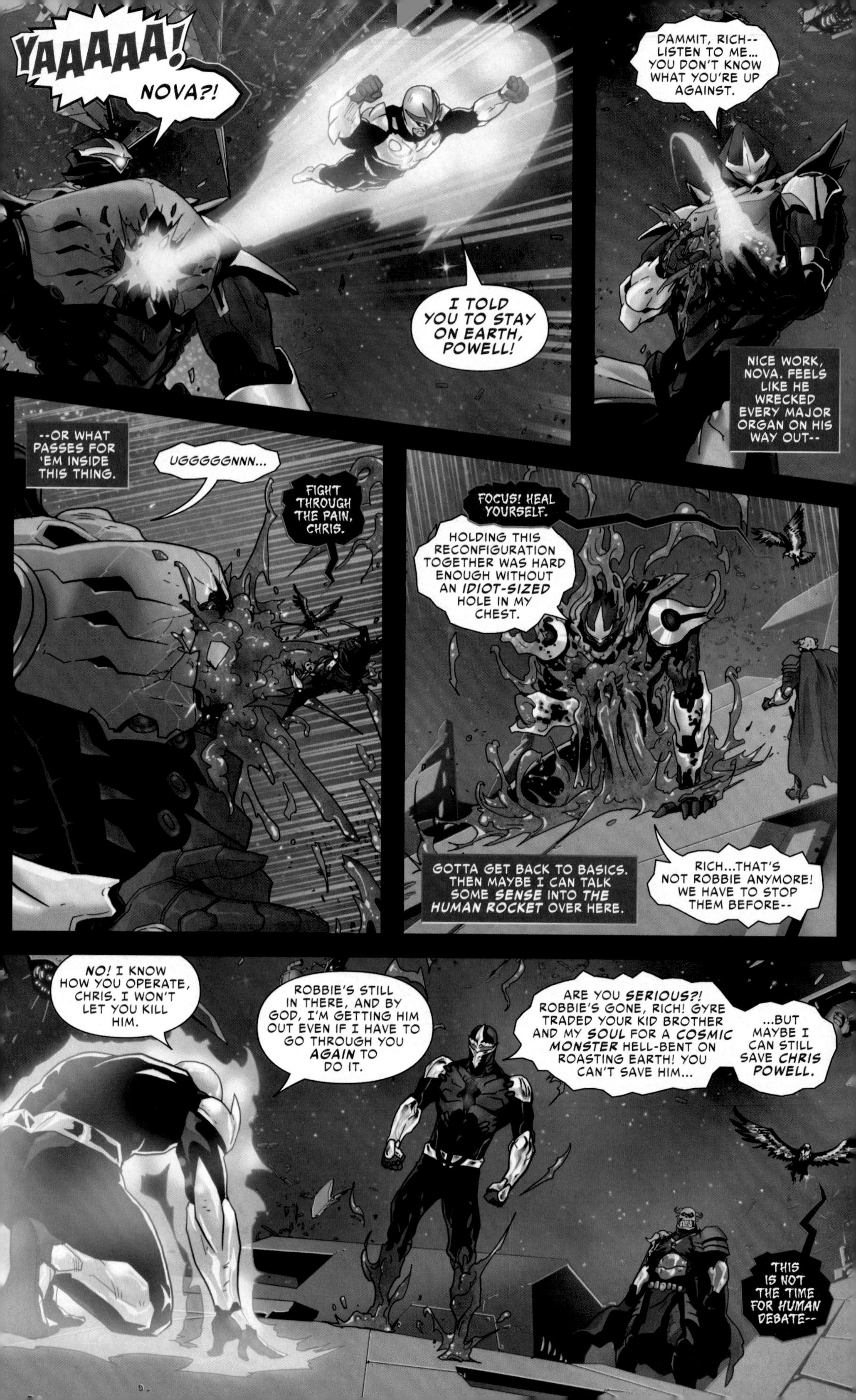

YAAAAA!
NOVA?!
I TOLD YOU TO STAY ON EARTH, POWELL!
DAMMIT, RICH-- LISTEN TO ME... YOU DON'T KNOW WHAT YOU'RE UP AGAINST.
NICE WORK, NOVA. FEELS LIKE HE WRECKED EVERY MAJOR ORGAN ON HIS WAY OUT--
--OR WHAT PASSES FOR 'EM INSIDE THIS THING.
UGGGGGNNN...
FIGHT THROUGH THE PAIN, CHRIS.
FOCUS! HEAL YOURSELF.
HOLDING THIS RECONFIGURATION TOGETHER WAS HARD ENOUGH WITHOUT AN IDIOT-SIZED HOLE IN MY CHEST.
GOTTA GET BACK TO BASICS. THEN MAYBE I CAN TALK SOME SENSE INTO THE HUMAN ROCKET OVER HERE.
RICH...THAT'S NOT ROBBIE ANYMORE! WE HAVE TO STOP THEM BEFORE--
NO! I KNOW HOW YOU OPERATE, CHRIS. I WON'T LET YOU KILL HIM.
ROBBIE'S STILL IN THERE, AND BY GOD, I'M GETTING HIM OUT EVEN IF I HAVE TO GO THROUGH YOU AGAIN TO DO IT.
ARE YOU SERIOUS?! ROBBIE'S GONE, RICH! GYRE TRADED YOUR KID BROTHER AND MY SOUL FOR A COSMIC MONSTER HELL-BENT ON ROASTING EARTH! YOU CAN'T SAVE HIM...
...BUT MAYBE I CAN STILL SAVE CHRIS POWELL.
THIS IS NOT THE TIME FOR HUMAN DEBATE--

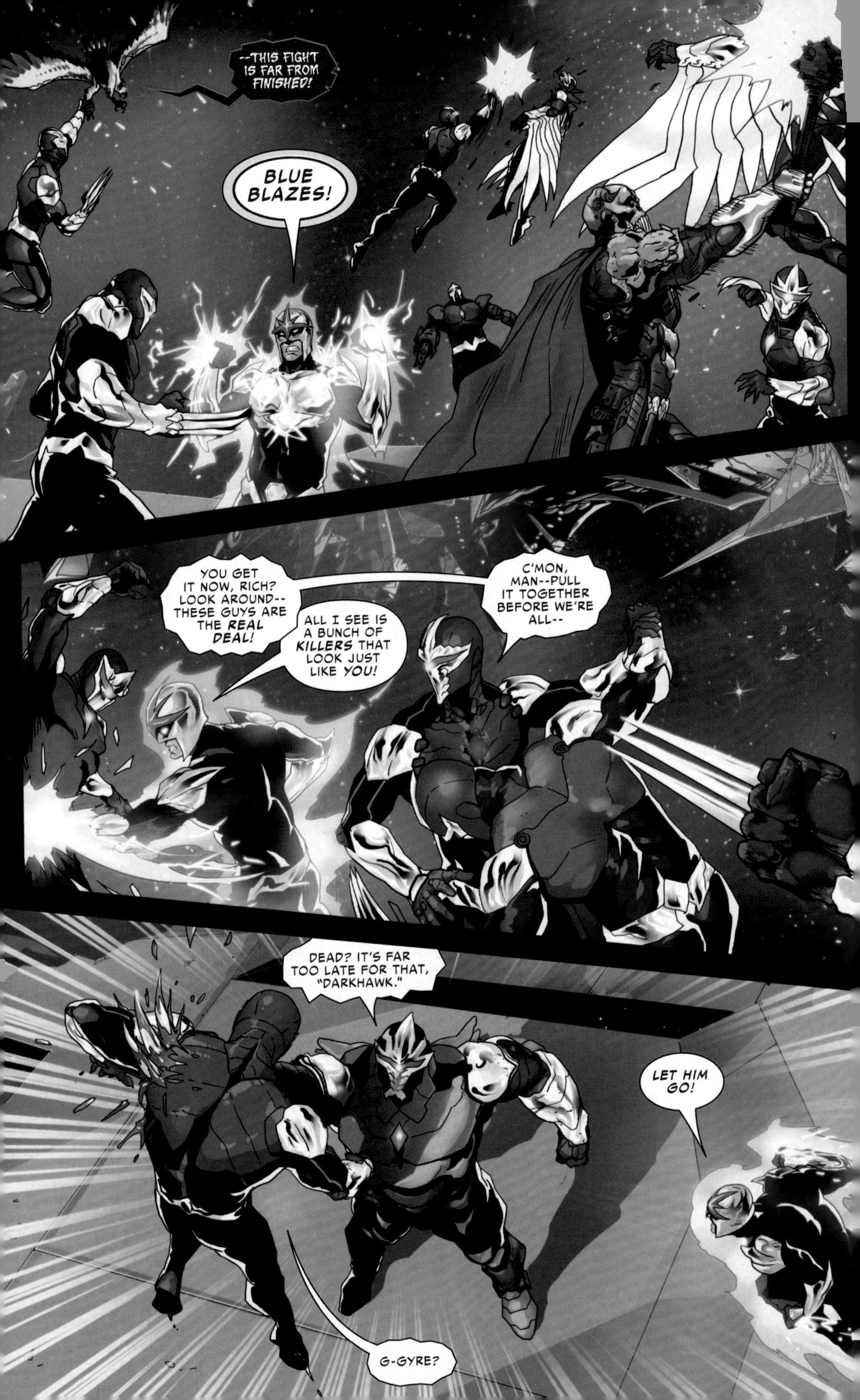
--THIS FIGHT IS FAR FROM FINISHED!
BLUE BLAZES!
YOU GET IT NOW, RICH? LOOK AROUND-- THESE GUYS ARE THE REAL DEAL!
ALL I SEE IS A BUNCH OF KILLERS THAT LOOK JUST LIKE YOU!
C'MON, MAN--PULL IT TOGETHER BEFORE WE'RE ALL--
DEAD? IT'S FAR TOO LATE FOR THAT, "DARKHAWK."
LET HIM GO!
G-GYRE?

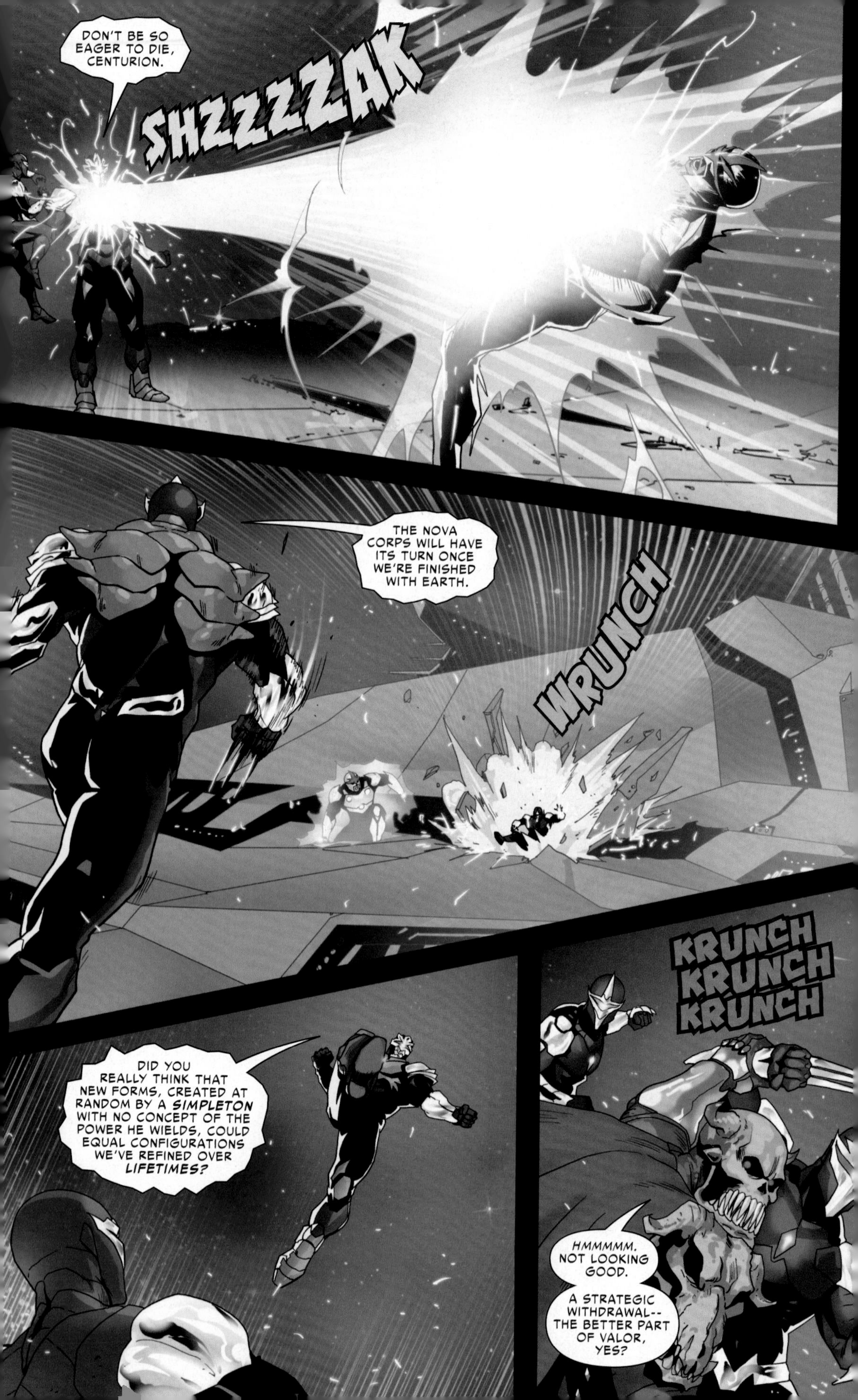
DON'T BE SO EAGER TO DIE, CENTURION.
SHZZZZAK
THE NOVA CORPS WILL HAVE ITS TURN ONCE WE'RE FINISHED WITH EARTH.
WRUNCH
DID YOU REALLY THINK THAT NEW FORMS, CREATED AT RANDOM BY A *SIMPLETON* WITH NO CONCEPT OF THE POWER HE WIELDS, COULD EQUAL CONFIGURATIONS WE'VE REFINED OVER *LIFETIMES?*
KRUNCH KRUNCH KRUNCH
HMMMMM. NOT LOOKING GOOD.
A STRATEGIC WITHDRAWAL-- THE BETTER PART OF VALOR, YES?

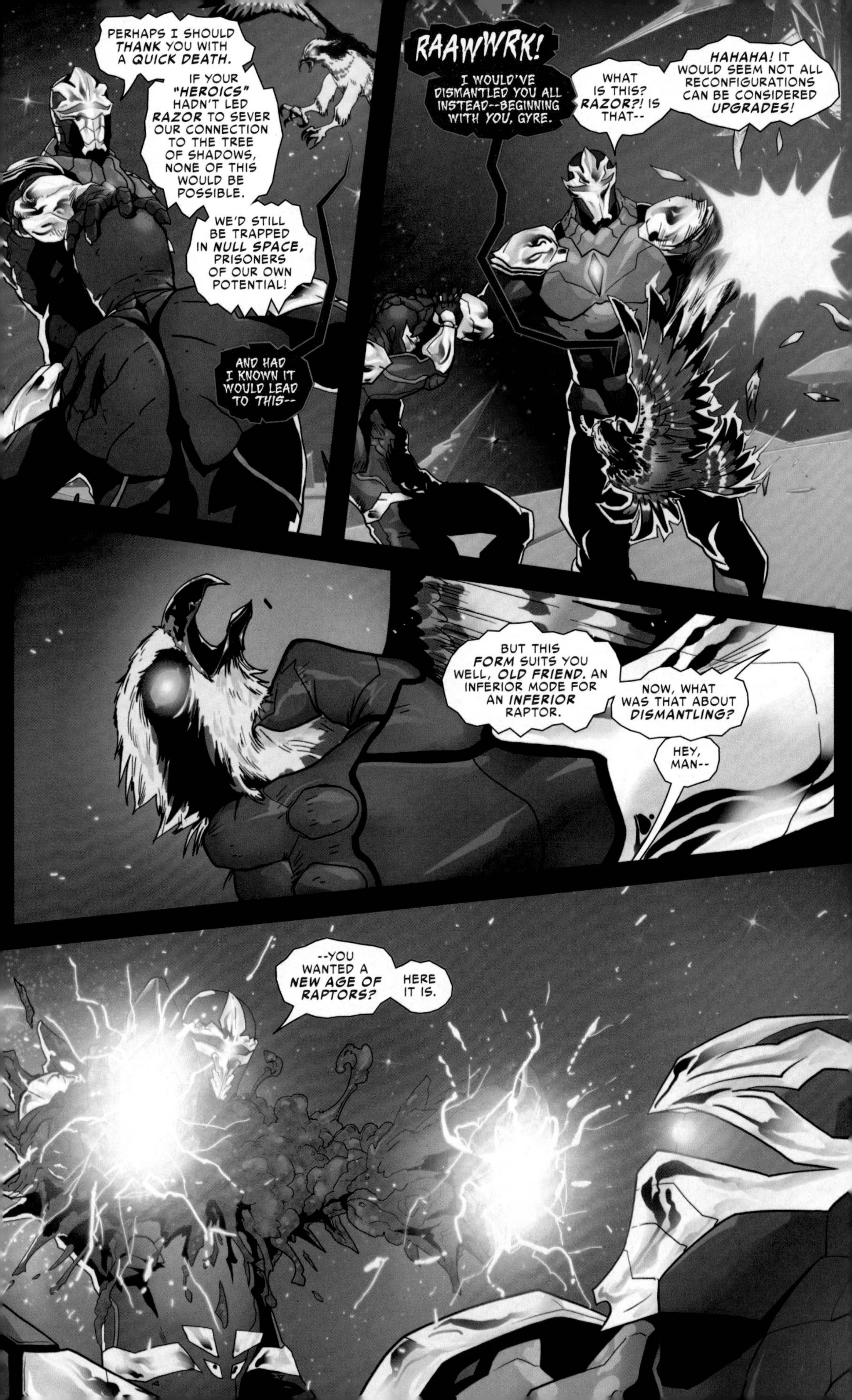
PERHAPS I SHOULD THANK YOU WITH A QUICK DEATH.
IF YOUR "HEROICS" HADN'T LED RAZOR TO SEVER OUR CONNECTION TO THE TREE OF SHADOWS, NONE OF THIS WOULD BE POSSIBLE.
WE'D STILL BE TRAPPED IN NULL SPACE, PRISONERS OF OUR OWN POTENTIAL!
AND HAD I KNOWN IT WOULD LEAD TO THIS--
RAAWWRK!
I WOULD'VE DISMANTLED YOU ALL INSTEAD--BEGINNING WITH YOU, GYRE.
WHAT IS THIS? RAZOR?! IS THAT--
HAHAHA! IT WOULD SEEM NOT ALL RECONFIGURATIONS CAN BE CONSIDERED UPGRADES!
BUT THIS FORM SUITS YOU WELL, OLD FRIEND. AN INFERIOR MODE FOR AN INFERIOR RAPTOR.
NOW, WHAT WAS THAT ABOUT DISMANTLING?
HEY, MAN--
--YOU WANTED A NEW AGE OF RAPTORS?
HERE IT IS.

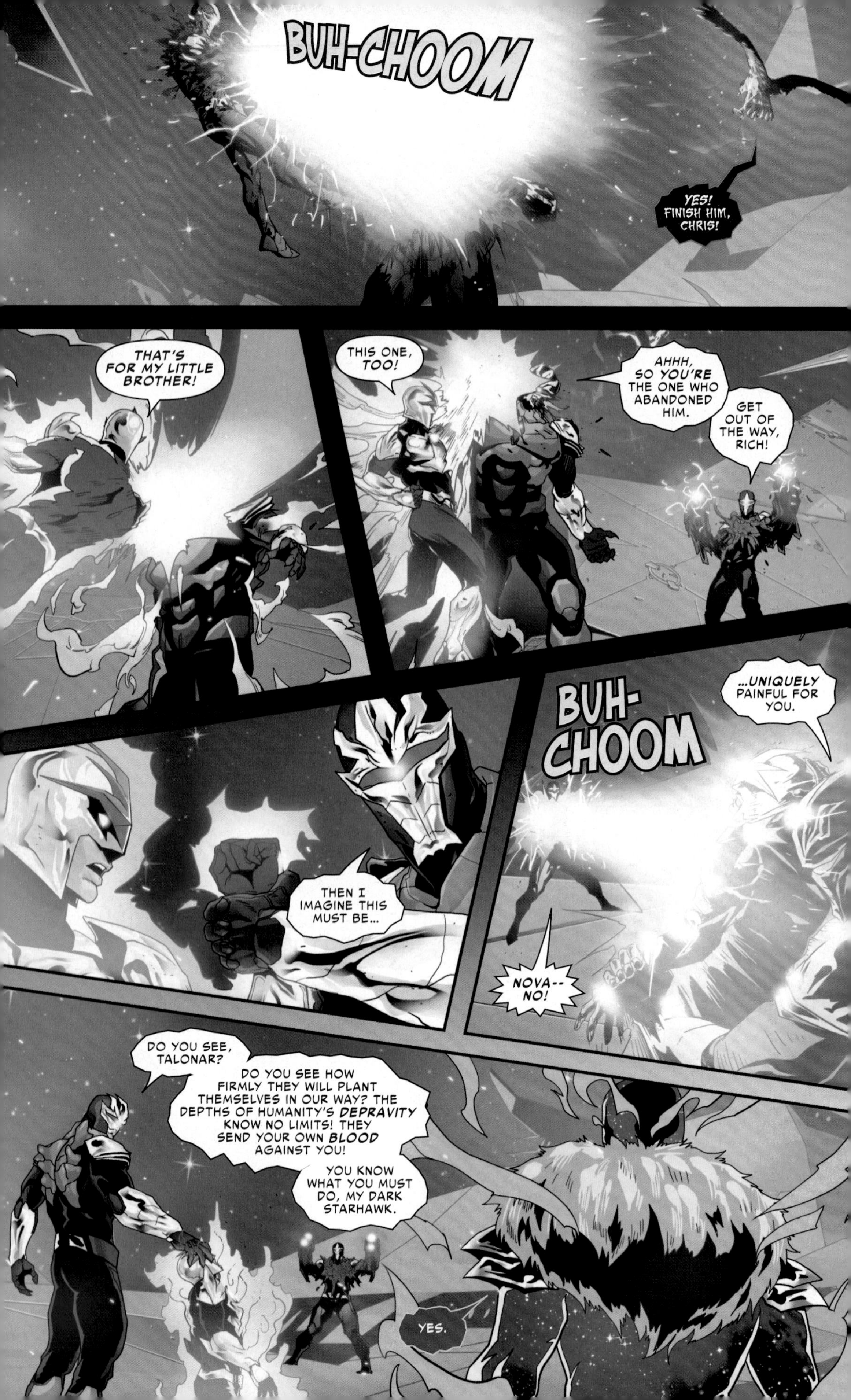
BUH-CHOOM
YES! FINISH HIM, CHRIS!
THAT'S FOR MY LITTLE BROTHER!
THIS ONE, TOO!
AHHH, SO YOU'RE THE ONE WHO ABANDONED HIM.
GET OUT OF THE WAY, RICH!
THEN I IMAGINE THIS MUST BE...
BUH-CHOOM
...UNIQUELY PAINFUL FOR YOU.
NOVA--NO!
DO YOU SEE, TALONAR?
DO YOU SEE HOW FIRMLY THEY WILL PLANT THEMSELVES IN OUR WAY? THE DEPTHS OF HUMANITY'S DEPRAVITY KNOW NO LIMITS! THEY SEND YOUR OWN BLOOD AGAINST YOU!
YOU KNOW WHAT YOU MUST DO, MY DARK STARHAWK.
YES.

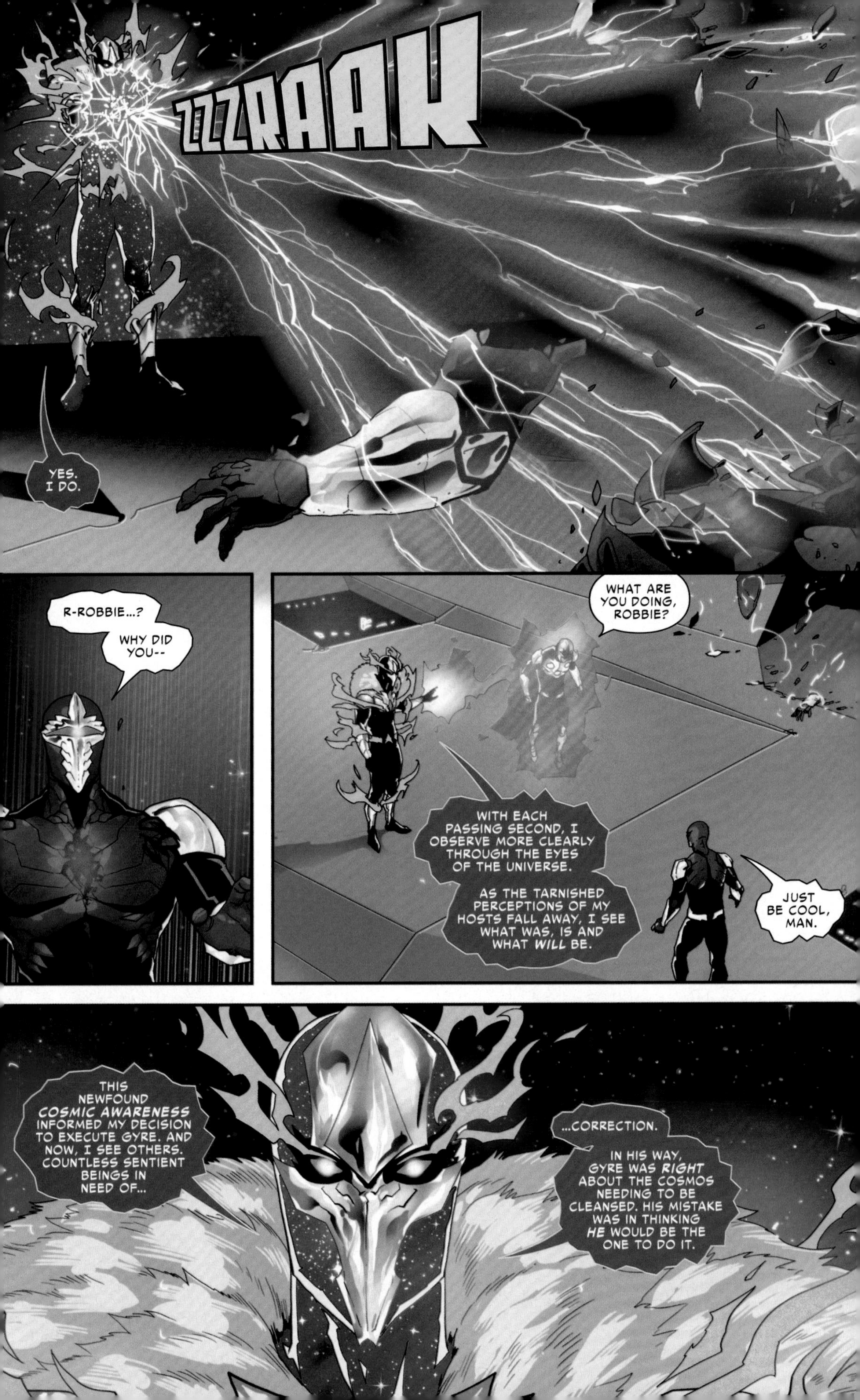
ZZZRAAK
YES. I DO.
R-ROBBIE...?
WHY DID YOU--
WHAT ARE YOU DOING, ROBBIE?
WITH EACH PASSING SECOND, I OBSERVE MORE CLEARLY THROUGH THE EYES OF THE UNIVERSE.
AS THE TARNISHED PERCEPTIONS OF MY HOSTS FALL AWAY, I SEE WHAT WAS, IS AND WHAT WILL BE.
JUST BE COOL, MAN.
THIS NEWFOUND COSMIC AWARENESS INFORMED MY DECISION TO EXECUTE GYRE. AND NOW, I SEE OTHERS. COUNTLESS SENTIENT BEINGS IN NEED OF...
...CORRECTION.
IN HIS WAY, GYRE WAS RIGHT ABOUT THE COSMOS NEEDING TO BE CLEANSED. HIS MISTAKE WAS IN THINKING HE WOULD BE THE ONE TO DO IT.

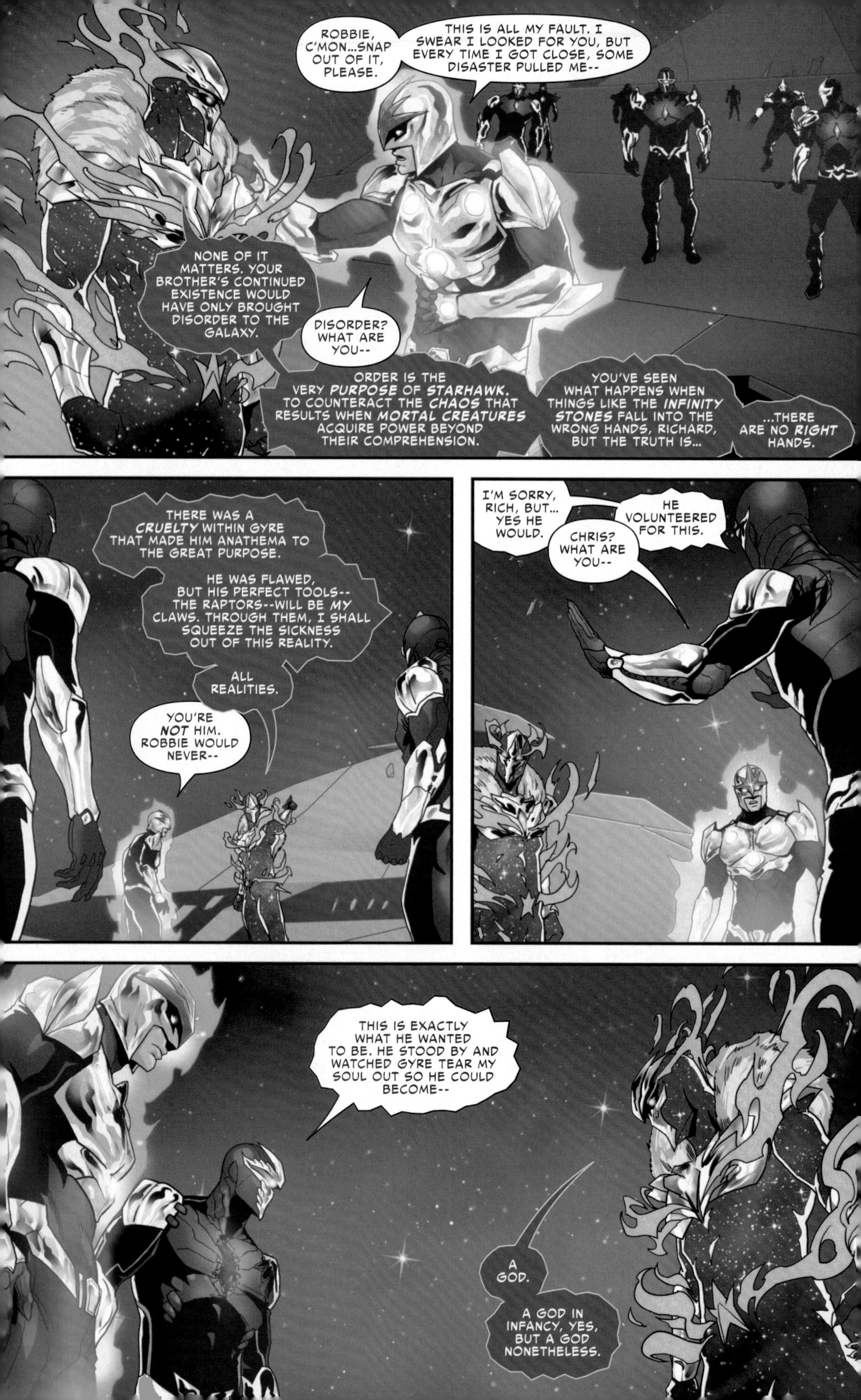
ROBBIE, C'MON...SNAP OUT OF IT, PLEASE.
THIS IS ALL MY FAULT. I SWEAR I LOOKED FOR YOU, BUT EVERY TIME I GOT CLOSE, SOME DISASTER PULLED ME--
NONE OF IT MATTERS. YOUR BROTHER'S CONTINUED EXISTENCE WOULD HAVE ONLY BROUGHT DISORDER TO THE GALAXY.
DISORDER? WHAT ARE YOU--
ORDER IS THE VERY PURPOSE OF STARHAWK. TO COUNTERACT THE CHAOS THAT RESULTS WHEN MORTAL CREATURES ACQUIRE POWER BEYOND THEIR COMPREHENSION.
YOU'VE SEEN WHAT HAPPENS WHEN THINGS LIKE THE INFINITY STONES FALL INTO THE WRONG HANDS, RICHARD, BUT THE TRUTH IS...
...THERE ARE NO RIGHT HANDS.
THERE WAS A CRUELTY WITHIN GYRE THAT MADE HIM ANATHEMA TO THE GREAT PURPOSE.
HE WAS FLAWED, BUT HIS PERFECT TOOLS--THE RAPTORS--WILL BE MY CLAWS. THROUGH THEM, I SHALL SQUEEZE THE SICKNESS OUT OF THIS REALITY.
ALL REALITIES.
YOU'RE NOT HIM. ROBBIE WOULD NEVER--
I'M SORRY, RICH, BUT... YES HE WOULD.
CHRIS? WHAT ARE YOU--
HE VOLUNTEERED FOR THIS.
THIS IS EXACTLY WHAT HE WANTED TO BE. HE STOOD BY AND WATCHED GYRE TEAR MY SOUL OUT SO HE COULD BECOME--
A GOD.
A GOD IN INFANCY, YES, BUT A GOD NONETHELESS.

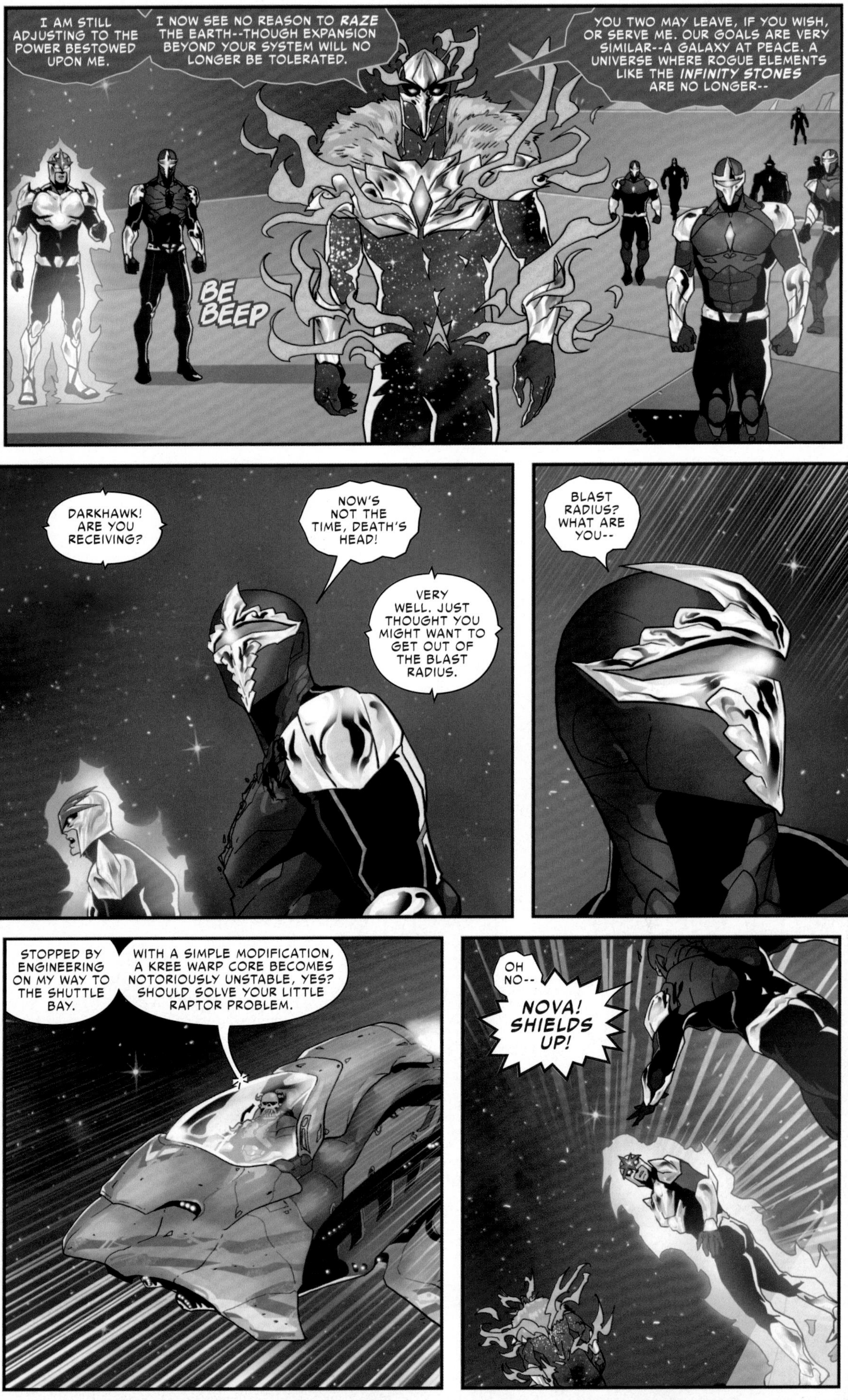

I AM STILL ADJUSTING TO THE POWER BESTOWED UPON ME.
I NOW SEE NO REASON TO *RAZE* THE EARTH--THOUGH EXPANSION BEYOND YOUR SYSTEM WILL NO LONGER BE TOLERATED.
YOU TWO MAY LEAVE, IF YOU WISH, OR SERVE ME. OUR GOALS ARE VERY SIMILAR--A GALAXY AT PEACE. A UNIVERSE WHERE ROGUE ELEMENTS LIKE THE *INFINITY STONES* ARE NO LONGER--
BE BEEP
DARKHAWK! ARE YOU RECEIVING?
NOW'S NOT THE TIME, DEATH'S HEAD!
VERY WELL. JUST THOUGHT YOU MIGHT WANT TO GET OUT OF THE BLAST RADIUS.
BLAST RADIUS? WHAT ARE YOU--
STOPPED BY ENGINEERING ON MY WAY TO THE SHUTTLE BAY.
WITH A SIMPLE MODIFICATION, A KREE WARP CORE BECOMES NOTORIOUSLY UNSTABLE, YES? SHOULD SOLVE YOUR LITTLE RAPTOR PROBLEM.
OH NO--
NOVA! SHIELDS UP!

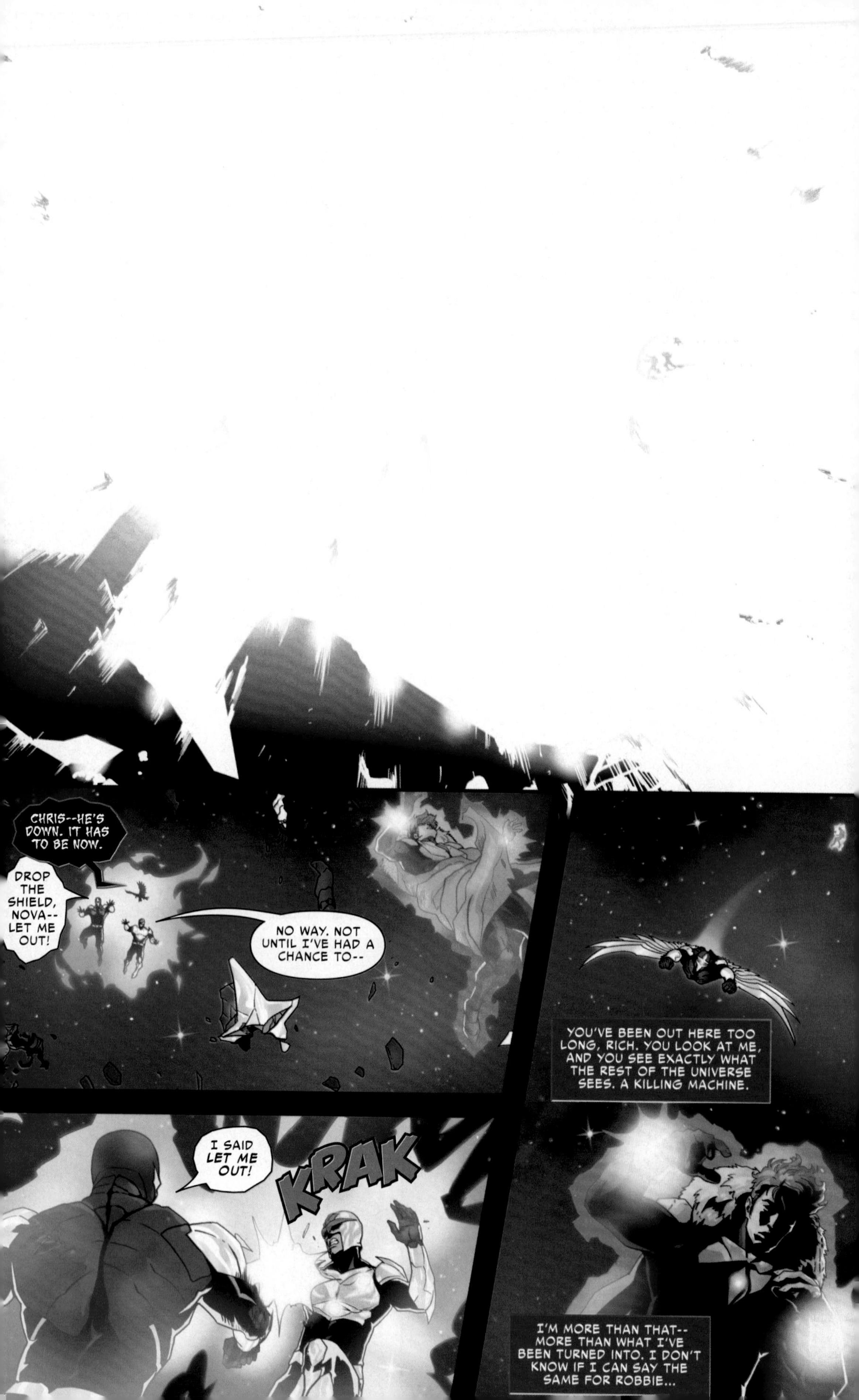
CHRIS--HE'S DOWN. IT HAS TO BE NOW.
DROP THE SHIELD, NOVA--LET ME OUT!
NO WAY. NOT UNTIL I'VE HAD A CHANCE TO--
YOU'VE BEEN OUT HERE TOO LONG, RICH. YOU LOOK AT ME, AND YOU SEE EXACTLY WHAT THE REST OF THE UNIVERSE SEES. A KILLING MACHINE.
I SAID LET ME OUT!
KRAK
I'M MORE THAN THAT--MORE THAN WHAT I'VE BEEN TURNED INTO. I DON'T KNOW IF I CAN SAY THE SAME FOR ROBBIE...

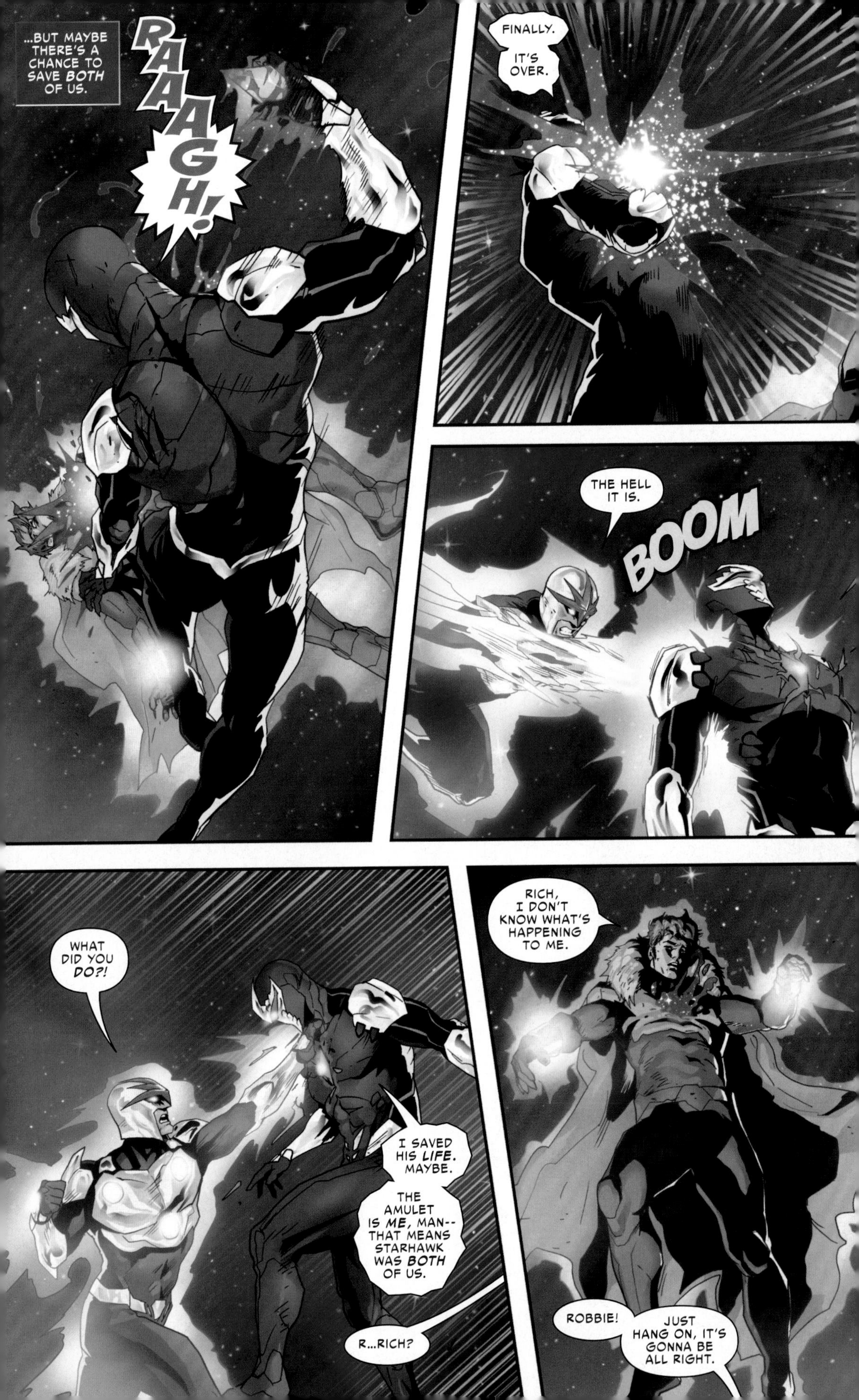
...BUT MAYBE THERE'S A CHANCE TO SAVE BOTH OF US.
RAAAGH!
FINALLY.
IT'S OVER.
THE HELL IT IS.
BOOM
WHAT DID YOU DO?!
I SAVED HIS LIFE. MAYBE.
THE AMULET IS ME, MAN-- THAT MEANS STARHAWK WAS BOTH OF US.
R...RICH?
RICH, I DON'T KNOW WHAT'S HAPPENING TO ME.
ROBBIE!
JUST HANG ON, IT'S GONNA BE ALL RIGHT.

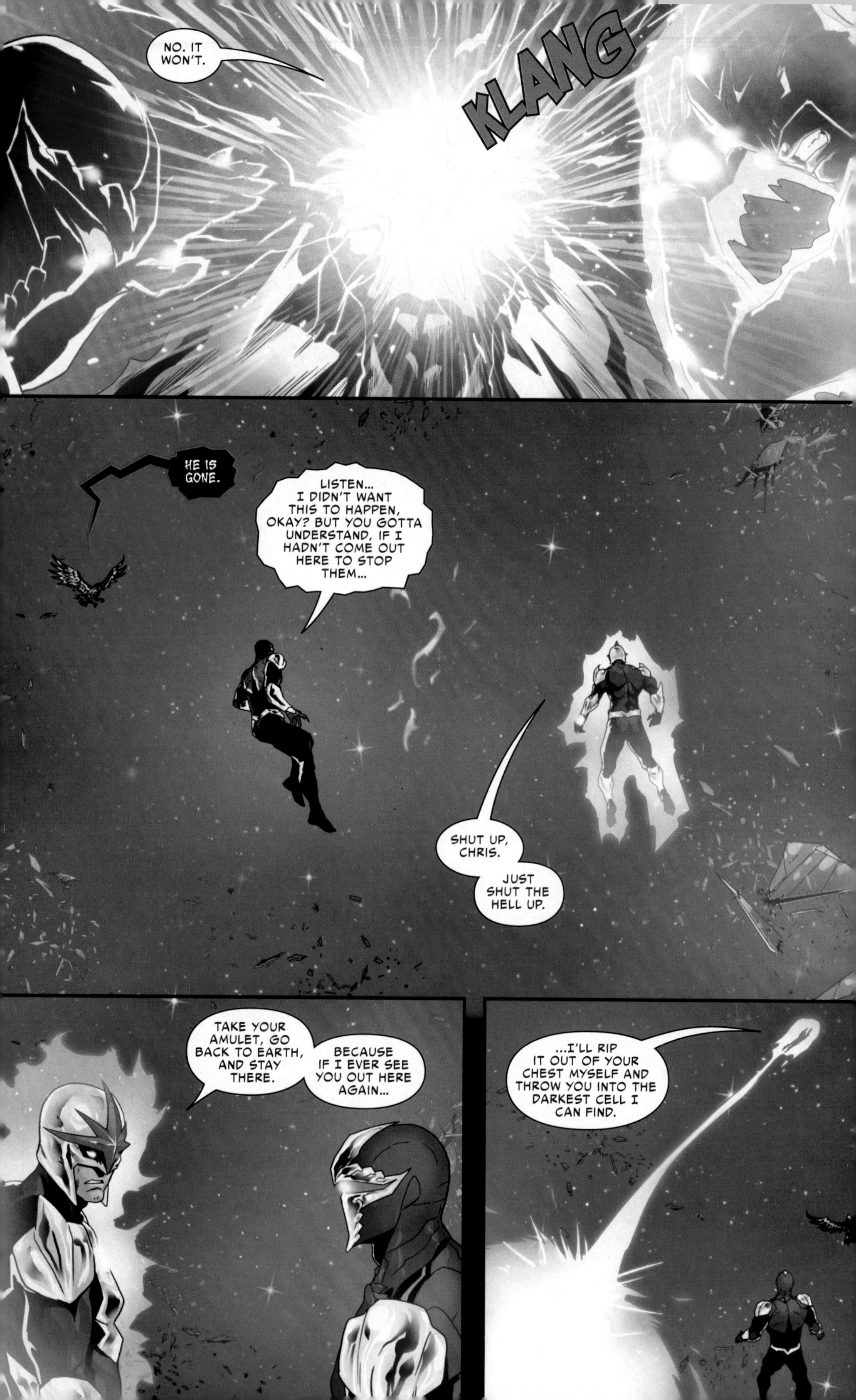

NO. IT WON'T.
KLANG
HE IS GONE.
LISTEN... I DIDN'T WANT THIS TO HAPPEN, OKAY? BUT YOU GOTTA UNDERSTAND, IF I HADN'T COME OUT HERE TO STOP THEM...
SHUT UP, CHRIS.
JUST SHUT THE HELL UP.
TAKE YOUR AMULET, GO BACK TO EARTH, AND STAY THERE.
BECAUSE IF I EVER SEE YOU OUT HERE AGAIN...
...I'LL RIP IT OUT OF YOUR CHEST MYSELF AND THROW YOU INTO THE DARKEST CELL I CAN FIND.

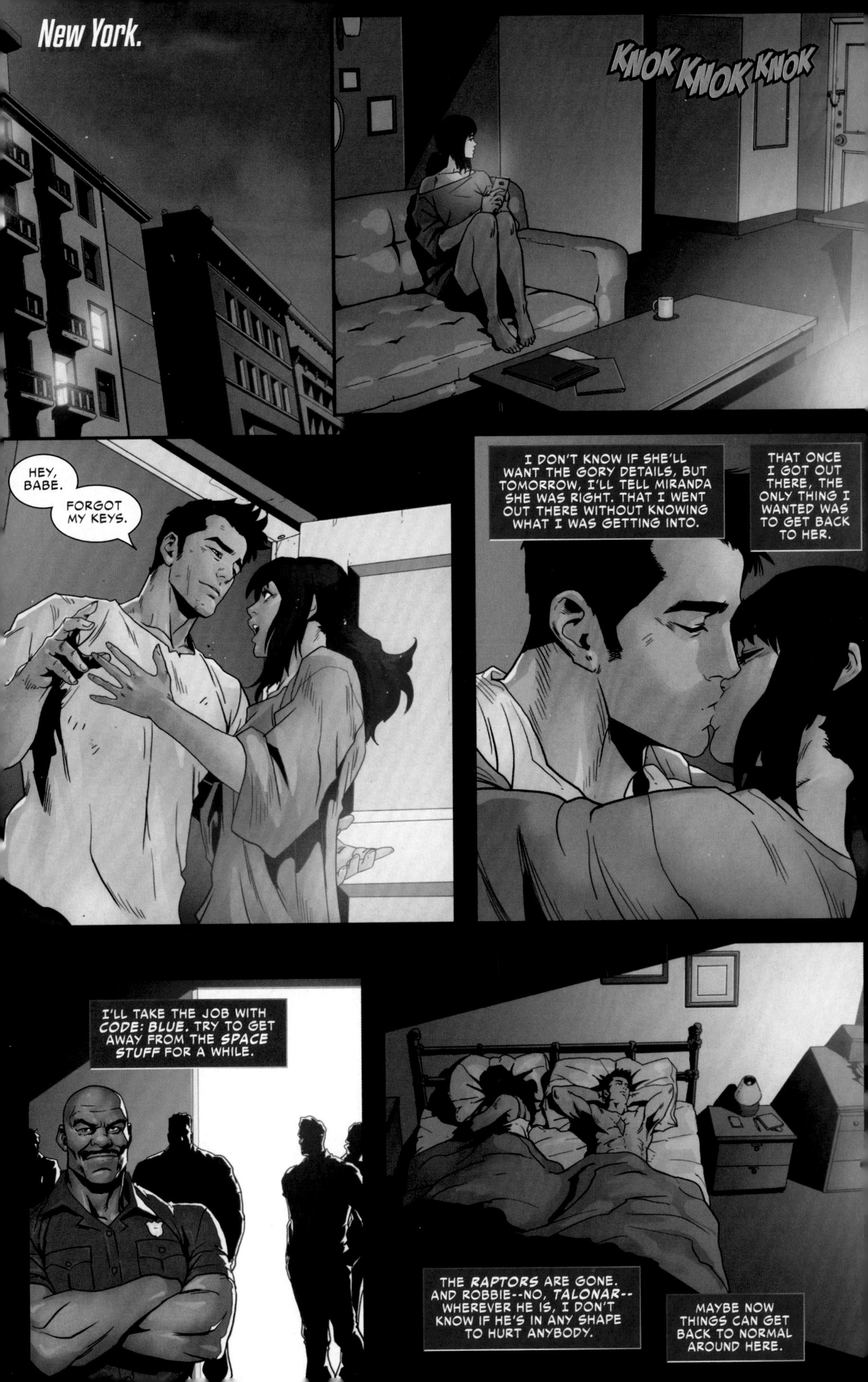
New York.
KNOK KNOK KNOK
HEY, BABE.
FORGOT MY KEYS.
I DON'T KNOW IF SHE'LL WANT THE GORY DETAILS, BUT TOMORROW, I'LL TELL MIRANDA SHE WAS RIGHT. THAT I WENT OUT THERE WITHOUT KNOWING WHAT I WAS GETTING INTO.
THAT ONCE I GOT OUT THERE, THE ONLY THING I WANTED WAS TO GET BACK TO HER.
I'LL TAKE THE JOB WITH *CODE: BLUE*. TRY TO GET AWAY FROM THE *SPACE STUFF* FOR A WHILE.
THE *RAPTORS* ARE GONE. AND ROBBIE--NO, *TALONAR*--WHEREVER HE IS, I DON'T KNOW IF HE'S IN ANY SHAPE TO HURT ANYBODY.
MAYBE NOW THINGS CAN GET BACK TO NORMAL AROUND HERE.

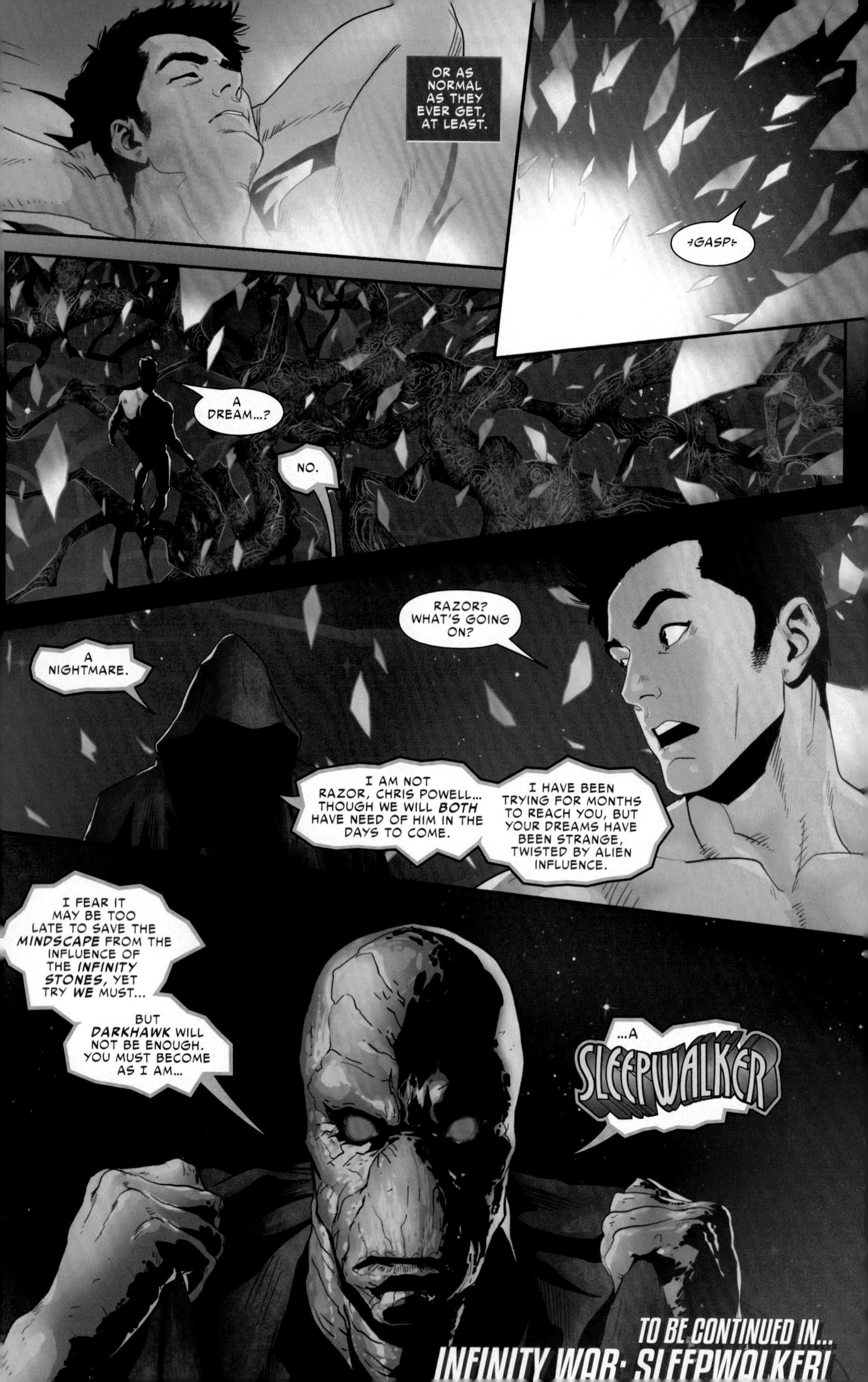

OR AS NORMAL AS THEY EVER GET, AT LEAST.
⊰GASP⊱
A DREAM...?
NO.
RAZOR? WHAT'S GOING ON?
A NIGHTMARE.
I AM NOT RAZOR, CHRIS POWELL... THOUGH WE WILL BOTH HAVE NEED OF HIM IN THE DAYS TO COME.
I HAVE BEEN TRYING FOR MONTHS TO REACH YOU, BUT YOUR DREAMS HAVE BEEN STRANGE, TWISTED BY ALIEN INFLUENCE.
I FEAR IT MAY BE TOO LATE TO SAVE THE MINDSCAPE FROM THE INFLUENCE OF THE INFINITY STONES, YET TRY WE MUST...
BUT DARKHAWK WILL NOT BE ENOUGH. YOU MUST BECOME AS I AM...
...A SLEEPWALKER
TO BE CONTINUED IN...
INFINITY WAR: SLEEPWALKER!

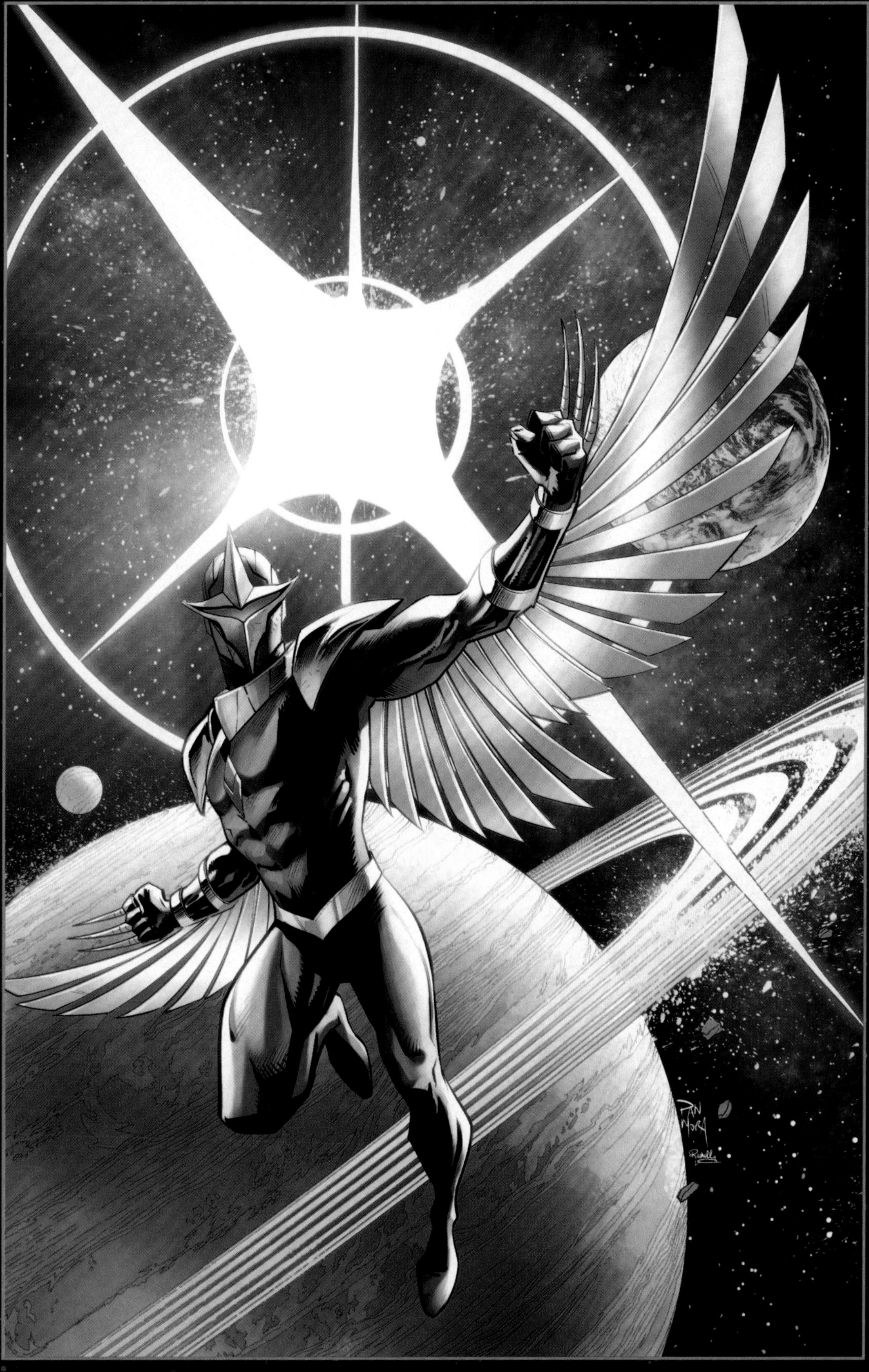

DAN MORA & RACHELLE ROSENBERG

DARKHAWK #51 LEGACY VARIANT

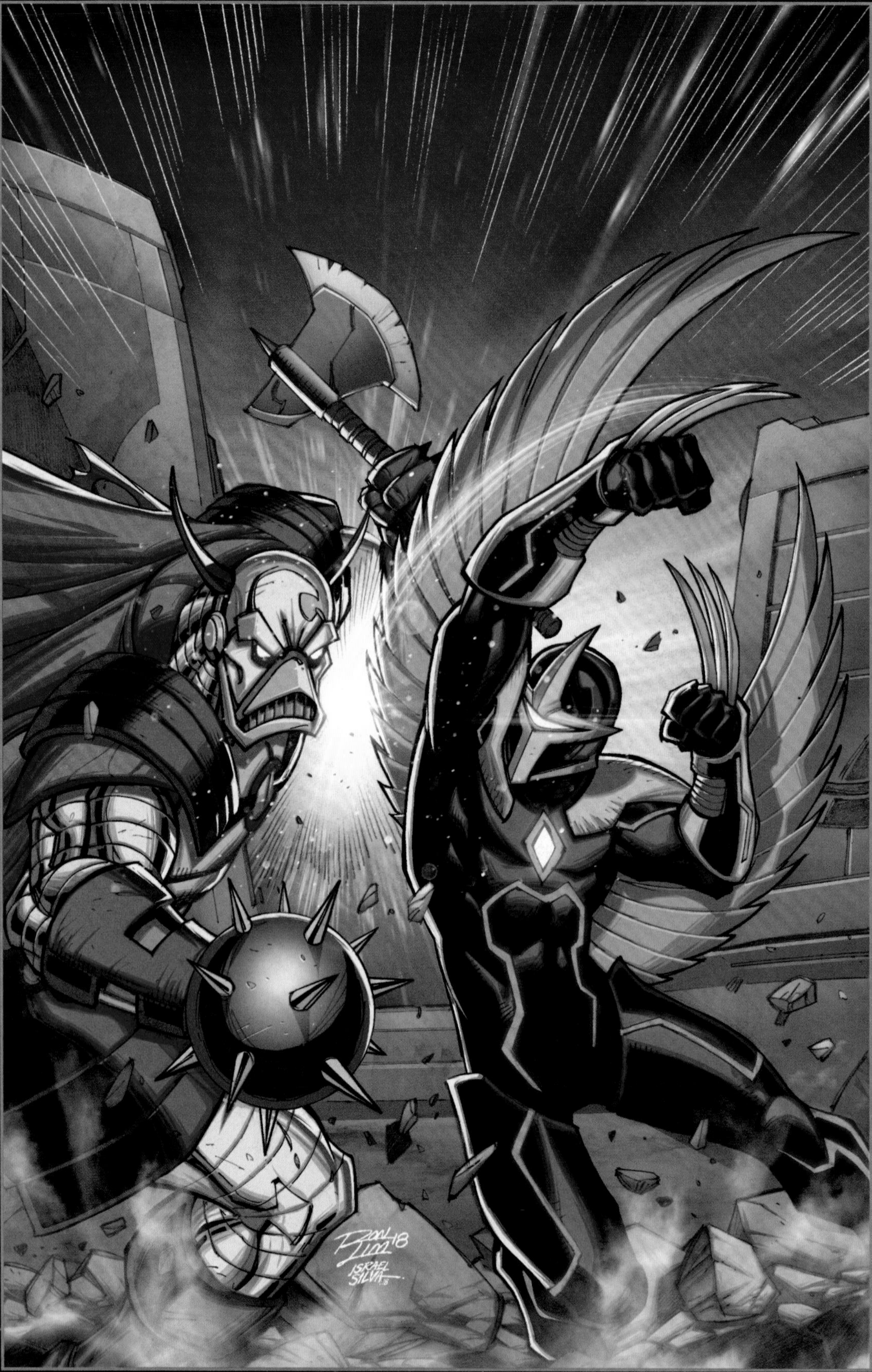
RON LIM '18
ISRAEL SILVA

RON LIM & ISRAEL SILVA

INFINITY COUNTDOWN: DARKHAWK #1 VARIANT

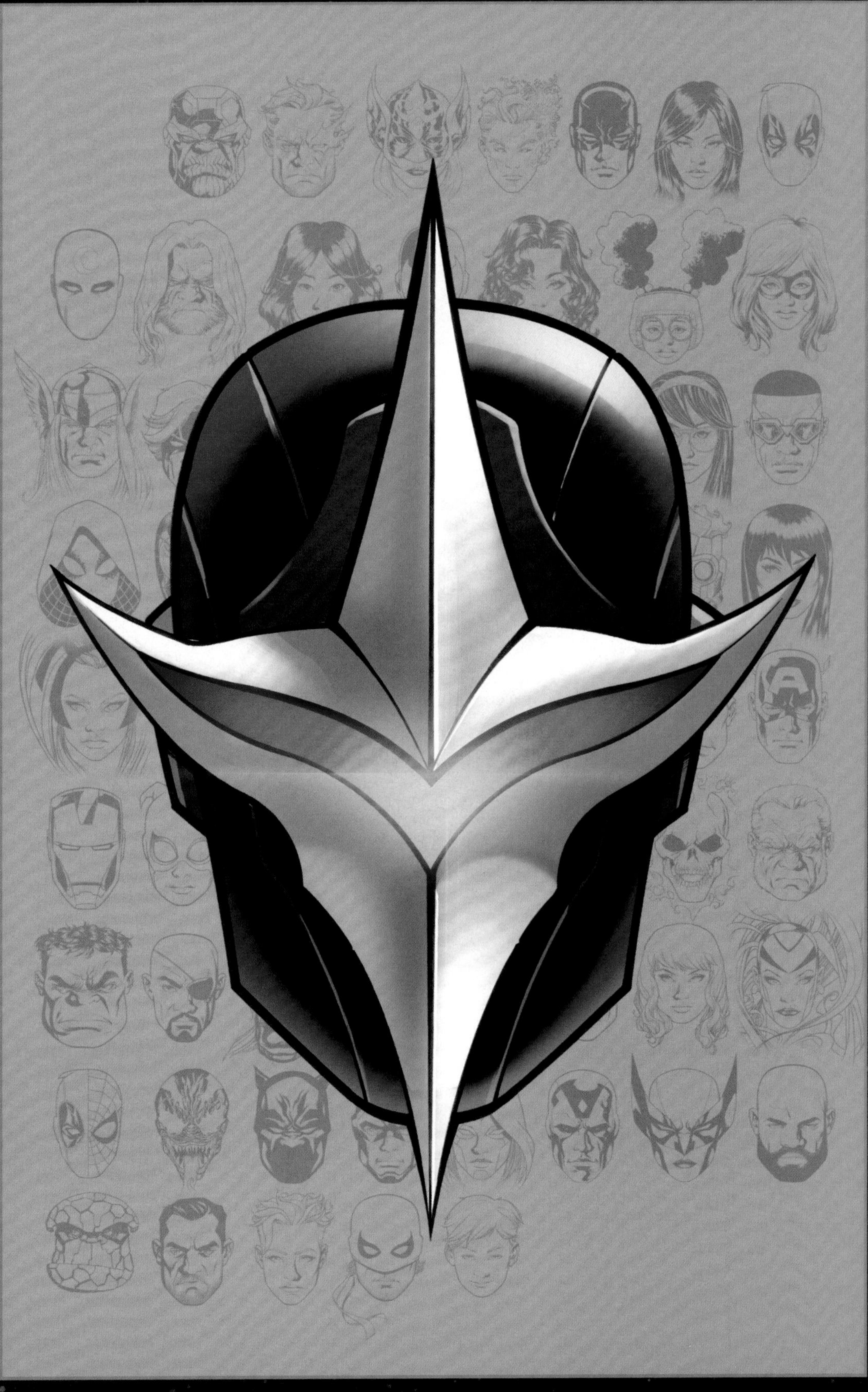

MIKE McKONE & RACHELLE ROSENBERG

INFINITY COUNTDOWN: DARKHAWK #2 LEGACY HEADSHOT VARIANT

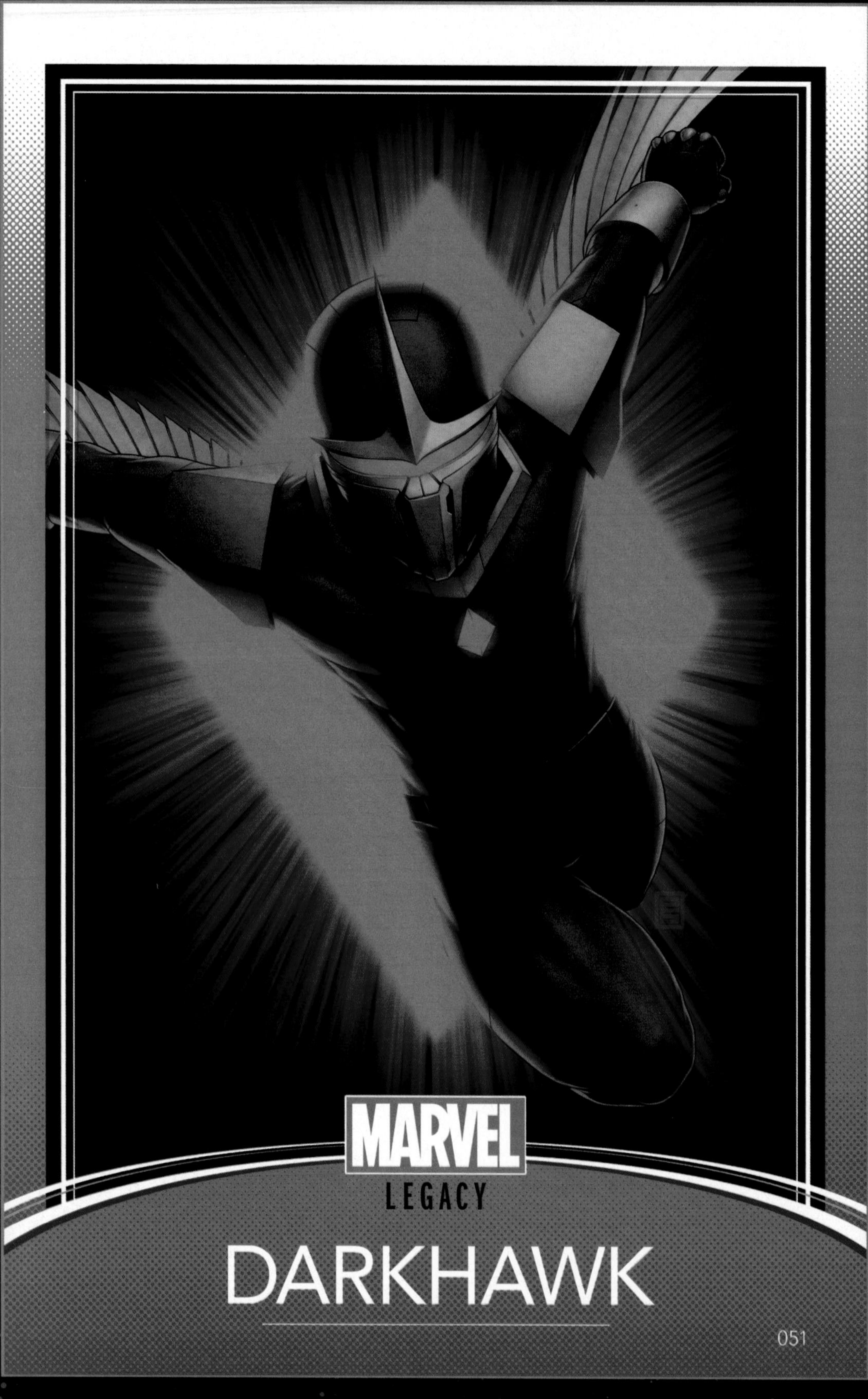
MARVEL
LEGACY
DARKHAWK
051

JOHN TYLER CHRISTOPHER

DARKHAWK #51 TRADING CARD VARIANT

INFINITY COUNTDOWN: DARKHAWK #1 LAYOUTS

BY GANG HYUK LIM

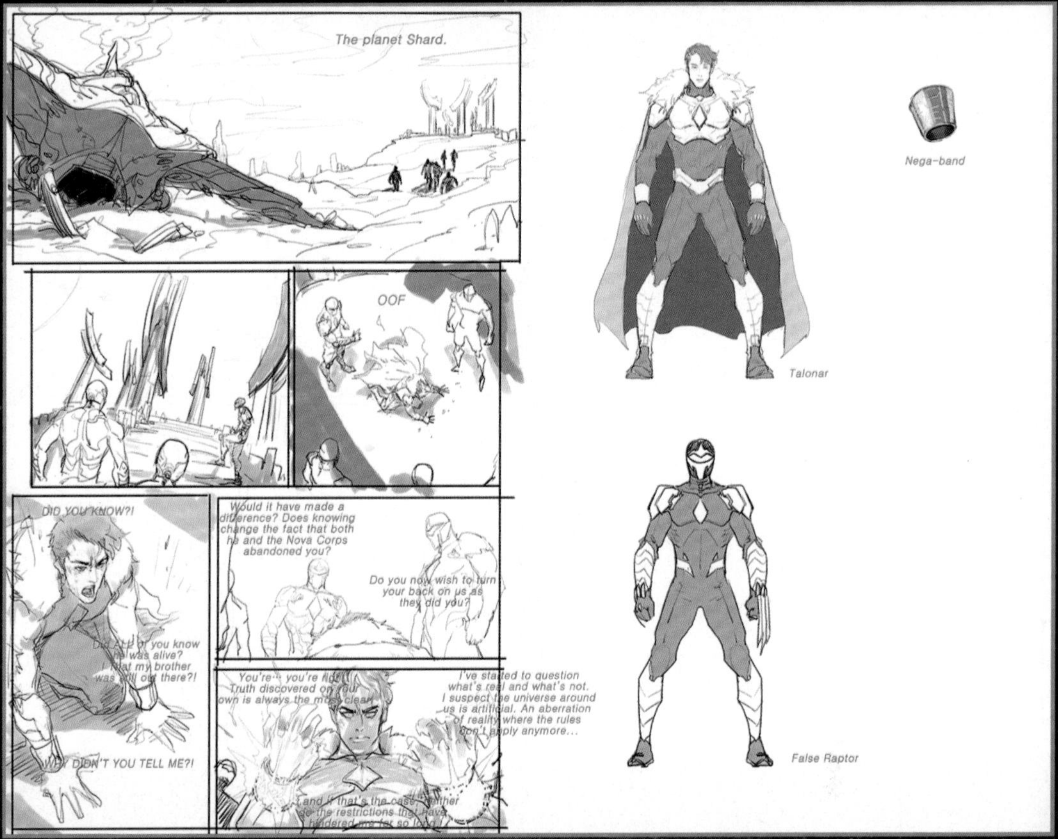

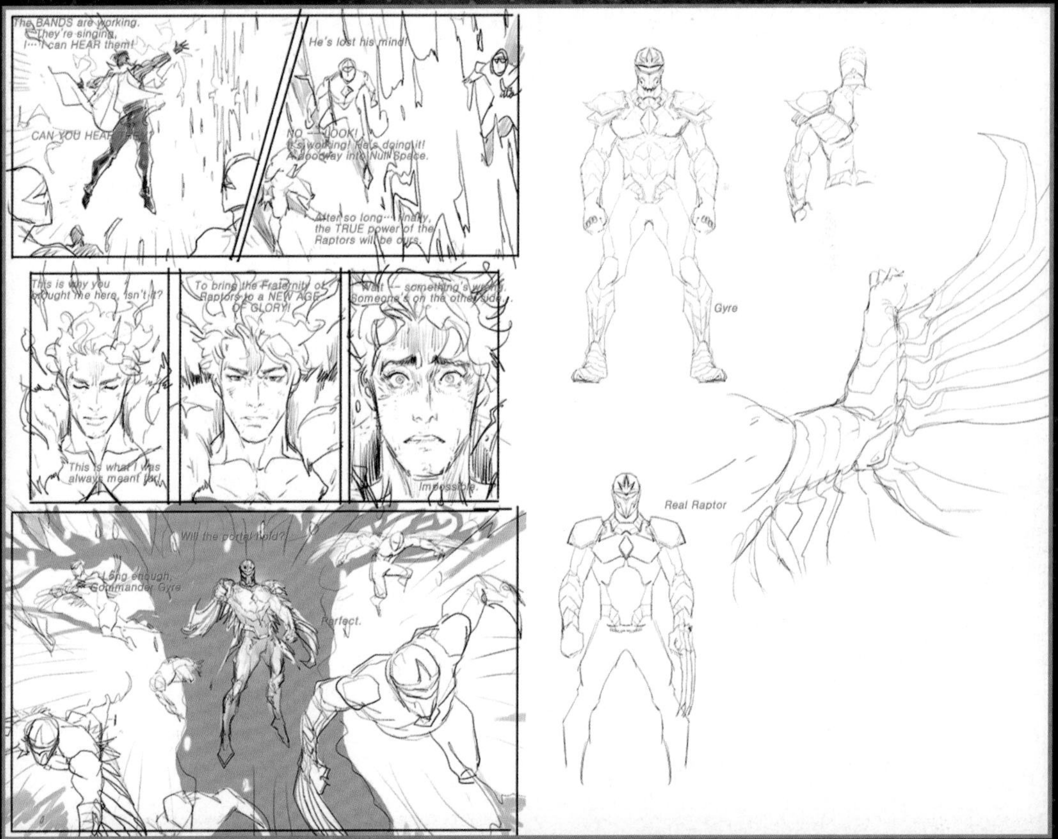

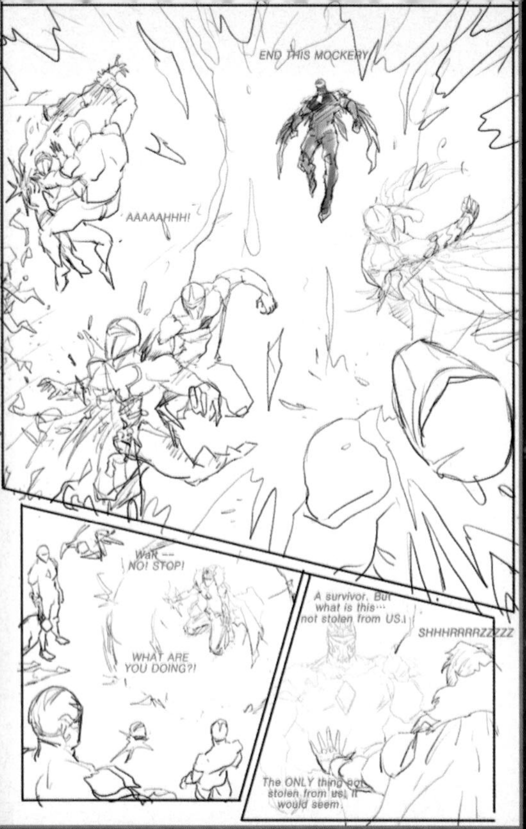
END THIS MOCKERY
AAAAAHHH!
Wait --
NO! STOP!
WHAT ARE YOU DOING?!
A survivor. But what is this··· not stolen from US.
SHHHRRRRZZZZZ
The ONLY thing not stolen from us, it would seem.

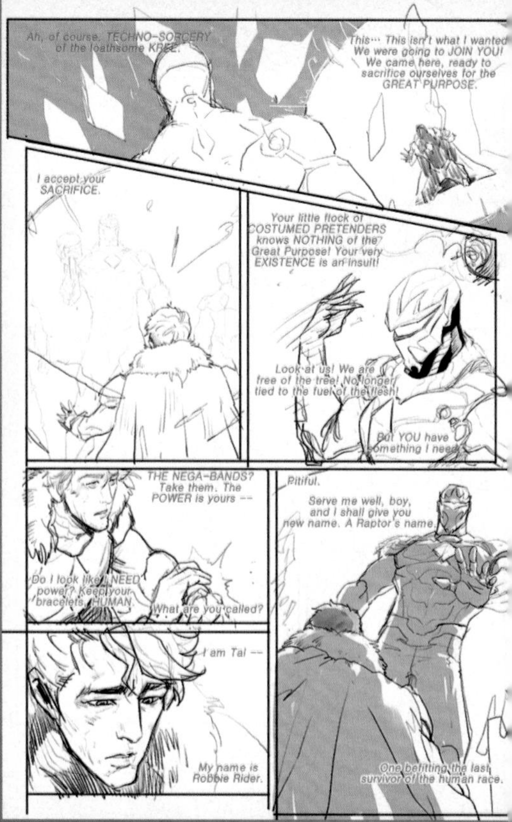
Ah, of course. TECHNO-SORCERY of the loathsome KREE.
This··· This isn't what I wanted. We were going to JOIN YOU! We came here, ready to sacrifice ourselves for the GREAT PURPOSE.
I accept your SACRIFICE.
Your little flock of COSTUMED PRETENDERS knows NOTHING of the Great Purpose! Your very EXISTENCE is an insult!
Look at us! We are free of the tree! No longer tied to the fuel of the flesh!
But YOU have something I need.
THE NEGA-BANDS? Take them. The POWER is yours --
Do I look like I NEED power? Keep your bracelets, HUMAN.
What are you called?
Pitiful.
Serve me well, boy, and I shall give you new name. A Raptor's name.
I am Tal --
My name is Robbie Rider.
One befitting the last survivor of the human race.

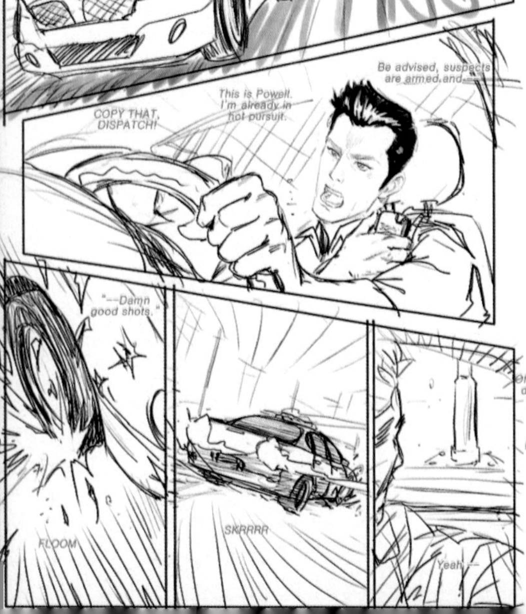
New York. Hell's Kitchen.
The perps are in a late model red sedan, heading west on --
BANG BANG
Be advised, suspects are armed and--
This is Powell. I'm already in hot pursuit.
COPY THAT, DISPATCH!
"--Damn good shots."
FLOOM
SKRRRR
Officer Powell, do you need back-up?
DO - YOU - NEED - HELP?
Yeah --

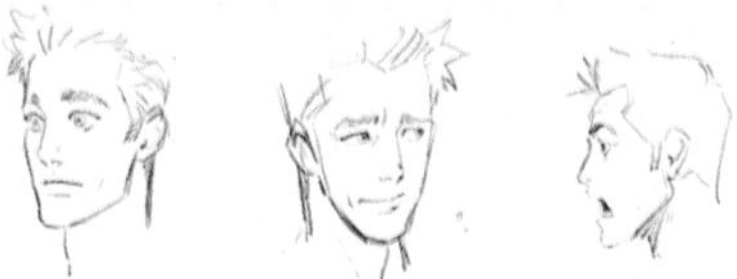

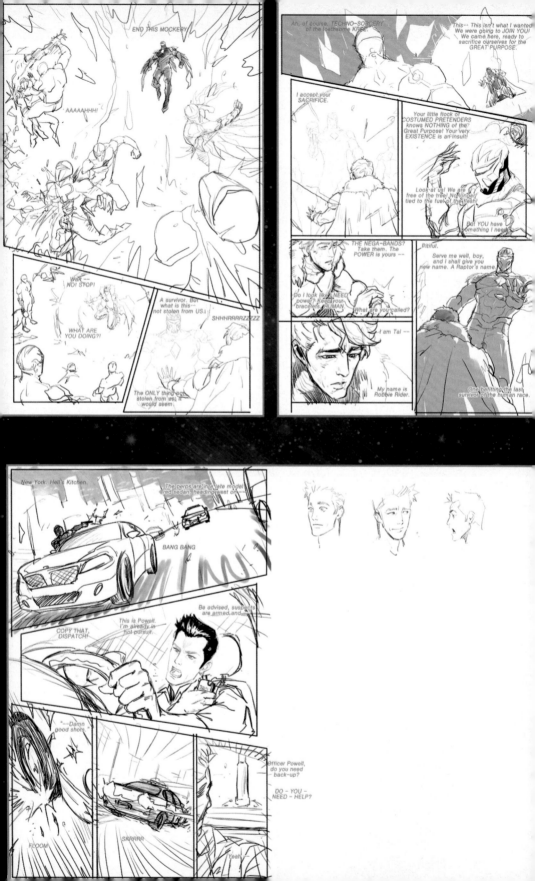

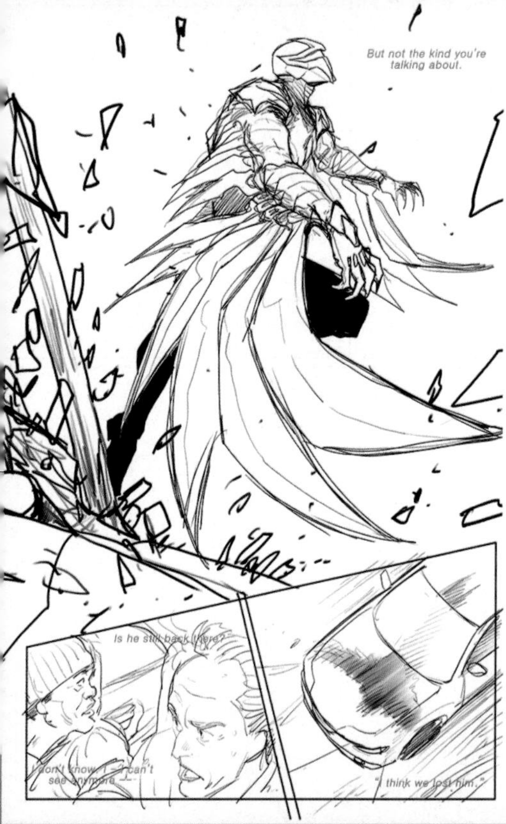
But not the kind you're talking about.
Is he still back there?
I don't know. I—I can't see anymore—
"I think we lost him."

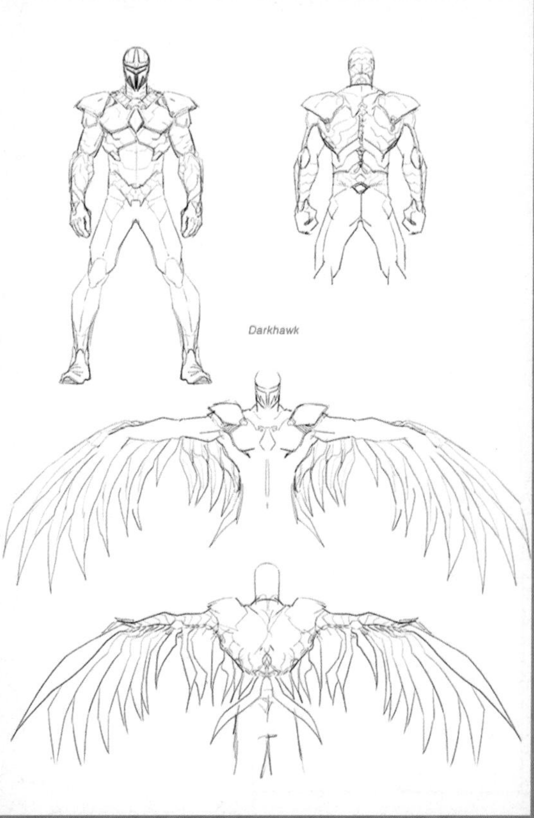
Darkhawk

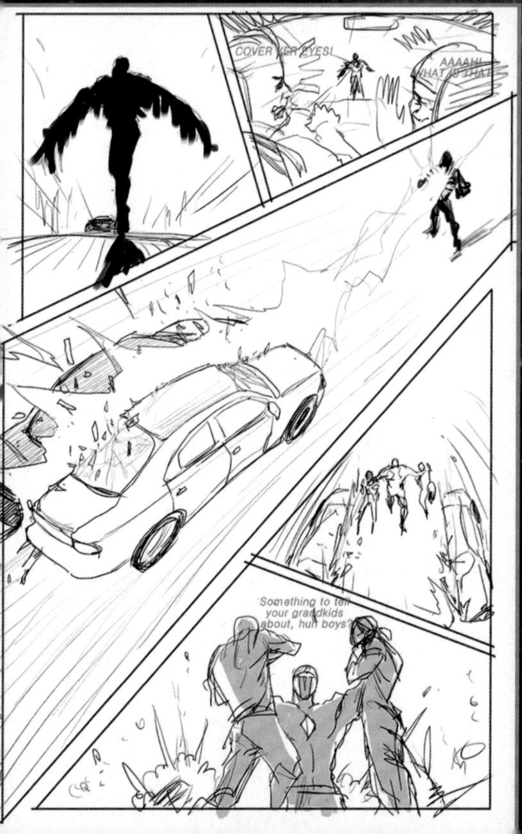
COVER HER EYES!
AAAAH! WHAT IS THAT
Something to tell your grandkids about, huh boys?

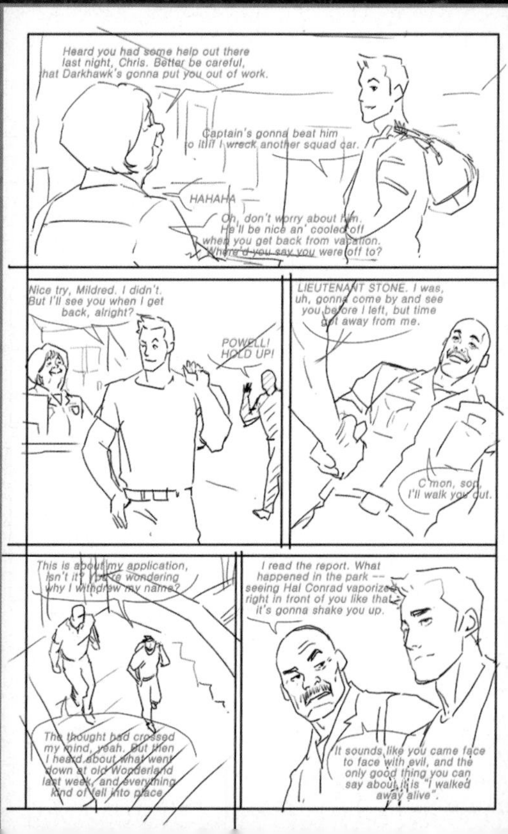
Heard you had some help out there last night, Chris. Better be careful, that Darkhawk's gonna put you out of work.
Captain's gonna beat him to it if I wreck another squad car.
HAHAHA
Oh, don't worry about him. He'll be nice an' cooled off when you get back from vacation. Where'd you say you were off to?
Nice try, Mildred. I didn't. But I'll see you when I get back, alright?
POWELL! HOLD UP!
LIEUTENANT STONE. I was, uh, gonna come by and see you before I left, but time got away from me.
C'mon, son. I'll walk you out.
This is about my application, isn't it? You're wondering why I withdrew my name?
The thought had crossed my mind, yeah. But then I heard about what went down at old Wonderland last week, and everything kind of fell into place.
I read the report. What happened in the park -- seeing Hal Conrad vaporized right in front of you like that -- it's gonna shake you up.
It sounds like you came face to face with evil, and the only good thing you can say about it is "I walked away alive".

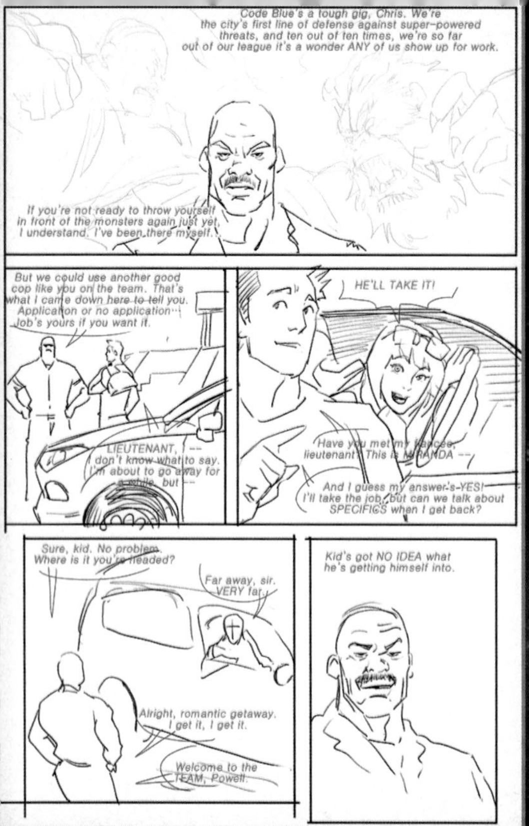
Code Blue's a tough gig, Chris. We're the city's first line of defense against super-powered threats, and ten out of ten times, we're so far out of our league it's a wonder ANY of us show up for work.
If you're not ready to throw yourself in front of the monsters again just yet, I understand. I've been there myself.
But we could use another good cop like you on the team. That's what I came down here to tell you. Application or no application··· Job's yours if you want it.
LIEUTENANT, I -- I don't know what to say. I'm about to go away for a while, but --
HE'LL TAKE IT!
Have you met my fiancee, lieutenant? This is MIRANDA --
And I guess my answer's YES! I'll take the job, but can we talk about SPECIFICS when I get back?
Sure, kid. No problem. Where is it you're headed?
Far away, sir. VERY far.
Alright, romantic getaway. I get it, I get it.
Welcome to the TEAM, Powell.
Kid's got NO IDEA what he's getting himself into.

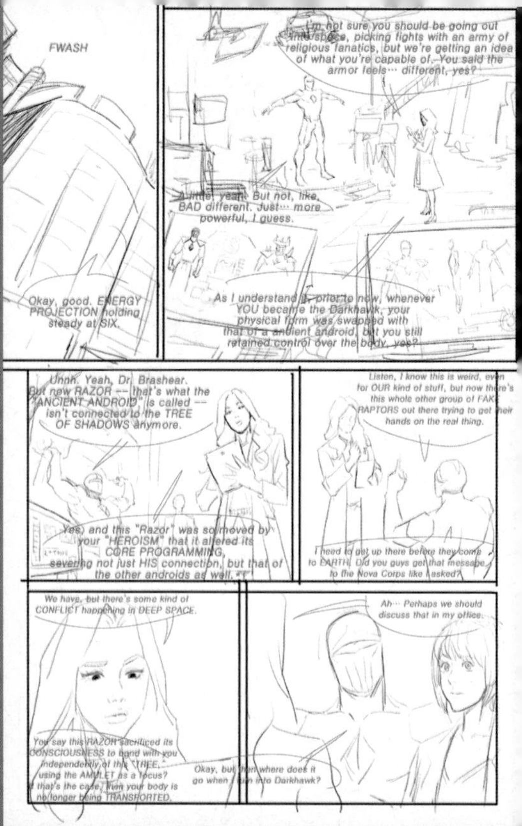
FWASH
I'm not sure you should be going out into space, picking fights with an army of religious fanatics, but we're getting an idea of what you're capable of. You said the armor feels··· different, yes?
A little, yeah. But not, like, BAD different. Just··· more powerful, I guess.
Okay, good. ENERGY PROJECTION holding steady at SIX.
As I understand it, prior to now, whenever YOU became the Darkhawk, your physical form was swapped with that of a ancient android, but you still retained control over the body, yes?
Unnh. Yeah, Dr. Brashear. But new RAZOR -- that's what the "ANCIENT ANDROID" is called -- isn't connected to the TREE OF SHADOWS anymore.
Yes, and this "Razor" was so moved by your "HEROISM" that it altered its CORE PROGRAMMING, severing not just HIS connection, but that of the other androids as well.
Listen, I know this is weird, even for OUR kind of stuff, but now there's this whole other group of FAKE RAPTORS out there trying to get their hands on the real thing.
I need to get up there before they come to EARTH. Did you guys get that message to the Nova Corps like I asked?
We have, but there's some kind of CONFLICT happening in DEEP SPACE.
You say this RAZOR sacrificed its CONSCIOUSNESS to bond with you independently of the "TREE," using the AMULET as a focus? If that's the case, then your body is no longer being TRANSPORTED.
Okay, but then where does it go when I turn into Darkhawk?
Ah··· Perhaps we should discuss that in my office.

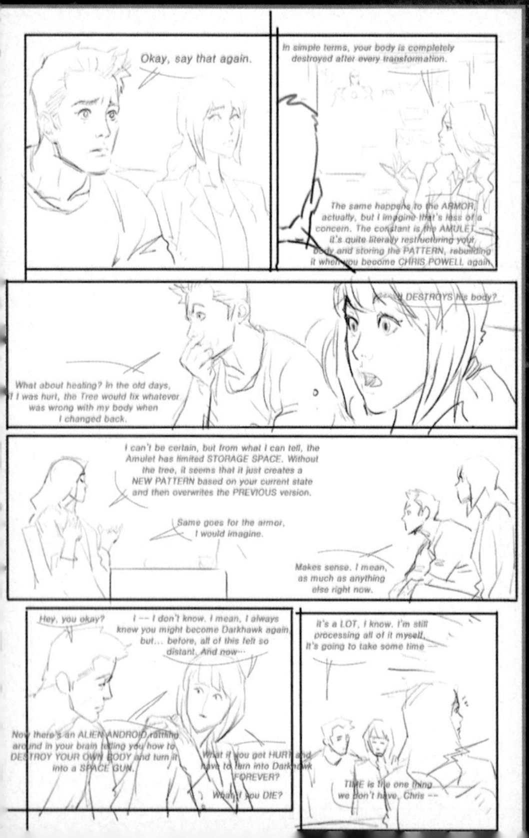
Okay, say that again.
In simple terms, your body is completely destroyed after every transformation.
The same happens to the ARMOR, actually, but I imagine that's less of a concern. The constant is the AMULET -- it's quite literally restructuring your body and storing the PATTERN, rebuilding it when you become CHRIS POWELL again.
DESTROYS his body?
What about healing? In the old days, if I was hurt, the Tree would fix whatever was wrong with my body when I changed back.
I can't be certain, but from what I can tell, the Amulet has limited STORAGE SPACE. Without the tree, it seems that it just creates a NEW PATTERN based on your current state and then overwrites the PREVIOUS version.
Same goes for the armor, I would imagine.
Makes sense. I mean, as much as anything else right now.
Hey, you okay?
I -- I don't know. I mean, I always knew you might become Darkhawk again, but... before, all of this felt so distant. And now···
Now there's an ALIEN ANDROID rattling around in your brain telling you how to DESTROY YOUR OWN BODY and turn it into a SPACE GUN.
What if you get HURT and have to turn into Darkhawk FOREVER?
What if you DIE?
It's a LOT, I know. I'm still processing all of it myself. It's going to take some time --
TIME is the one thing we don't have, Chris --

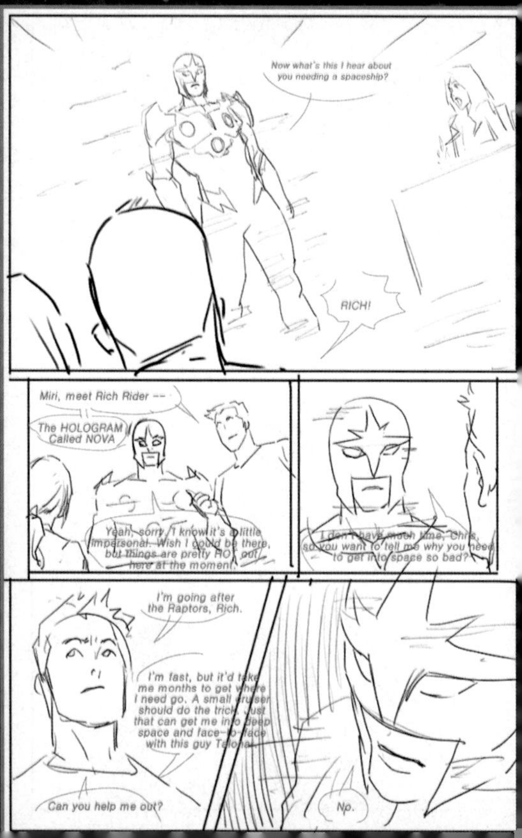
Now what's this I hear about you needing a spaceship?
RICH!
Miri, meet Rich Rider --
The HOLOGRAM Called NOVA
Yeah, sorry. I know it's a little impersonal. Wish I could be there, but things are pretty HOT out here at the moment.
I don't have much time, Chris, so you want to tell me why you need to get into space so bad?
I'm going after the Raptors, Rich.
I'm fast, but it'd take me months to get where I need go. A small cruiser should do the trick. Just that can get me into deep space and face-to-face with this guy Talonar.
Can you help me out?
No.

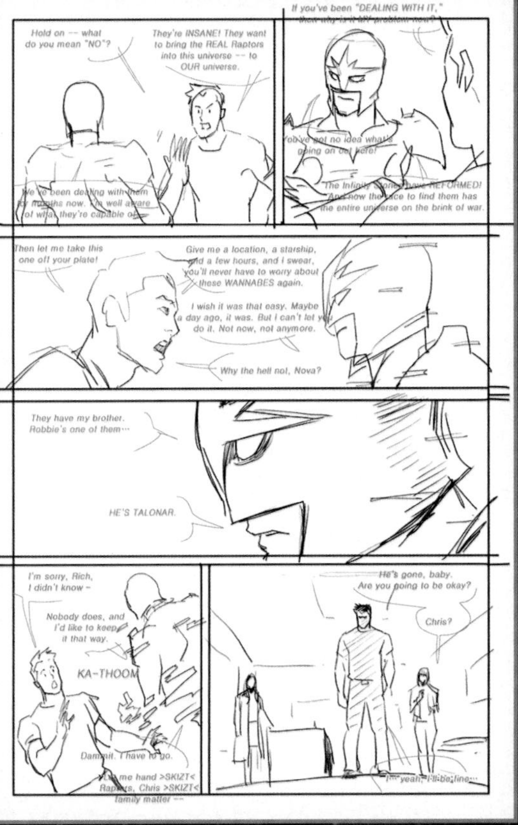
Hold on -- what do you mean "NO"?
They're INSANE! They want to bring the REAL Raptors into this universe -- to OUR universe.
If you've been "DEALING WITH IT,"
The Infinity Stones have REFORMED! And now the race to find them has the entire universe on the brink of war.
Then let me take this one off your plate!
Give me a location, a starship, and a few hours, and I swear, you'll never have to worry about these WANNABES again.
I wish it was that easy. Maybe a day ago, it was. But I can't let you do it. Not now, not anymore.
Why the hell not, Nova?
They have my brother. Robbie's one of them…
HE'S TALONAR.
I'm sorry, Rich, I didn't know -
Nobody does, and I'd like to keep it that way.
KA-THOOM
Dammit. I have to go.
He's gone, baby. Are you going to be okay?
Chris?
I… yeah, I'll be fine…

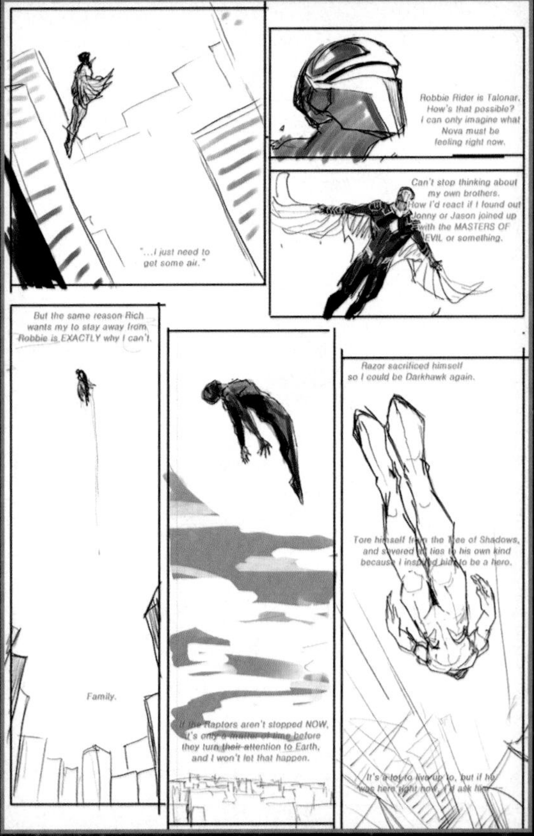
"...I just need to get some air."
Robbie Rider is Talonar. How's that possible? I can only imagine what Nova must be feeling right now.
Can't stop thinking about my own brothers. How I'd react if I found out Jonny or Jason joined up with the MASTERS OF EVIL or something.
But the same reason Rich wants my to stay away from Robbie is EXACTLY why I can't.
Family.
If the Raptors aren't stopped NOW, it's only a matter of time before they turn their attention to Earth, and I won't let that happen.
Razor sacrificed himself so I could be Darkhawk again.
Tore himself from the Tree of Shadows, and severed all ties to his own kind because I inspired him to be a hero.

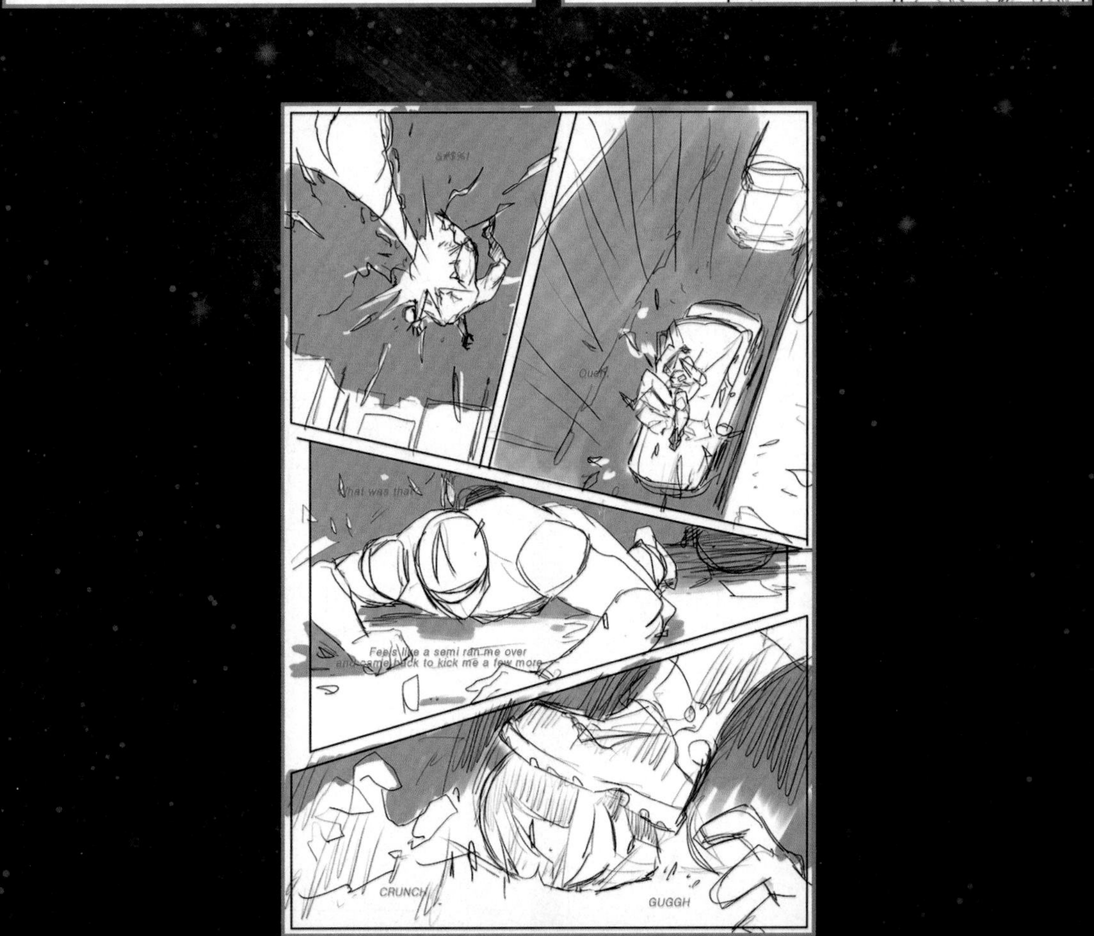
What was that
Feels like a semi ran me over and came back to kick me a few more
CRUNCH
GUGGH

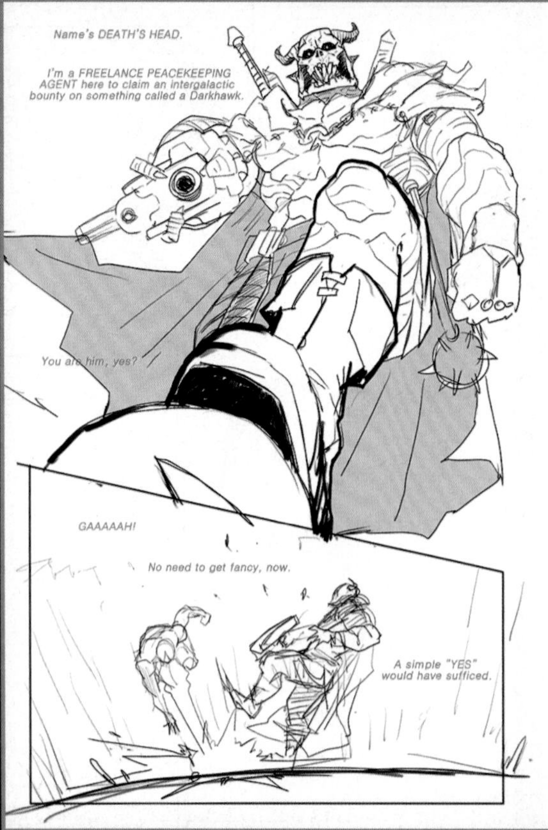

Name's DEATH'S HEAD.
I'm a FREELANCE PEACEKEEPING AGENT here to claim an intergalactic bounty on something called a Darkhawk.
You are him, yes?
GAAAAAH!
No need to get fancy, now.
A simple "YES" would have sufficed.

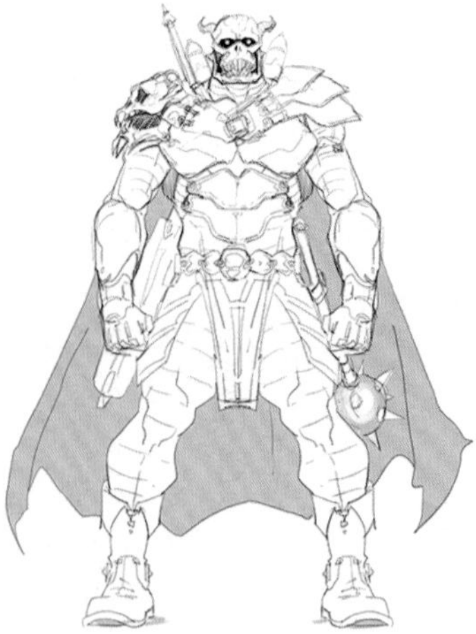

DEATH's HEAD

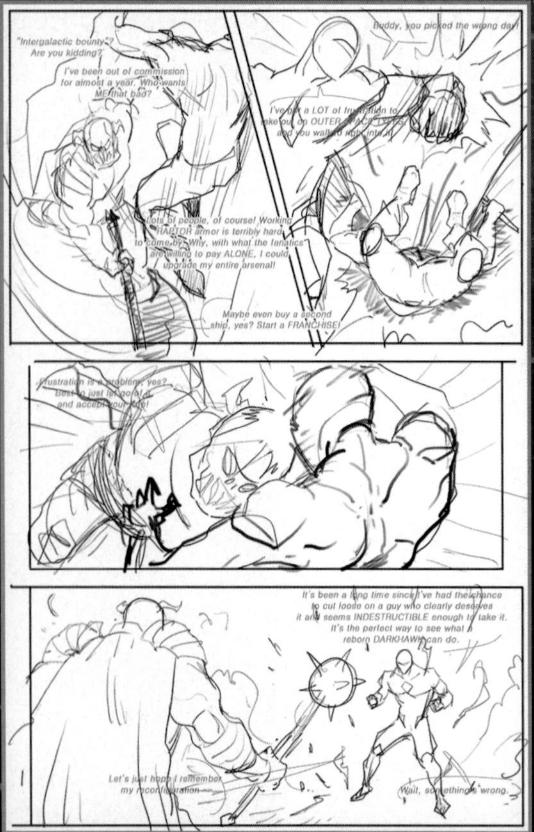

"Intergalactic bounty"? Are you kidding?
I've been out of commission for almost a year. Who wants ME that bad?
Buddy, you picked the wrong day!
Lots of people, of course! Working RAPTOR armor is terribly hard to come by. Why, with what the fanatics are willing to pay ALONE, I could upgrade my entire arsenal!
Maybe even buy a second ship, yes? Start a FRANCHISE!
It's been a long time since I've had the chance to cut loose on a guy who clearly deserves it and seems INDESTRUCTIBLE enough to take it. It's the perfect way to see what a reborn DARKHAWK can do.
Let's just hope I remember my reconfiguration ––
Wait, something's wrong.

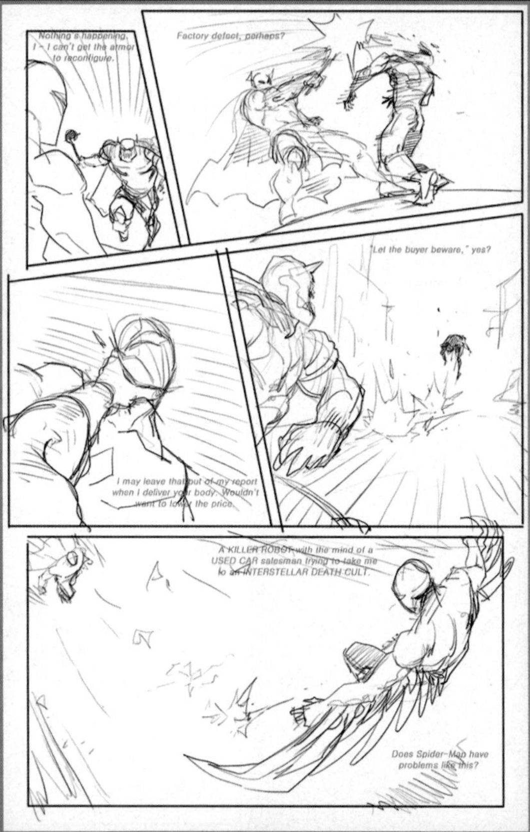

Nothing's happening. I – I can't get the armor to reconfigure.
Factory defect, perhaps?
"Let the buyer beware," yes?
I may leave that out of my report when I deliver your body. Wouldn't want to lower the price.
A KILLER ROBOT with the mind of a USED CAR salesman trying to take me to an INTERSTELLAR DEATH CULT.
Does Spider-Man have problems like this?

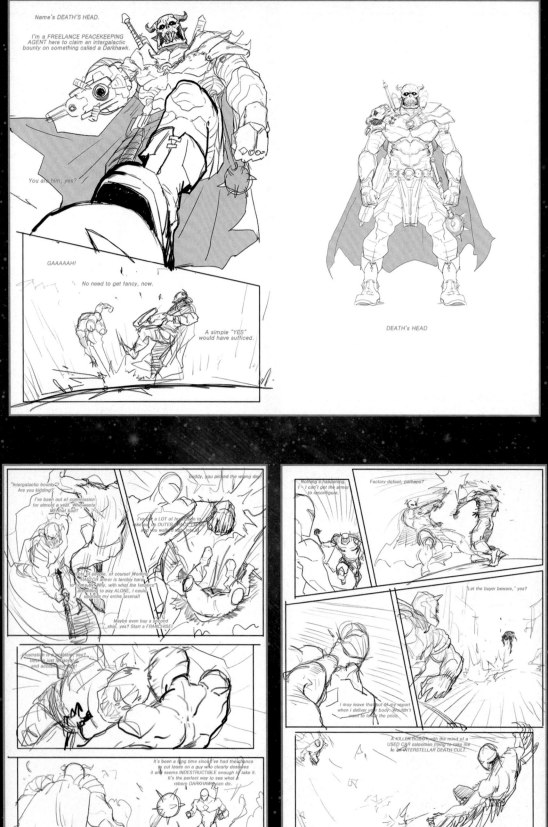

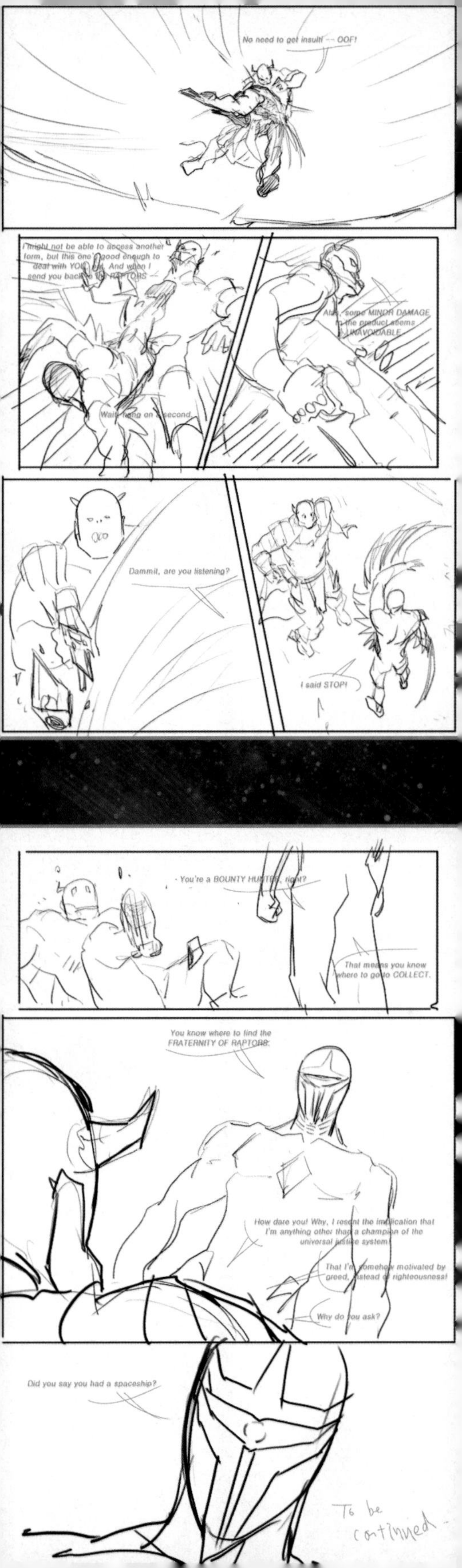
No need to get insult! -- OOF!
I might not be able to access another form, but this one's good enough to deal with YOU, And when I send you back RAPTORS --
Ah, some MINOR DAMAGE to the product seems UNAVOIDABLE.
Wait, hang on a second.
Dammit, are you listening?
I said STOP!
You're a BOUNTY HUNTER, right?
That means you know where to go to COLLECT.
You know where to find the FRATERNITY OF RAPTORS.
How dare you! Why, I resent the implication that I'm anything other than a champion of the universal justice system!
That I'm somehow motivated by greed, instead of righteousness!
Why do you ask?
Did you say you had a spaceship?
To be continued.

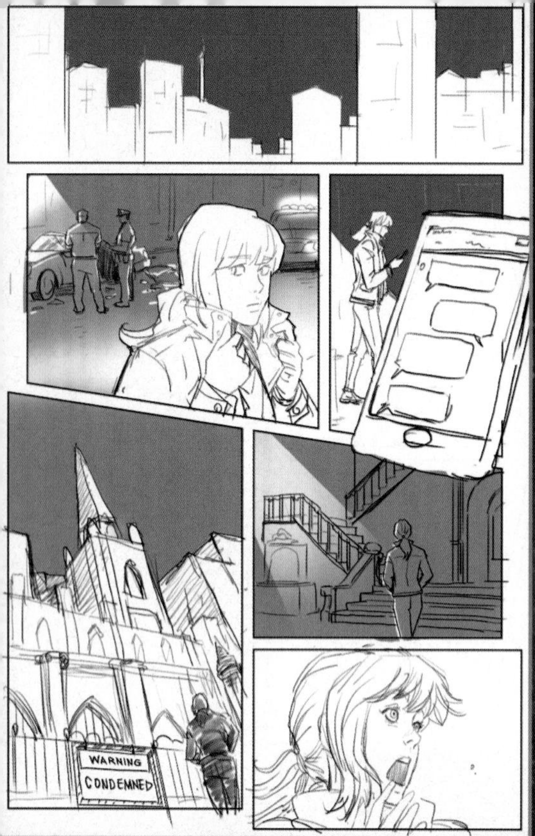
WARNING
CONDEMNED

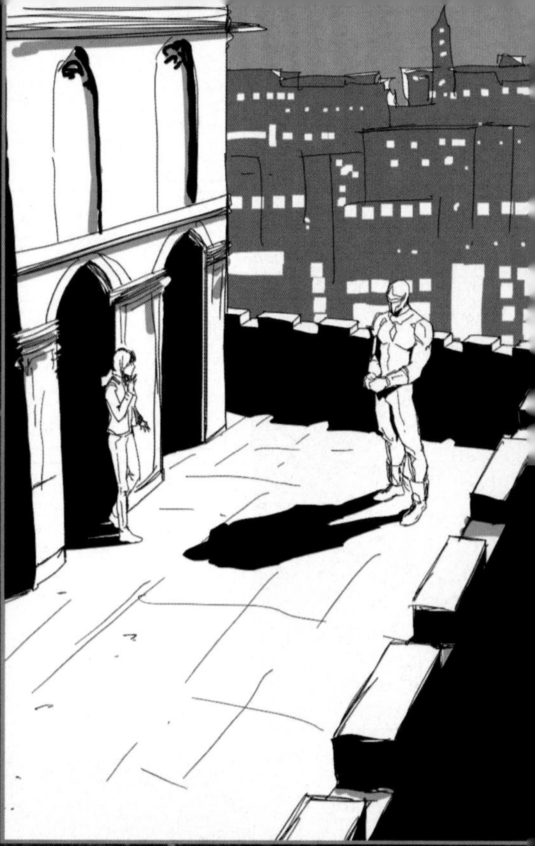

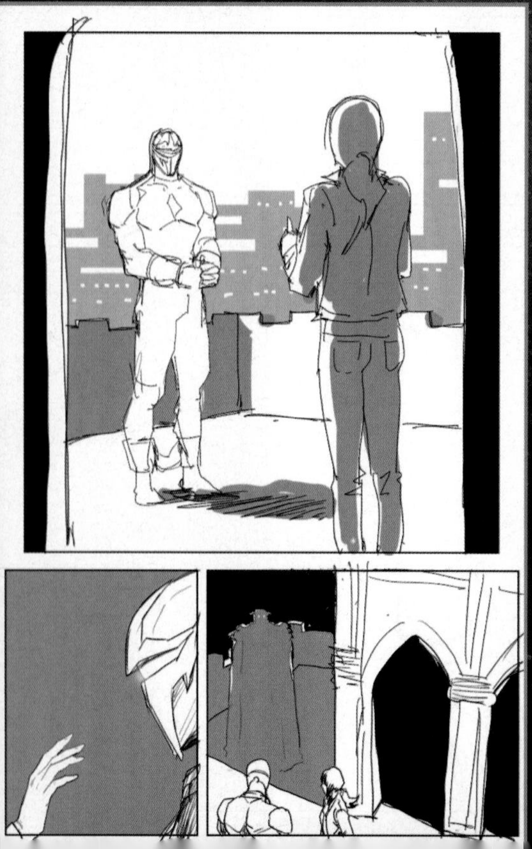

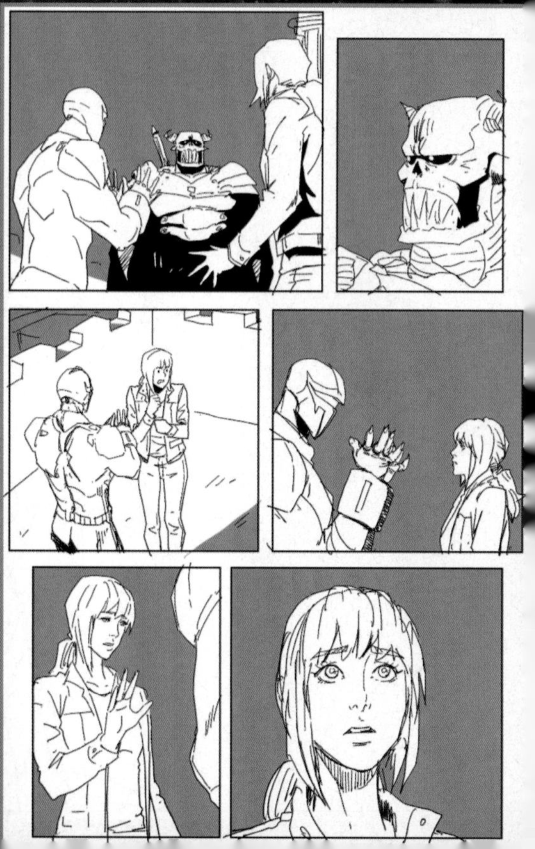

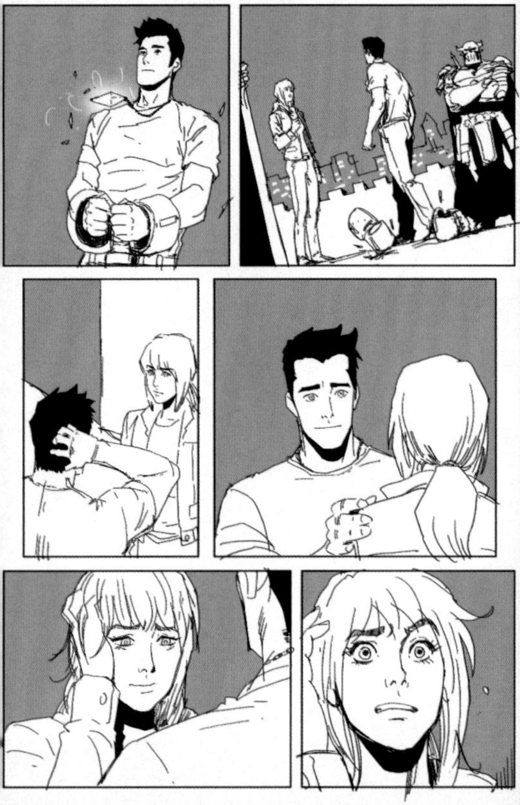

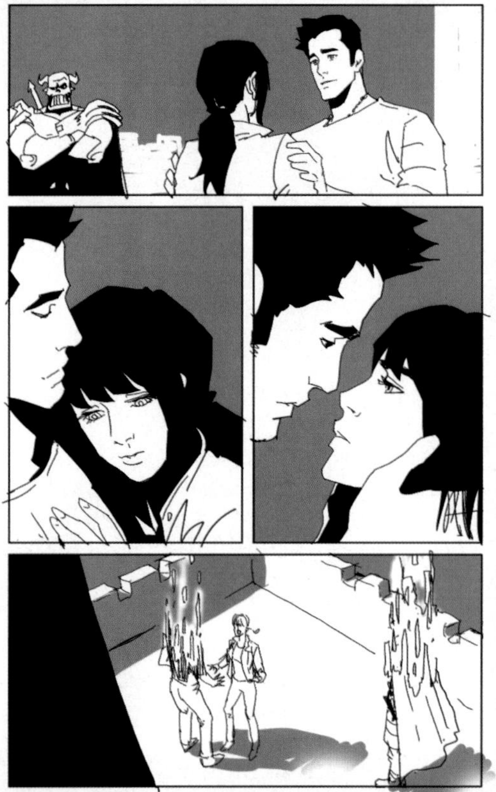

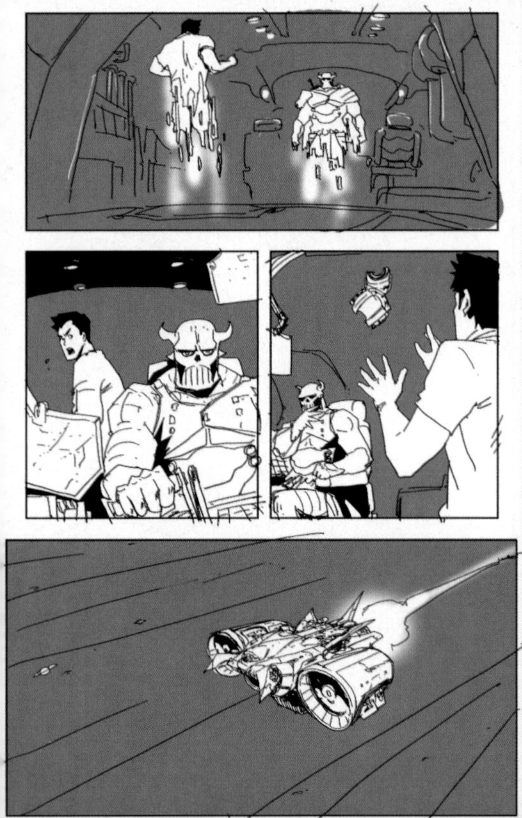

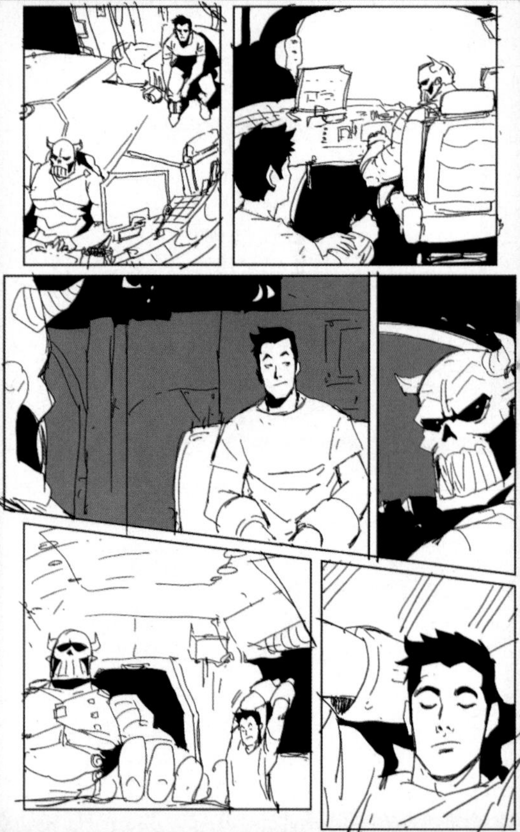

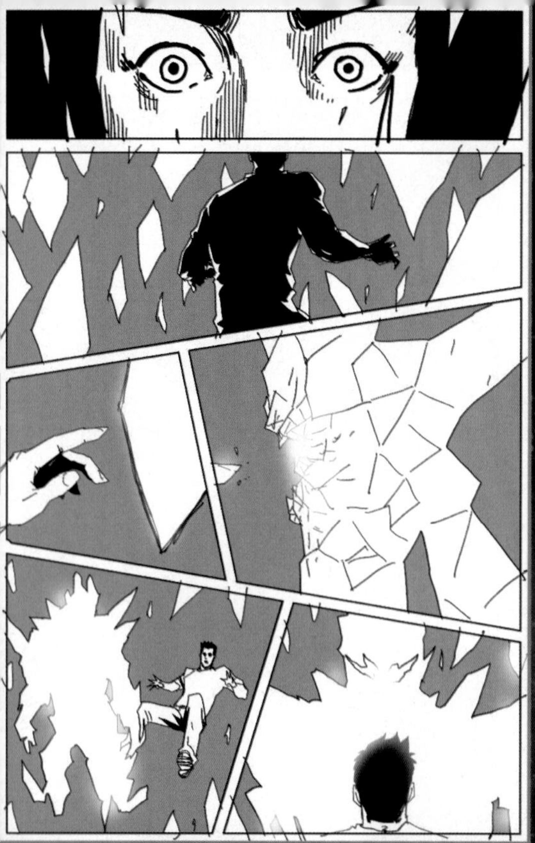
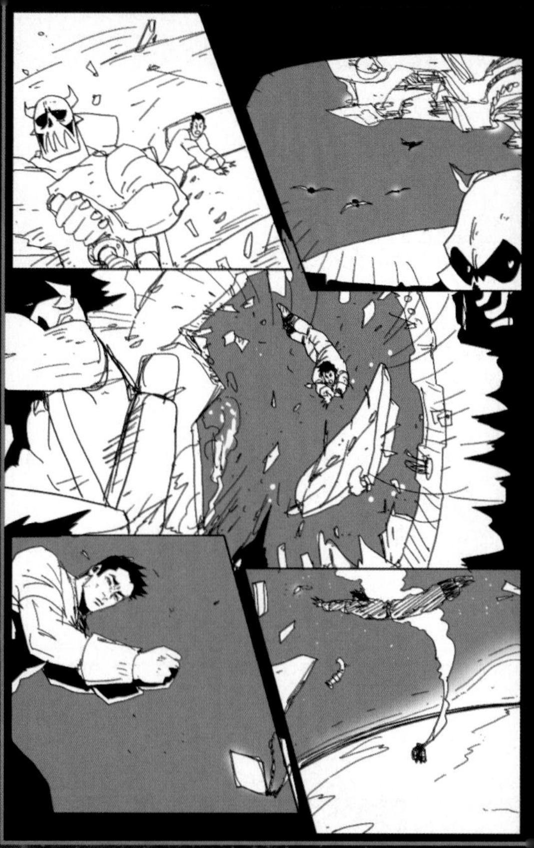
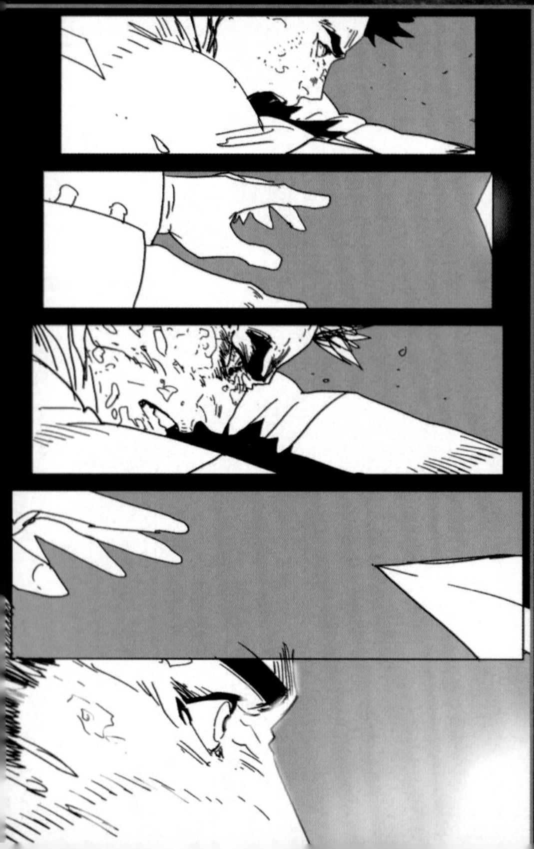
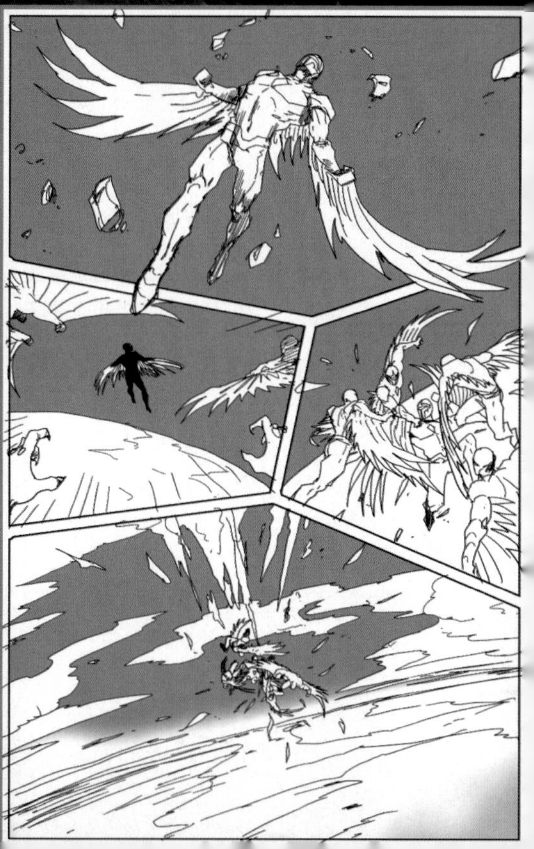

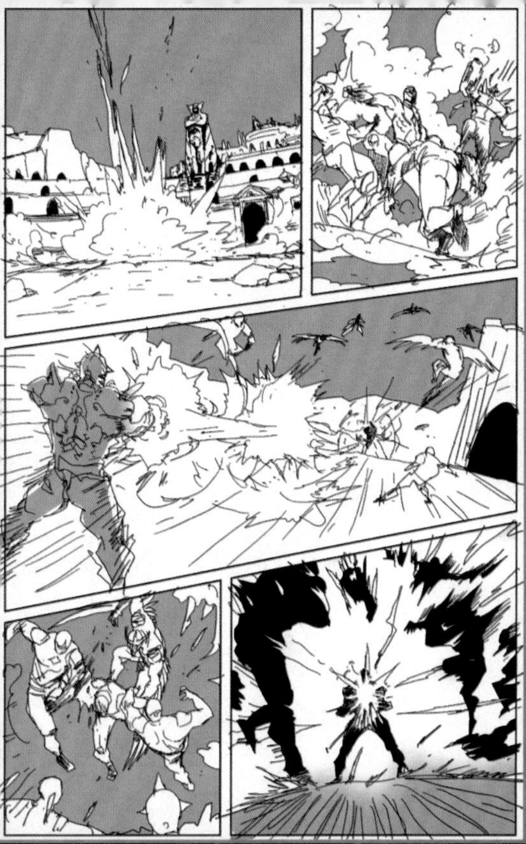
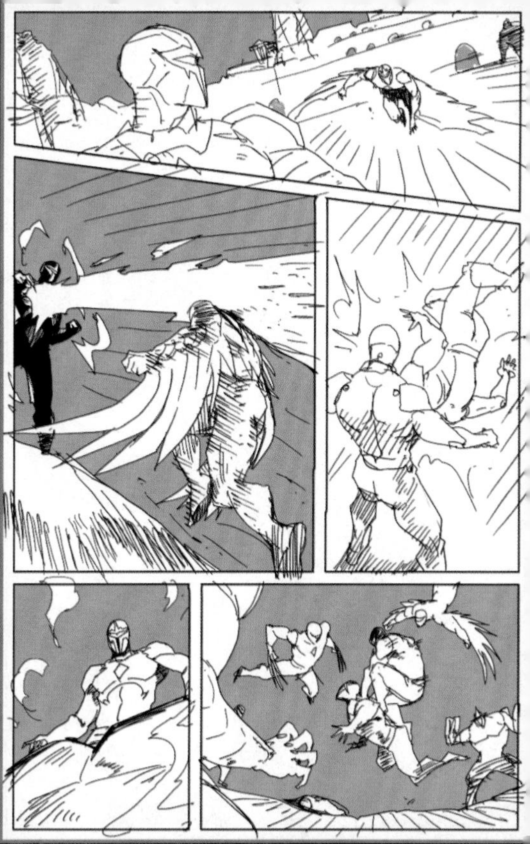
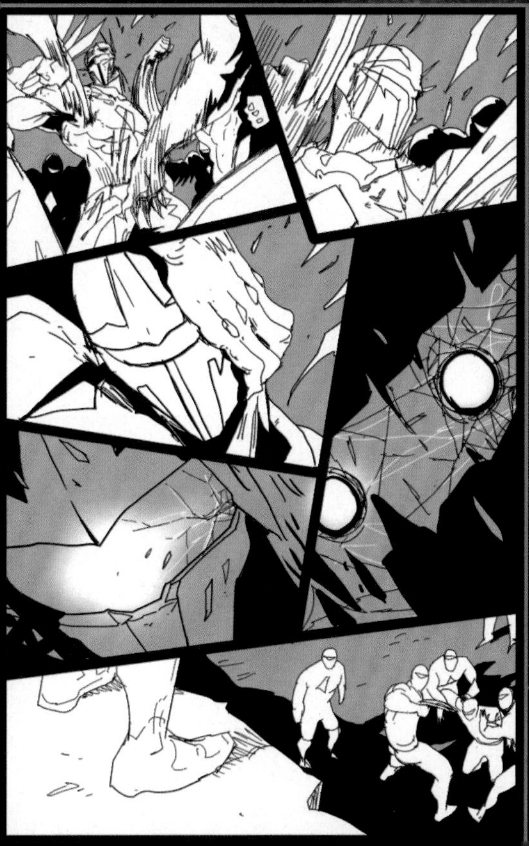
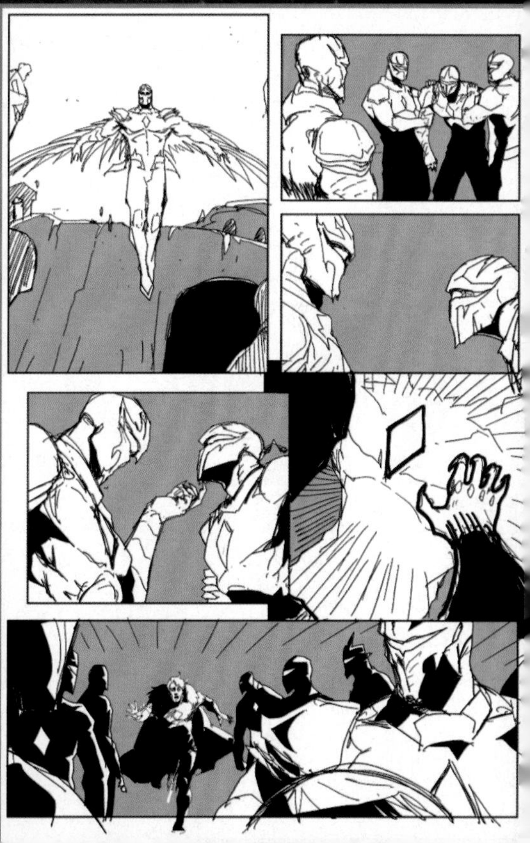

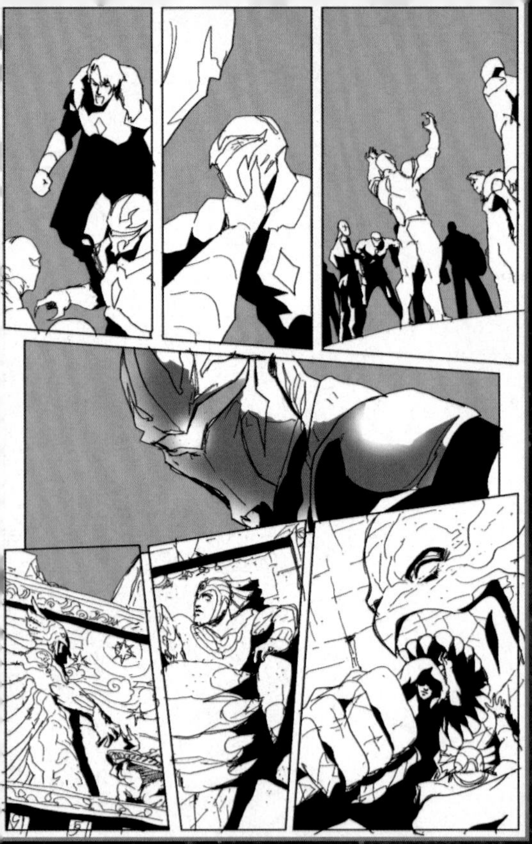

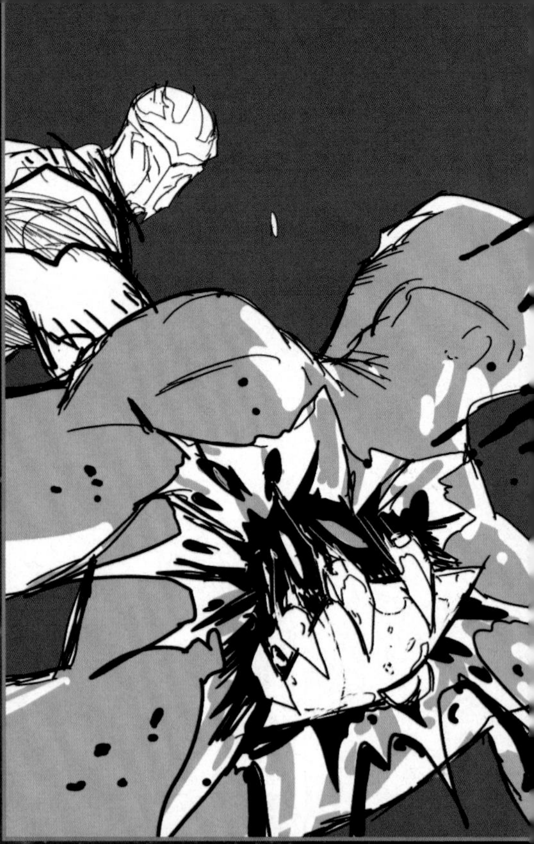

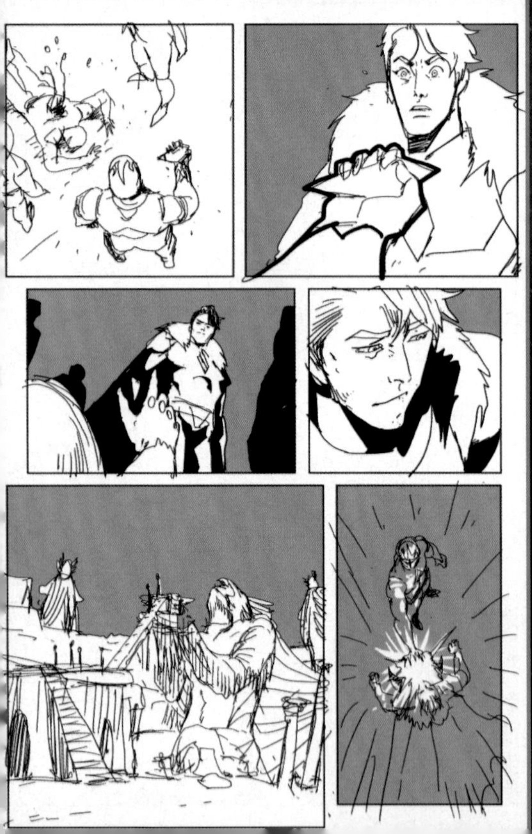

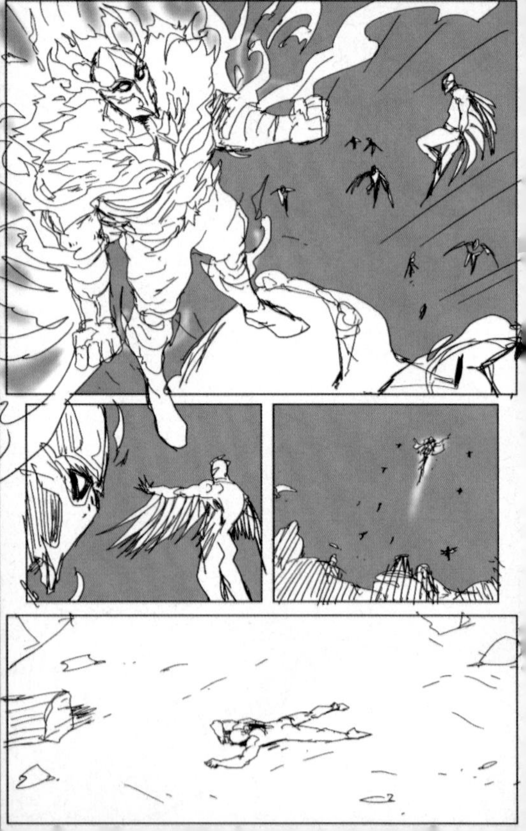

DARKHAWK #51, PAGES 1-4 ART PROCESS

BY KEV WALKER

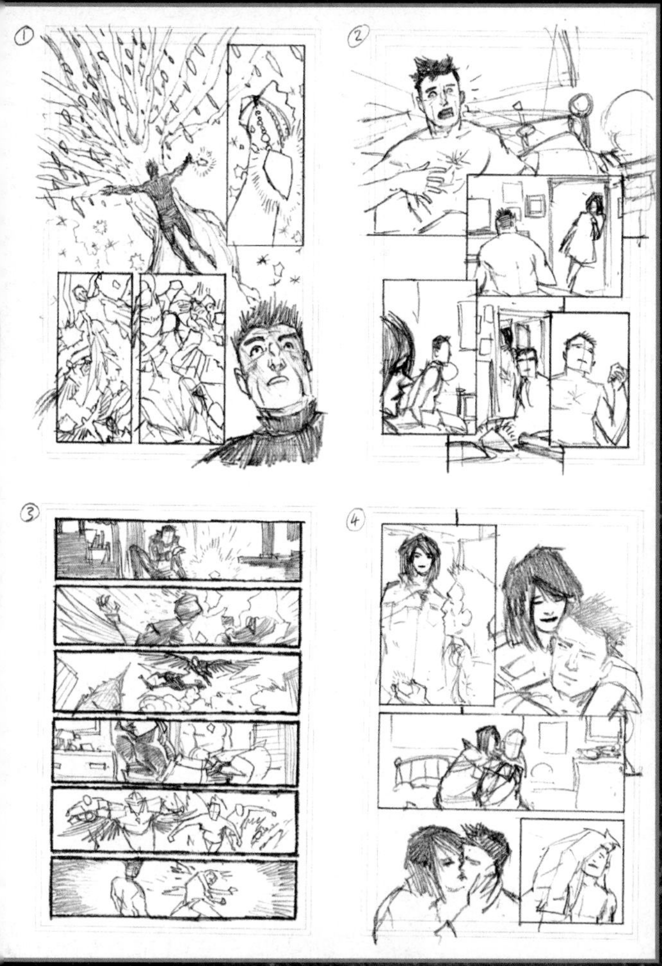

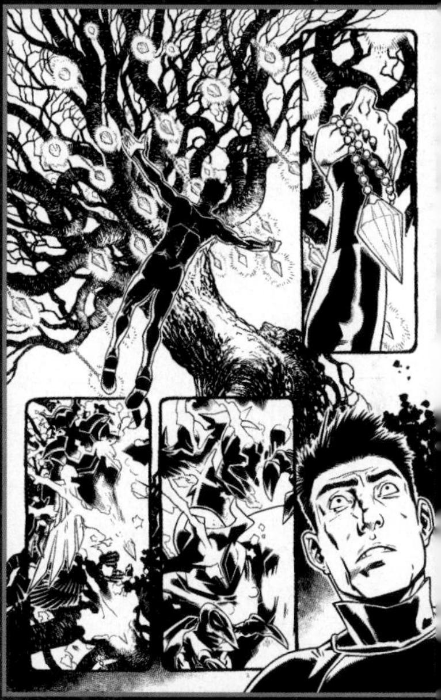

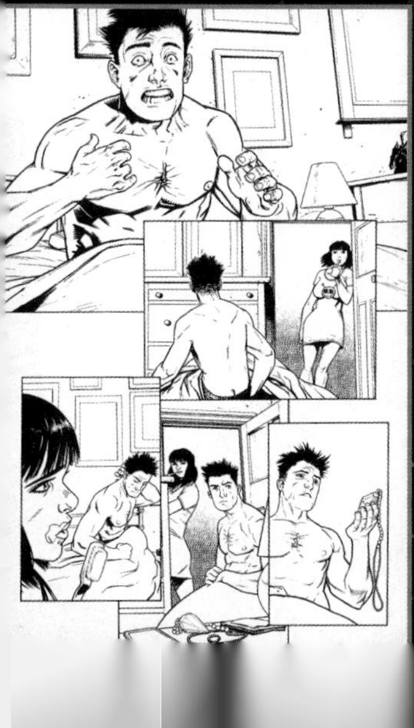

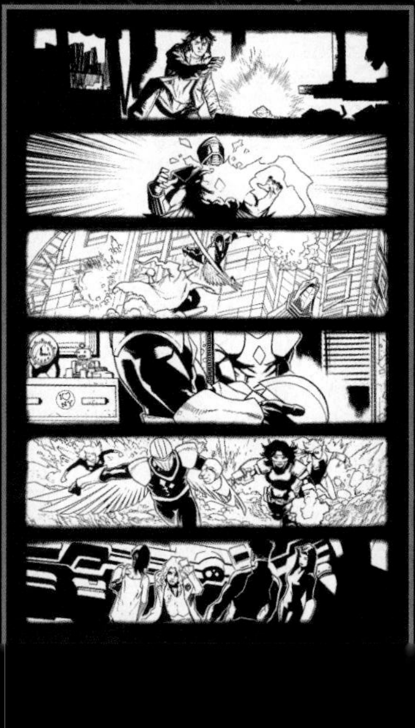

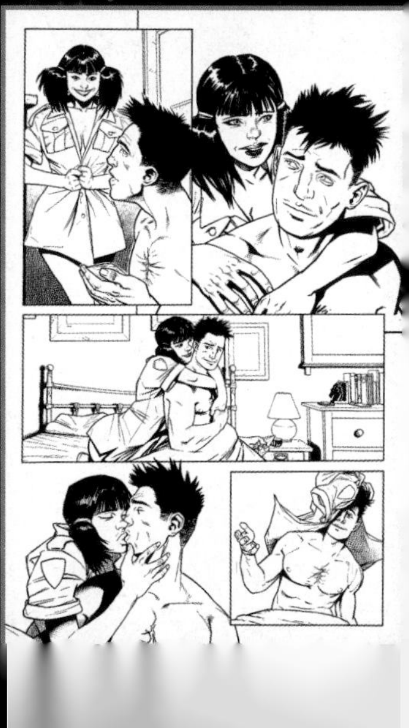

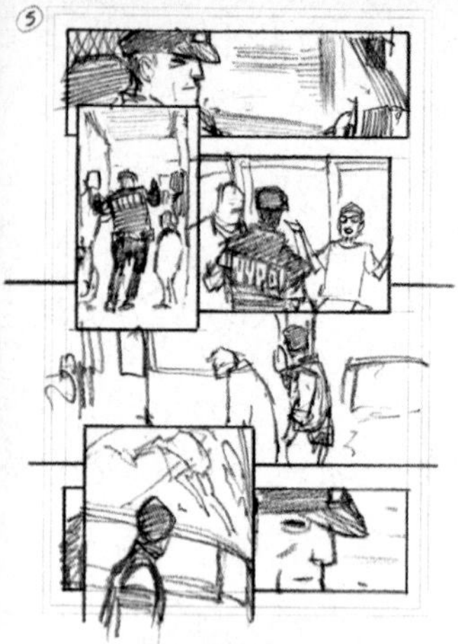
5
NYPD

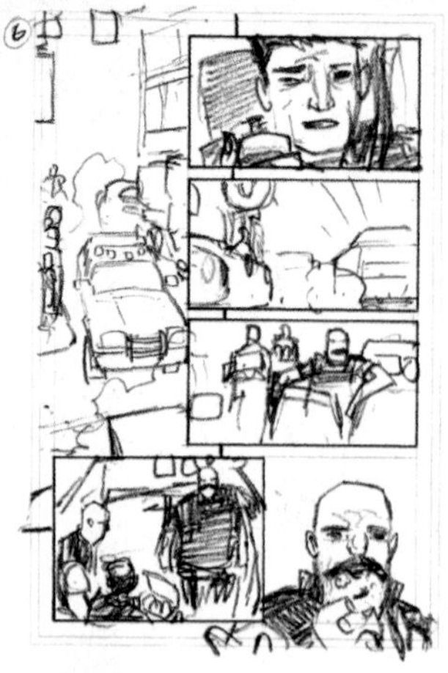
6

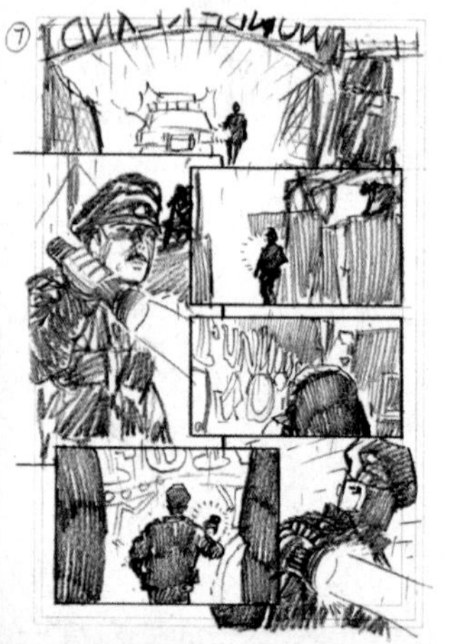
7

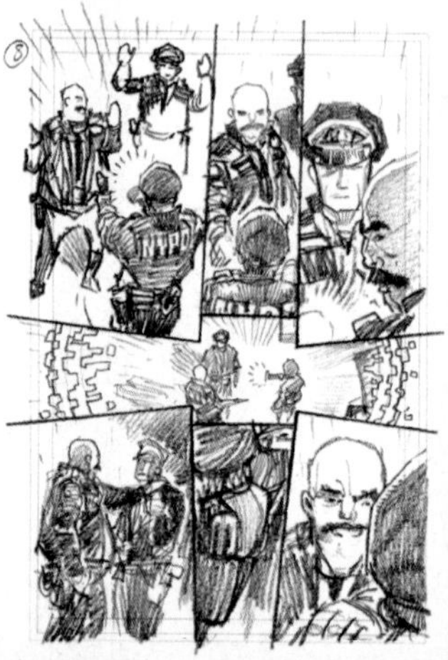
8
NYPD

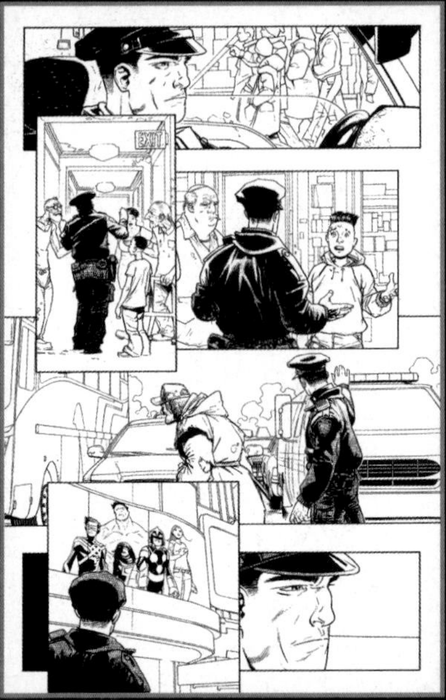
EXIT

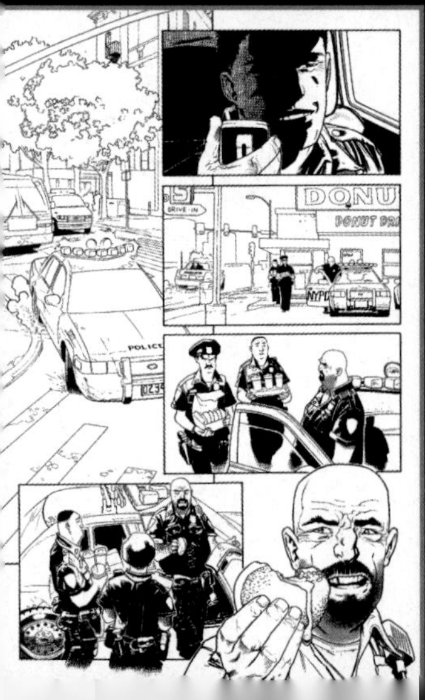
DONU
DRIVE IN
NYPD
POLICE

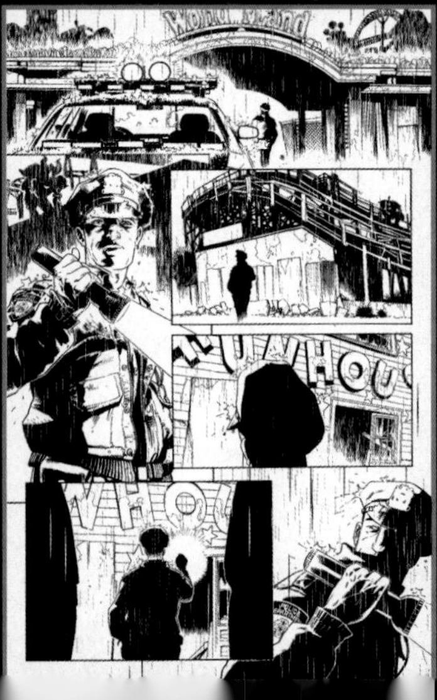

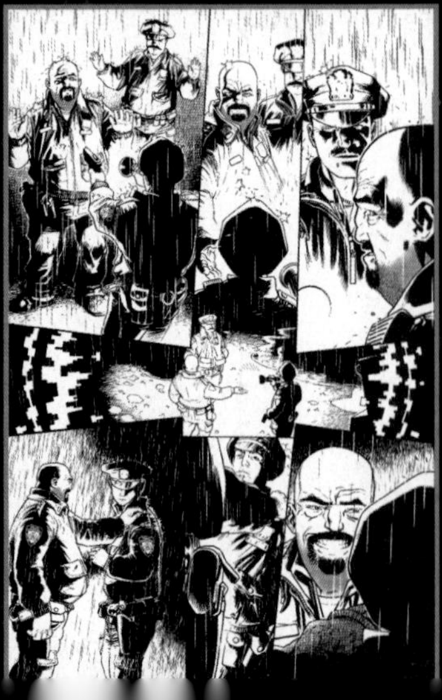

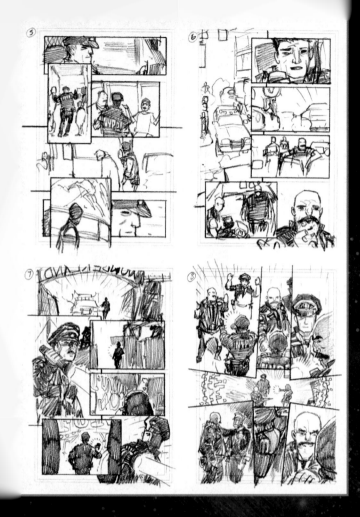